Entry Strategies for International Markets

Revised and Expanded

Franklin R. Root

LEXINGTON BOOKS
An Imprint of Macmillan, Inc.
NEW YORK

Maxwell Macmillan Canada
TORONTO

Maxwell Macmillan International
NEW YORK   OXFORD   SINGAPORE   SYDNEY

Library of Congress Cataloging-in-Publication Data

Root, Franklin R.
    Entry strategies for International markets / Franklin R. Root. —
Rev. and expanded ed.
        p.   cm.
    Includes index.
    ISBN 0-02-926903-2 (cloth) — ISBN 0-02-926904-0 (pbk.)
    1. Export marketing.   2. International business enterprises-
-Management.   I. Title.
HF1416.R66   1994
658.8'48—dc20   93-40129
                                                                      CIP

Lexington Books
An Imprint of Macmillan, Inc.
866 Third Avenue, New York, N.Y. 10022

Maxwell Macmillan Canada, Inc.
1200 Eglinton Avenue East
Suite 200
Don Mills, Ontario M3C 3N1

Macmillan, Inc. is part of the Maxwell Communication
Group of Companies.

Printed in the United States of America

printing number
1   2   3   4   5   6   7   8   9   10

to Joyce

| Contents |

| Tables |

| Figures |

| Preface |

This book is written for managers who are actively pursuing international market opportunities or want to do so, and for students in university courses on international business and marketing, especially courses oriented toward managerial decision making in the global marketplace. It should also interest public officials who must deal with international companies and can therefore benefit from a greater understanding of them.

The grand theme is the need for managers to design and execute international market entry strategies that aim to achieve a sustainable presence in foreign markets. This theme is incorporated in an entry-planning model that identifies key decisions and their relationships. The model also serves to structure the book, enabling a comprehensive yet integrated treatment of all forms of market entry: exporting, investment, licensing, and many contractual arrangements. Throughout the text comparisons have been drawn (and even forced) among alternative entry modes and international marketing plans. To my knowledge, this integration has not been achieved by any other publication.

The book starts with an overview of the forces now transforming the international economy into a global economy. Managers need to learn how to cope with new business environments created by the global economy whether their companies are big or small, domestic or international. The book then goes on to focus on three fundamental questions: (1) How should managers decide which international markets to enter, if any? (2) How should managers decide their mode of international market entry? (3) How should managers decide their international marketing plan—their product, channel, price, and promotion strategies?

Chapters 2 through 8 tackle these questions in the context of a single product (or product line) and a single target market. Chapter 9 then looks at entry strategies from the perspective of cultural differences, which are a distinctive feature of international business. Chapter 10 closes the book with the design of entry strategies for global competitive advantage in multinational enterprise systems, addressing issues relating to organization, planning, strategic alliances, and tomorrow's global managers.

This book is directly traceable to my executive seminars on international market entry strategies. To the hundreds of executives here and abroad who have passed through these seminars wih me, I am warmly grateful for our time together. Your questions and comments have immeasurably enriched my approach to the subject. If this normative treatment of international market entry strategies impresses readers with its pragmatic tone, I have only you to thank.

CHAPTER 1

The New Global Economy

Challenges and Opportunities

A new global economy is emerging to confront business enterprises of the West with extraordinary threats to their survival, coupled with the unprecedented opportunities for growth and profits. China, South Korea, Mexico, and other nations are assuming leading economic roles as the old industrial countries lose their relative economic strength. The United States—no longer the dominant economic power it was in the three decades following World War II—has become the first among equals, able to lead by example but not by command. From a broad historical perspective, the transformation of the international economy represents a geographical extension of the industrial revolution that started in Great Britain more than two centuries ago. The previous comparable extension took place in the half century before World War I, when the global industrial map was profoundly altered by the rise to prominence of the United States, Germany, and Japan.

This book examines how companies can design entry strategies for international markets in the new global economy. But before turning to that subject, we need to understand the dynamic forces building the new global economy.

Forces Transforming the International Economy

Accelerating rates of technological change, interacting with accelerating rates of globalization, are causing a migration of traditional industries from the industrial countries of Europe, Japan, and the United States to the developing countries of Asia, Latin America, and (most recently) eastern Europe. At the same time, the industrial countries are undergoing a painful reallocation of resources from traditional capital and labor intensive industries to new technology and skill-intensive industries. These massive resource shifts are creating a global economy with new competitors and new markets. The forces of innovation and globalization interact in many ways; suffice it to point out that remarkable improvements in the speed, availability, and cost-effectiveness of international communications are reinforcing globalization, which in turn is forcing the pace of innovation.

The evidence of accelerating technological innovation surrounds us. Today more scientists and engineers are engaged in R & D than in all the past combined. The flow of technological innovations has been depicted as a series of bursting tides, with each higher than the last.[1] Certainly we are now living through a bursting technological tide: electronic products of all sorts, lasers and fiber optics, biogenetics, superconductivity, and other technologies are continuing to form the industrial foundation for the twenty-first century. These new industries, centered on electronics technology, differ strikingly from their traditional predecessors. They are global from the start, with products (commonly services) whose high unit costs make transportation costs an insignificant barrier to international trade. Because they are knowledge and service intensive rather than resource and capital-intensive, the new industries are also footloose, capable of quickly relocating production anywhere in the world through international investment and other entry modes. Their most distinctive feature is a critical dependence on technological innovation.

The signs of accelerating globalization are all around us. International trade has been growing at twice the rate of gross world product for several decades, and international flows of services have grown more rapidly than flows of tangible products. Starting in the 1970s, international financial flows have exploded with the progressive integration of money and capital markets in the leading industrial countries. One sign of globalization that can be seen in the United States is its international trade: since the 1960s, U.S. exports of manufactured products have grown from less than 10 percent of U.S. manufacturing output to more than 20 percent, while imports of manufactured products have grown from 5 percent to more than 25 percent of domestic output. All of the industrial countries are far more dependent on imports of manufactures (as measured by the import penetration ratio—imports of finished manufactured products as a percentage of total supplies) than at any time since the World War II and, with the exception of Japan, at any time since 1899.[2]

A second and more significant sign of globalization is massive foreign direct investment undertaken by multinational enterprises to create international production networks. Since the early 1980s, foreign direct investment flows have risen four times faster than world output.[3] The international production of goods and services now dominates international trade: nearly 80 percent of U.S.-Japanese trade, 40 percent of U.S.–European Community (EC) trade, and 55 percent of EC-Japan trade are between parent companies and their foreign subsidiaries.[4] This intracorporate trade demonstrates that the new global economy is also an economy of global enterprise.

The twin forces of technological innovation and globalization are narrowing international technology gaps and bringing about a convergence of demand preferences across the industrial countries. These processes, in turn, are compressing the duration of international product life cycles. As their real per capita incomes approach parity, demand preferences in the industrial countries are converging for both industrial and consumer goods and services. This convergence has already sharply cut the time it takes for a new product introduced in one country to gain acceptance in other countries (known as international demand lag).

In the 1950s, the extraordinary technological lead of U.S. companies enabled them to dominate foreign markets and treat the American market as their own. But since that time, the American lead has steadily shrunk as European and Japanese firms acquired U.S. technology (through licensing and other channels) and built their own R & D capabilities. By the 1980s, many European and

Japanese companies had moved from being technological imitators to being technological innovators.

Although the closing of technology gaps has not occurred at the same pace in all industries, the cases of the computer and integrated circuit are instructive. In 1953, when IBM launched its 701 computer, the U.S. lead time over Japan was 4 years. By 1970, when IBM launched its 370 computer, the lead time had fallen to 1.2 years. In 1980, when IBM introduced the 3085x, the lead time had become zero as Japanese firms achieved technological parity. The closing of a technology gap was even more dramatic in the case of semiconductors. In 1948, when the transistor was first introduced, the U.S. lead over Japan was 5 years. By 1970 the lead had narrowed to 1.5 years, and by 1982 it had been reversed, as Japanese firms launched the 256K chip 1 year in advance of American firms. By the mid-1980s, Japanese companies held 60 percent of the U.S. semiconductor market for 64K RAM chips and 85 percent of the market for 256K chips.[5]

Today the progressive narrowing of international technology gaps is most dramatically displayed in the manufacture and export of high-tech products by South Korea, Taiwan, Singapore, Brazil, Mexico, and other newly industrializing countries (NICs). For the most part these countries do not yet originate technology, but they are rapidly enhancing their capabilities to quickly imitate technology created by the industrial countries.

Shrinking demand and imitation lags have contracted product life cycles.[6] In the early 1980s the life cycles of most manufactured products lasted about 6 years, and even for consumer electronics they were seldom less than 3 years. But a decade later, life cycles for many products are down to months rather than years; high-tech specialty products quickly become high-tech commodities. As products move more swiftly through their life cycles, companies need to speed up entry into domestic and foreign markets if they are to recoup R & D expenditures and make profits. In addition to adapting market strategies to changing competitive situations, companies also need to adapt *production* to different phases of the product life cycle. As a company's product reaches maturity, the ability to manufacture it at low cost and high quality becomes ever more vital for market success.

Key National Actors in the Global Economy

To further readers' understanding of the new global economy, we offer a review of its the key national participants.

The Triad: Dominating the Global Economy

The Triad is made up of the United States, Japan, and the European Community (EC).[7] Although its dominance is almost certain to diminish as the NICs (including China) continue their economic expansion, the Triad will remain at the center of the global economy into the 21st century. The combined gross domestic product (GDP) of the Triad is two-thirds that of the entire world (allocated as follows: United States, 26 percent; EC, 25 percent; and Japan, 14 percent). The Triad generates about four-fifths of the world's exports and imports, and trade among the three Triad members accounts for two-thirds of the world's trade.[8] The Triad's overwhelming importance in international trade is matched by its role in foreign direct investment (FDI), accounting for more than three-fourths of the world's annual outflow of FDI and about two-thirds of its annual inflow. Furthermore, as was true of trade, about two-thirds of the world's FDI flow occurs within the Triad itself.

Figure 1 depicts the total FDI stocks (the cumulative book value of all past investment) held by each Triad member in other members as of the late 1980s. Observe that the United States is the leading host country, with EC investment valued at $193.9 billion and Japanese investment valued at $53.4 billion (for a total DFI of $247.3 billion). The EC ranks second as an FDI host with $143.6 billion, while Japan comes in a poor third with a mere $19.6 billion. When ranked as home countries—that is, as sources of investment—the EC comes first with $195.6 billion (almost all located in the United States), the United States second with $149 billion, and Japan third with $65.9 billion. The striking imbalance between Japan as a host and home country is attributable to the restrictions that kept FDI out of Japan until the 1980s and to present institutional obstacles preventing the acquisition of Japanese firms by U.S. and European investors.

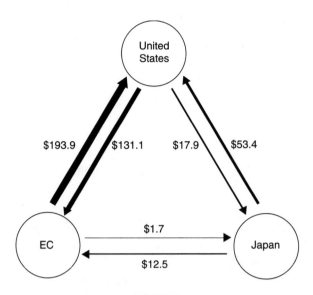

FIGURE 1

*Intra-Triad Foreign Direct Investment: Outward Stocks in
1988 (Billions of Dollars)*

Source: Adapted from United Nations Center on Transnational Corporations,
World Investment Report: The Triad in Foreign Direct Investment
(New York: United Nations, 1991), p. 40, figure 2.

It is no coincidence that the role of the Triad in international trade matches its role in foreign direct investment. The two roles are closely linked, as trade leads to investment and investment leads to trade in a dynamic, interactive process. FDI may be regarded as a proxy for international production, because it is mainly used by companies to establish foreign subsidiaries that produce goods and services for sale in local and international markets.[9] The U.S. subsidiaries of foreign companies account for one-fifth of U.S. exports and one-third of U.S. imports; at the same time, the foreign subsidiaries of U.S. parent companies account for nearly one-third of U.S. exports and one-fifth of U.S. imports. Overall, foreign subsidiaries are responsible for about half of U.S. exports and imports.[10]

The geographical distribution of FDI falls into regional clusters centered on each Triad member. For most countries outside the Triad, a single Triad member accounts for more than half of their FDI. This pattern reflects the strategies of international firms to build up regionally integrated networks of subsidiaries in countries clustered geographically around their home countries: Japanese firms in Asian countries, EC firms in European countries, and U.S. firms in the countries of North and South America. This regional clustering, however, is not absolute: the United States is the leading direct investor in Pakistan and the Philippines, and the EC leads direct investors in Brazil, Peru, Indonesia, and Vietnam.[11] Keep in mind that the United States is the principal direct investor in the EC and Japan, and the EC is the principal direct investor in the United States. That is to say, the pattern of intra-Triad FDI is global.

One final observation on the Triad: overall, its members protect against imports in about the same degree. The trade-weighted average of their import duties is around 5 percent, and nontariff trade barriers cover about one-quarter of their imports.[12] Trade liberalization in the Triad depends critically on the outcome of the Uruguay Round sponsored by the General Agreement on Tariffs and Trade (GATT). The Triad members follow a much more open policy on FDI; as of the early 1990s, each member maintains regulations restraining foreign investment only in some industries related to natural resources and defense. Nonetheless, it is easier for Japanese firms to invest in the United States and the EC than for firms in the latter countries to invest in Japan. The obstacle in Japan is structural: Japanese firms are organized into industrial groups (known as *keiretsu*) that resist outsiders.[13]

The European Community: Completing the Common Market

The distinctive purpose of the EC is the creation of a common market involving the abolition of all restrictions on the movement of goods, services, persons, and capital among the member countries.[14] In the 1960s, the EC made rapid progress in getting rid of import duties on intra-EC trade in industrial products and setting up a common external tariff for non-EC products.[15] Many nontariff trade barriers, however, continued to prevent the formation of EC markets. By the 1980s, European business leaders were arguing strongly for a single market. In a world going global, they feared that their companies would not be able to match American and Japanese competitors in the absence of a home market as big as those in the United States and Japan. In the mid-1980s, the EC responded to this anxiety with an effort to wipe out all remaining barriers to trade, investment, and enterprise within the common market. To do so, some three hundred directives eliminating specific barriers were scheduled to go into effect at the end of 1992; hence the effort came to be known as *Europe '92.*

An EC-sponsored study known as the Cecchini report estimated that Europe '92 would add about 5 percent to the EC's gross domestic product. It was predicted that the opening of procurement by government agencies in public sectors (notably communications, energy, and transportation) to all EC firms; the liberalization of financial services provided by banks, insurance, and securities firms; the elimination of border controls; and the supply-side effects of firms responding to the new EC market would intensify pan-European competition, stimulating new investment and lower costs. Individual firms would be able to cut costs by exploiting more fully national comparative advantages, economies of scale, and learning effects. At the same time, stronger competitive pressures would force firms to cut their price/cost margins; competitive rivalry would also compel firms to innovate and to restructure operations to raise productivity. Consequently, consumers would gain from lower prices, higher quality, and more product choice.

Europe '92 is now in effect, but it actually began several years earlier as both EC and foreign companies responded to the prospect of a single pan-European market. Industries that could benefit from scale economies but had been prevented from doing so by intra-EC barriers—banking, telecommunications, construction, major appliances, food, beverages, household nondurables, publishing, transportation, and business services—had already experienced painful shakeouts. By early 1993 firms in those industries were moving into other EC countries by acquiring local firms, entering into contractual arrangements with them, or investing in new subsidiaries.

Individual companies need to respond with different strategies, depending on specific circumstances. But big or small, domestic or international, EC or non-EC, all companies now face a pan-European market and pan-European competition. Even U.S. companies that have stayed at home may feel the effects of Europe '92 as EC firms gain in competitive strength in world markets.[16]

As an illustration of the forces set loose by Europe '92, consider how Whirlpool and Maytag responded to the pan-European market in home appliances. The U.S. home appliance market is mature, so U.S. appliance companies must go abroad for growth: in 1988, Whirlpool (with sales about $7 billion) and Maytag (with sales of about $3 billion) made costly acquisitions in Europe. But the results for the two companies have been very different. Whirlpool has been successful in Europe, gaining about one-fifth of the home appliance market; Maytag has lost money in Europe.

This contrast points to the importance of making the right acquisition. Whirlpool bought 53 percent of the appliance business of Philips N.V. (the Netherlands) in 1989, and the remainder two years later, for a total outlay of nearly $1 billion. At the time, Philips ranked third in European appliance sales. Whirlpool then cut costs by closing twelve of twenty-eight European warehouses, with ten to twelve slated to follow. Whirlpool is hoping to get the same economies of scale in Europe that it gets in the United States, where two giant plants make more than half the washers and dryers sold in the country.

It also launched a massive advertising campaign to build the Whirlpool name (the Philips name can be used only until 1999) and to promote a pan-European marketing strategy. Whirlpool believes that home appliances are an emerging global industry that will be dominated by four or five giant companies. Counting on the integration of the heretofore fragmented European market, Whirlpool has already scored successes with its pan-European strategy. Based on market research, it introduced the VIP Crisp microwave oven, which also performs like a conventional oven; hence it can fry bacon and eggs for Britishers, and crisp pizza crusts for Italians. VIP Crisp is now the best-selling microwave oven in Europe. By the end of the 1990s, Whirlpool anticipates that more than half of its sales will be abroad.

Unlike Whirlpool, which has penetrated most of the European market, Maytag has only established a beachhead. In 1989, Maytag bought the Hoover Company (U.K.) for close to $1 billion. Hoover's appliance business was centered in the United Kingdom and ranked only tenth in European appliance sales; consequently,

Hoover provides only one-seventh of Maytag's sales, while Philips provides one-third of Whirlpool's sales. Maytag has since begun restructuring Hoover, but cutting costs is not enough to make a pan-European strategy work. Maytag needed to market its appliances across Europe, but it did not have the resources to match the distribution systems of other appliance manufacturers. Because of this, in 1993 Maytag formed an alliance with Bosch-Siemens (Germany), Europe's second-ranked appliance maker, to market each other's products, collaborate on R & D, and consolidate some distribution systems.[17]

The United States and the North American Free Trade Agreement

In 1992 the United States, Canada, and Mexico concluded negotiations on the North American Free Trade Agreement (NAFTA), which would abolish trade and investment barriers among the three countries. Formal government approval is needed before the agreement can go into effect. With $6 trillion in gross domestic product and 360 million consumers, the North American free trade area would rival the European Community as the world's biggest single market. In general, import duties and quantitative trade restrictions would be phased out over a five- to ten-year period. The precursor of NAFTA is the U.S.-Canadian Free Trade Agreement (FTA), which went into effect in 1989.

The NAFTA signatories have two features, in particular, that distinguish them from the European Community nations. The United States would dominate with nine-tenths of the combined North American gross domestic product; there is no such dominant power in the EC. Also, a large gap would exist between the United States and Canada, on the one hand, and Mexico, on the other, in levels of economic development. In the EC, gaps are much smaller.

Studies by economists point to rather modest *static* (or allocation) benefits of NAFTA, because tariffs on U.S.-Mexican trade are moderate (averaging 6 percent for the United States and 13 percent for Mexico), and most nontariff trade barriers are already being phase out. Also, restrictions on U.S.-Canadian trade are moving toward zero under the FTA. Economists, however, anticipate much larger *dynamic* (or growth) benefits: a sustained rise in FDI in Mexico by U.S. and other multinational firms would generate higher industrial activity and income in Mexico that, in turn, would stimulate imports of capital and consumer goods coming mainly from the United States, which accounts for over two-thirds of Mexico's foreign trade. This positive growth effect—extending over several decades—would benefit all the member countries.[18]

NAFTA promises to create many opportunities for U.S. companies in the Mexican market. In autos and trucks, the United States would end its tariffs immediately, while Mexico phases them out over ten years. The outlook is for U.S. exports of autos and trucks to rise substantially, along with the sales in Mexico of products from U.S.-owned plants. In computers, computer components, and electronics, Mexican duties on 90 percent of U.S. exports would end in five years. The outlook is for both U.S. exports and imports to rise more than 15 percent as more components come from North America. In pharmaceuticals, Mexican duties on 85 percent of imports from the United States would end, and patent protection in Mexico would broaden in coverage. The outlook is for U.S. exports to rise as U.S. firms become free to bid on Mexican government contracts.

In textiles and apparel, duties would end in six years on products made from yarn produced in North America. The outlook is for U.S. apparel imports from Mexico to rise 60 percent over the long term, while U.S. apparel exports to Mexico rise 30 percent. In machine tools, Mexico's tariffs would end on more than three-quarters of its imports from the United States, and the remaining tariffs would be phased out over five years. The outlook is for U.S. exports to rise 9 percent in the first year of the agreement.[19]

Japan: The Challenge of Market Entry

Earlier we discussed Japan as one leg of the Triad, observing that it was a difficult market to enter than the United States and the European Community. But it would be wrong for U.S. and EC managers to conclude that entry barriers exclude them from Japan.

With a few exceptions, import and investment restrictions no longer prevent foreign firms from entering business sectors in

Japan. Of course, competition is fierce, and consumers are extraordinarily demanding of quality and services. Although Japan is
no longer a closed market, it remains a very tough market to enter.
Nonetheless, many U.S. and EC companies have demonstrated
that with the right product and the right marketing strategy, they
can compete in Japan—and prosper. In 1988 Apple Computers
(U.S.) sold only a few thousand Macintosh computers in Japan,
but in 1991 the company sold 120,000, moving from a 1 percent
share of the market to 6 percent. This success was mostly owing to
Japanese-language software that became available only three
years ago.

Another success story is TRW (U.S.), whose sales of auto parts
to Japanese auto companies worldwide rose sevenfold over seven
years, reaching $500 million (or 10 percent of its total sales) in
1991. TRW took an indirect approach to the Japanese market.
First, it invested heavily in joint ventures with Japanese auto parts
companies to supply the U.S. plants of the Japanese auto firms.
Toyota and Nissan. After the latter started using TRW parts in
their U.S.-made autos, it became relatively easy for TRW to take
the next step of supplying the same companies back in Japan. The
core of TRW's competitive advantage is its air-bag technology; the
company now sells air-bag triggering sensors for half the cars
Japanese firms market abroad, and for one-third of the cars they
market in Japan.

A third success story is Xerox Corporation (U.S.), a manufacturer of photocopying machines. The company designed its new
Model 5100 to duplicate the Japanese *kanji* language characters
and also handle the thin paper used in Japan. Now the Model
5100, able to make high-quality reproductions faster than any
Japanese-made copier, is the top-selling high-speed copier in
Japan, with close to 90 percent of the high-speed market.

Probably the classic example of an American business success in
Japan is Aflac, Inc., the world's leading seller of cancer insurance.
In 1991 this company had revenues of $3.3 billion, of which an
astounding three-quarters came from operations in Japan. Entry
into Japan was triggered in 1970 when Aflac discovered that cancer was a leading cause of death in the country, but that no company offered cancer insurance. It took four years for Aflac to get a
license from the Japanese Ministry of Finance, but then it received

an eight-year monopoly to sell cancer insurance in Japan. As of the early 1990s the company has 90 percent of the Japanese market for cancer insurance.

The roll call of successful foreign firms in Japan is indeed long. To name a few more U.S. companies: Johnson & Johnson dominates the dental floss and toothbrush markets, Warner-Lambert nearly monopolizes the mouthwash markets with its Listerine, Coca-Cola earns more selling its soda in Japan than in the United States, Schick has 70 percent of the safety-blade market, McDonald's holds 30 percent of the fast-food hamburger market, and Procter & Gamble has one-fifth of the disposable diaper market. Managers of these and other successful American companies in Japan stress the need for a long-term commitment and patience. But the rewards can be great in a country of 125 million generally affluent consumers.[20]

Eastern Europe and China: The Transition from Centrally Planned to Market Economies

For decades the countries of Eastern Europe and China managed their economies through central plans that ignored market forces and restricted transactions with other economies.[21] Now these countries, with one-quarter of the world's people, are engaged in an unprecedented effort to transform their planned economies into market-based systems that would fully participate in the global economy. This effort will probably continue for decades, and we can only speculate on its outcome. In one way or another, however, the transformation process will profoundly affect the global economy in the years ahead.

The failure of central planning provoked the collapse of the Soviet Union at the end of 1991 and the dissolution of communist regimes in other eastern European countries a few years earlier. Democratic governments have now come to power, committed to building market economies. A communist regime remains in power in China, but that regime started a "marketization" of China's economy in the late 1970s, more than a decade earlier than the revolutions in eastern Europe.

Economists agree on the reforms needed to transform a centrally planned economy into a market economy. The reform package includes (1) macroeconomic stabilization; (2) establishment of competitive markets through price and wage liberalization, convertibility of the currency for exports and imports of goods and services, and the abolition of international trade restrictions; (3) privatization of state-owned enterprises, and (4) creation of a legal framework (particularly for property rights) and institutional frameworks (financial and others) necessary to the functioning of a market economy. Economists disagree on the *sequence* of reforms, however, as their recommendations range from the "big bang" approach (doing everything at once) to a gradualist approach (doing one thing at a time in a certain sequence). Whatever the approach, reform demands painful adjustments; inflation, unemployment, and income distribution are likely to worsen before economic growth and higher productivity bring higher living standards to consumers. In practice, China and Hungary are following a gradualist approach; Poland, a big-bang approach. Russia started with a big-bang approach but was forced to abandon it in the face of political opposition.

Economic reform has proceeded furthest in China.[22] By the early 1990s less than 10 percent of the Chinese economy remained covered by the central plan; it had become the third biggest economy in the world, exceeded only by the U.S. and Japanese economies. If China's economy continues to grow at the annual rate of 9 percent recorded in the 1980s, it will become the world's leading economy by 2010 or so. (At a 9 percent annual growth rate, GDP increases fivefold in nineteen years.) Also, an export-led growth strategy has made China a major player in the world economy. The biggest risk facing Western firms in China is political: will economic growth, with its rising standards of living, compel the central government to move toward democracy? Or will the government resist political reform, causing protests (such as in Tiananmen Square in 1989), social turmoil, and even civil war?

Putting fears of political risk aside, foreign companies are now investing in China at an extraordinary rate.[23] Motorola (U.S.) is spending $400 million to build plants to manufacture pagers, cellular telephones, advanced microprocessors, walkie-talkie systems, and other electronic products. AT&T (U.S.) has a $1 billion agreement to manufacture switches, wireless phones, and integrated circuits. NEC (Japan) is constructing a microwave telecommunications factory. Volkswagen (Germany) is spending

$315 million to double the output of pickup trucks in its joint venture near Shanghai. Asea Brown Boveri (Sweden/Switzerland) has invested $400 million in a coal-fired power station under construction in Guangdong province. Total (France) holds a 20 percent share in a $450 million refinery. Coca-Cola, one of the first U.S. companies to invest in China, is adding ten new bottling plants, located mainly in interior cities, to its twelve existing plants in cities on China's east coast. Yaohan Department Store (Japan) is constructing in Shanghai the largest department store in Asia. Johnson & Johnson, a U.S. maker of baby care products, started with joint ventures in China but has since added a wholly run operation in Shanghai. Procter & Gamble (U.S.) opened a shampoo plant in Guangzhou in 1988, eventually manufacturing several products under its brand names.

In spite of optimism about China's economic future, Western firms face several pitfalls in doing business in China. For example, American Standard (U.S.) discovered that shipping toilets 700 miles from Qingyuan to Shanghai can take six weeks. The firm also found that some banks do not accept traveler's checks, and some are ignorant of letters of credit. It can also be difficult for a foreign company to convert yuans into dollars, making local profits problematic. Disagreements with joint venture partners are common; costs can be high; red tape can make it difficult to obtain export licenses or deal with state-owned enterprises; and tariffs are more than 100 percent on consumer products. Most foreign enterprises lose money for several years while building distribution networks, finding reliable local suppliers, and developing good working relations with local partners. Managers of foreign companies operating profitably in China say that success requires patience, persistence, and "old-fashioned" marketing.

In Eastern Europe, Poland, Hungary, and the Czech Republic are now well launched on economic reform. In contrast, prospects for reform in Russia are clouded by a bitter struggle for power between the executive branch of government and the legislative branch. Consequently, the government has failed to stabilize the economy; in 1992 prices rose more than 2,000 percent, and output fell by 20 percent.[24]

The transformation process in Eastern Europe is spawning many opportunities for Western firms. But in establishing operations in countries moving from planned to market economies, these firms face many obstacles, including obsolete plants, a dearth of advertising services, and a lack of trucks and warehouses for physical distribution. Also, they need to educate local managers and workers in the basics of a market economy, as well as in more efficient production and marketing methods. Furthermore, they face the risk of political uncertainty. Nonetheless, thousands of Western firms are investing in Eastern Europe, and many more are prepared to do so if obstacles lessen in the future.

One example of successful market entry in Eastern Europe is Unilever. In 1991 Unilever N.V., a British-Dutch consumer products company, bought a laundry detergent factory in Poland for $20 million. The factory's product, Pollena 2000, has now become the market share leader in the Polish detergent market. In Hungary, Unilever acquired an ice cream producer and on 80 percent stake in a manufacturer of soap, margarine, and detergents. It also bought a soap and margarine business in Czechoslovakia (now divided into the Czech and Slovak republics). In addition to the detergent company, Unilever owns Poland's largest margarine producer.

Unilever has found it difficult to obtain market information in Eastern Europe, even on such basic questions as average household income or the number of households with washing machines. Unilever's entry strategy is to get the greatest possible sales from local brands it acquires while introducing its own brands. In Poland, for instance, the company has no plans to phase out Pollena 2000 (which has been reformulated using Western technology), but it is also marketing OMO, one of its Western European detergent brands. Unilever believes that Eastern Europe cannot be ignored, and it expects its sales in that region to triple within five years.[25]

NICs in the Global Economy: The New Kids on the Block

The closing of technology gaps, easier access to international capital, and national endowments of low-cost, productive labor are transforming the economies of certain developing countries, notably in East Asia. Newly industrializing countries (NICs) are aggressively entering international markets with consumer electronics, automobiles, light aircraft, and other mature—yet high-technology—industrial products.[26] As the new kids on the block who want to want to best their older counterparts, these countries are fierce competitors in markets that were formerly the exclusive preserve of U.S., Japanese, and European firms. Continually sourcing high technology from Western companies, NIC companies are already a major force in high-performance computers and memory chips and are steadily encroaching on other markets, putting Western firms under growing competitive pressures. Rather than compete head-on with Western firms, the NICs are quick to exploit niches in the aerospace, software, telecommunications, robotics, biotechnology, and other markets that are not being covered by competitors.[27] But the NICs are not only competitive threats; their extraordinary rates of growth—the highest in the world—are creating extraordinary opportunities.

One American company taking advantage of opportunities in the Asian NICs (as well as in China and Japan) is Motorola, a manufacturer of mobile communications devices (cellular telephones, pagers, and two-way radios) and semiconductors (mainly microprocessors for computers and microcontrollers for consumer electronics). Motorola gets half of its worldwide sales ($11.3 billion in 1991) outside the United States. In the 1990s it expects sales in Asia to grow much faster than sales in the United States or Europe. The company first entered Asia in the 1960s when it established sales agencies in Japan and Hong Kong. Three decades later it has one marketing headquarters, three national headquarters, seven manufacturing plants, and eleven sales offices in ten Asian countries. In the early 1980s Motorola decided to expand its presence in Japan, mainly because of the size of the Japanese market (which accounts for about one-third of world demand for semiconductors) and the need to challenge Japanese competitors in their home market if they were to be countered elsewhere. The turning point occurred in 1987 when Motorola formed an alliance with Toshiba to set up a joint venture to manufacture semiconductor chips. The company is now looking for other Japanese partners to help get approvals and radio frequencies from the Japanese government.

In 1990 Motorola opened a chip design and manufacturing center in Hong Kong. The company's Asian division, covering the entire region except for Japan and run from the Hong Kong center, is now the most profitable and fastest-growing Motorola unit in the world. The head of this division identifies three key elements of Motorola's Asian strategy: (1) forming alliances with other companies to share investment costs (a new chip factory can cost $1 billion) and to obtain the full range of chips that customers want from the same supplier; (2) building personal connections, which are more important in Asia than elsewhere; and (3) expanding operations slowly with staffing by local nationals from the start.

Obsessed with quality, Motorola wants to cut manufacturing defects by 90 percent every two years throughout the 1990s and also save $1 billion in nonmanufacturing costs during the decade. The company works to get quality right from the start, because with six-month product life cycles there is no time to correct defects after market entry. Motorola keeps close tabs on its Japanese competitors through its separate division in Japan. The company spends heavily on research (8 percent of sales), much of which is intended to improve production rather than develop new products. Motorola believe it can compete worldwide only with new products manufactured at the highest quality standards and at the lowest cost.[28]

It has now become evident that developing countries benefit far more from outward-oriented trade policies than from inward-oriented policies. A World Bank study covering forty-one developing countries for the 1980–1990 period found that outward-oriented policies (few or minor trade controls, and exchange rates that do not discriminate between importable and exportable goods) led to significantly higher rates of growth in gross domestic product and manufactured exports than inward-oriented policies (high import protection and overvalued exchange rates that favor production for the domestic market).[29]

All of the NICs have followed outward-oriented trade policies. Their example, together with failure of communist planned economies, has encouraged developing countries everywhere to open up their economies to world markets. These countries have concluded that only freer markets can bring about economic development. India offers a striking example of this liberalization movement. Long a practitioner of inward-oriented policies, India in recent years has abolished industrial licensing for most industries, eliminated quotas on imports of industrial goods, made the rupee convertible for trade, and sold as much as 20 percent of several government-owned companies to private investors.[30] Although India has a long way to go to match China or the "little dragons" in East Asia, it has made a good start in opening up its economy. One indication of this is a sharp rise in the number of investment proposals from foreign firms. Other examples of liberalization are Argentina and Mexico, with the latter seeking to consolidate its liberalization through membership in NAFTA. In sum, liberalization is opening up markets in Asia and Latin America as at no time in the past.

Implications of the Global Economy

The global economy is creating business environments that differ radically from those of the past. To survive and prosper in the 1990s, companies will need to develop new strategies. For the truth is that today *all* business firms—small or large, domestic or international—must strive for profits and growth in an international economy that features enormous flows of products, technology, capital, and enterprise among countries. In this economy, no market is forever safe from foreign competition. And so even when companies stay at home, sooner or later they learn from hard experience that there are no domestic markets, only global markets.

The point is not that all companies should go international, but rather that all companies should plan for growth and survival in a world of global competition. Many companies will come to understand, however, that they can no longer attain their strategic objectives by remaining at home or if they fail to sustain their presence in foreign markets. This book is dedicated to such companies. We now turn to the design of successful entry strategies for international markets in a global economy.

Summary

1. A new global economy is now emerging to confront business enterprises of the West with extraordinary threats to their survival, coupled with unprecedented opportunities for growth and profits.
2. Accelerating rates of technological change, interacting with accelerating globalization, are causing a migration of tradi-

tional industries from the industrial countries of Europe,
Japan, and the United States to the developing countries of
Asia, Latin America, and—most recently—Eastern Europe.

3. At the same time, the industrial countries are undergoing a
   painful reallocation of resources from traditional capital
   and labor-intensive industries to new technology and skill-
   intensive industries.

4. These massive resource shifts are creating a new global
   economy with new competitors and new markets.

5. The twin forces of technological innovation and globalization are narrowing international technology gaps and
   bringing about a convergence of demand preferences
   across the industrial countries. These processes, in turn,
   are compressing the duration of international product life
   cycles.

6. The Triad (the United States, Japan, and the European
   Community) generates about four-fifths of the world's
   trade and about two-thirds of its annual FDI. The Triad
   will remain at the center of the global economy into the
   twenty-first century.

7. The distinctive purpose of the EC is the creation of a common market encompassing the abolition of all restrictions
   on the movement of goods, services, persons, and capital
   among the member countries. The program to carry out
   this task (Europe '92) went into effect at the end of
   1992.

8. In 1992, the United States, Canada, and Mexico concluded
   negotiations on NAFTA, which would abolish trade and
   investment barriers among the three countries. NAFTA
   promises to create many opportunities for U.S. companies
   in Mexico.

9. Japan is a more difficult market to enter than the United
   States or European Community, but it would be wrong for
   American and European managers to conclude that they
   cannot enter Japanese markets.

10. Eastern European countries and China are now engaged in
    an unprecedented effort to transform their planned
    economies into market economies. This transformation
    process is generating many opportunities for Western

firms, but the latter face several obstacles in exploiting them.

11. NICs, notably those in Asia, are aggressively moving into international markets that were formerly the exclusive preserve of U.S., Japanese, and European firms. The economic success of the NICs is encouraging other developing countries to emulate their outward-oriented trade policies.

12. In the new global economy, there is no place for companies to hide from foreign competitors. All companies need to plan for growth and survival in a world of global competition.

CHAPTER 2

Designing Entry Strategies
for International Markets

T his chapter introduces a study of entry strategies for the new global economy by offering a model that identifies the elements of entry strategies and their dynamic linkages. This model provides the analytical framework for subsequent chapters.

The Elements of Entry Strategy

Entry strategy for international markets is a comprehensive plan. It sets forth the objectives, goals, resources, and policies that will guide a company's international business operations over a future period long enough to achieve sustainable growth in world markets. For most companies the entry strategy time horizon is from three to five years, because it will take that long to achieve enduring market performance. For some companies the period may be shorter or longer, but whatever its length, the time horizon should be distant enough to compel managers to raise and answer questions about the long-run direction and scope of a company's international business. For convenience of exposition, we shall assume in this book that the entry strategy planning horizon is three to five years.

Although it is common to speak of a company's entry strategy as if it were a single plan, it is actually a composite of several individual product/market plans. Managers need to plan the entry strategy for *each* product in *each* foreign market, because it is foolhardy to assume that the response to a particular entry strategy would be the same across different products and different country markets. Once the individual (constituent) product/market plans are completed, they should be brought together and reconciled to form the corporate international entry strategy.

The constituent product/market entry strategies require decisions on (1) the choice of a *target product/market,* (2) the *objectives and goals* in the target market, (3) the choice of an *entry mode* to penetrate the target country, (4) the *marketing plan* to penetrate the target market, and (5) the *control system* to monitor performance in the target market. Figure 2 depicts these elements of an international market entry strategy.

Although the elements are shown as a logical sequence of activities and decisions in Figure 2, the design of a market entry strategy is actually iterative, with many feedback loops. Evaluation of alternative entry modes, for instance, may cause a company to revise target market objectives or goals or even to initiate the search

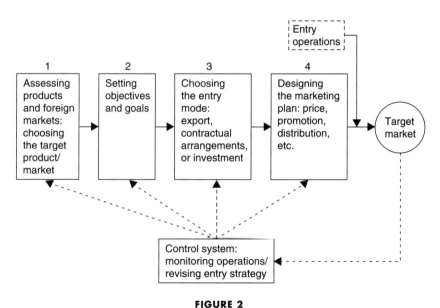

FIGURE 2

The Elements of an International Market Entry Strategy

for a new target market. Again, the formulation of the marketing plan may call into question an earlier preference for a particular entry mode. After operations begin, variances in market performance may lead to revisions in any or all of the first four elements, as indicated by the dashed lines emerging from the Control System box. In short, planning for international market entry is a continuing, open-ended process.

To managers in small and middle-size companies, planning entry strategies may appear to be something that only big companies can afford to do. These managers identify such planning with elaborate research techniques that are applied by specialists to a massive body of quantitative data. But this is a misconception of the entry planning process. What is truly important is the idea of planning entry strategies. Once management accepts this idea, it will find ways to plan international market entry, however limited company resources may be. To say that a company cannot afford to plan an entry strategy is to say that it cannot afford to think systematically about its future in world markets.

Without an entry strategy for a product/target market, a company has only a "sales" approach to foreign markets. Table 1 contrasts the sales and entry strategy approaches. Suffice it to say at this point that the sales approach may be narrowly justified for a first-entry company lacking in any international experience and doubtful of its ability to compete abroad. But a prolonged adherence to the sales approach will almost certainly doom a company's international business. That approach is simply not viable in a world of international competitors who plan and act to create foreign market positions for long-run success.

Classification of Entry Modes

An international market entry mode is an institutional arrangement that makes possible the entry of a company's products, technology, human skills, management, or other resources into a foreign country. For a domestic company that is, one already located in the country that contains its market, the question of entry mode as distinguished from market entry (the marketing plan) simply does not arise. In contrast, the international company initially stands outside both the foreign country and the market it con-

TABLE 1
*Entry Strategy Versus Sales Approach
to International Markets*

	Sales Approach	Entry Strategy Approach
Time horizons	Short run	Long run (3 to 5 years)
Target markets	No systematic selection	Selection based on analysis of market/sales potential
Dominant objective	Immediate sales	Build permanent market position
Resource commitment	Only enough to get immediate sales	What is necessary to gain permanent market position
Entry mode	No systematic choice	Systematic choice of most appropriate mode
New product development	Exclusively for home market	For both home and foreign markets
Product adaptation	Only mandatory adaptations (to meet legal/technical requirements) of domestic products	Adaptation of domestic products to foreign buyers' preferences, incomes, and use conditions
Channels	No effort to control	Effort to control in support of market objectives/goals
Price	Determined by domestic full cost with some ad hoc adjustments to specific sales situations	Determined by demand, competition, objectives, and other marketing policies, as well as cost
Promotion	Mainly confined to personal selling or left to middlemen	Advertising, sales promotion, and personal selling mix to achieve market objectives/goals

tains, and it must find a way to enter the country as well as a way to enter the market. Hence the international company must decide on both an entry mode and a marketing plan for each foreign target country.

From an economist's perspective, a company can arrange entry into a foreign country in only two ways. First, it can export its products to the target country from a production base outside that country. Second, it can transfer its resources in technology, capital, human skills, and enterprise to the foreign country, where they may be sold directly to users or combined with local resources (especially labor) to manufacture products for sale in local markets. Companies whose end products are services cannot produce them at home for sale abroad and must, therefore, use this second way to enter a foreign country.

From a management/operations perspective, these two forms of entry break down into several distinctive entry modes that offer different benefits and costs to the international company. The classification of entry modes used in this text is as follows:

Export Entry Modes
   Indirect
   Direct agent/distributor
   Direct branch/subsidiary
   Other

Contractual Entry Modes
   Licensing
   Franchising
   Technical agreements
   Service contracts
   Management contracts
   Construction/turnkey contracts
   Contract manufacture
   Countertrade arrangements
   Other

Investment Entry Modes
   Sole venture: new establishment
   Sole venture: acquisition
   Joint venture: new establishment/acquisition
   Other

Since these modes are described and evaluated in later chapters, we cite only their distinguishing features here. *Export entry modes* differ from the other two primary entry modes (contractual and investment) in that a company's final or intermediate product is manufactured outside the target country and subsequently transferred to it. Thus exporting is confined to physical products. Indirect exporting uses middlemen who are located in the company's own country and who actually do the exporting. In contrast, direct exporting does not use home country middlemen, although it may use target country middlemen. The latter leads to a distinction between direct agent/distributor exporting, which depends on target-country middlemen to market the exporter's product, and direct branch/subsidiary exporting, which depends on the company's own operating units in the target country. The latter form of exporting therefore requires equity investment in marketing institutions located in the target country.

Contractual entry modes are long-term nonequity associations between an international company and an entity in a foreign target country that involve the transfer of technology or human skills from the former to the latter. Contractual entry modes are distinguished from export modes because they are primarily vehicles for the transfer of knowledge and skills, although they may also create export opportunities. They are distinguished from investment entry modes because there is no equity investment by the international company. In a *licensing* arrangement, a company transfers to a foreign entity (usually another company) for a defined period of time the right to use its industrial property (patents, know-how, or trademarks) in return for a royalty or other compensation. Although similar, *franchising* differs from licensing in motivation, services, and duration. In addition to granting the right to use the company name, trademarks, and technology, the franchisor also assists the franchisee in organization, marketing, and general management under an arrangement intended to be permanent. Other contractual entry modes involve the transfer of services directly to foreign entities in return for monetary compensation (technical agreements, service contracts, management contracts, and construction/turnkey contracts) or in return for products manufactured with those services (contract manufacture and coproduction agreements). International companies frequently combine contractual entry modes with export or investment modes.

Investment entry modes involve ownership by an international company of manufacturing plants or other production units in the target country. In terms of the production stage, these subsidiaries may range all the way from simple assembly plants that depend entirely on imports of intermediate products from the parent company (and may be regarded as an extension of the export entry mode) to plants that undertake the full manufacture of a product. In terms of ownership and management control (which is the distinctive feature of this entry mode), foreign production affiliates may be classified as *sole ventures,* with full ownership and control by the parent company, or as *joint ventures,* with ownership and control shared between the parent company and one or more local partners, who usually represent a local company. An international company may start a sole venture from scratch (new establishment) or by acquiring a local company (acquisition).

Factors Influencing the Choice of the Entry Mode

A company's choice of its entry mode for a given product/target country is the net result of several often conflicting forces. The variety of forces, difficulties in measuring their strength, and the need to anticipate their direction over a future planning period combine to make the entry mode decision a complex process, with numerous trade-offs among alternative entry modes. To handle this complexity, managers need an analytical model that facilitates systematic comparisons among entry modes. This model is introduced in Chapter 7, after the reader has become familiar with the benefit/cost features of individual entry modes. For the present, we offer a general review of the external and internal factors that influence the choice of entry mode.

These factors are designated in Figure 3. The following comments are intended to be only suggestive of their influence.

External Factors

Market, production, and environmental factors in both the target and home countries can seldom be affected by management decisions. They are external to the company and may be regarded as parameters of the entry mode decision. Because no single external factor is likely to have a decisive influence on the entry mode for companies in general (although it may have for an individual company), one can only say that such factors encourage or discourage a particular entry mode.

Target Country Market Factors. The present and projected *size* of the target country market is an important influence on the entry mode. Small markets favor entry modes that have low break-even sales volumes (indirect and agent/distributor exporting, licensing, and some contractual arrangements). Conversely, markets with high sales potentials can justify entry modes with high break-even sales volumes (branch/subsidiary exporting and equity investment in local production).

Another dimension of the target market is its *competitive structure:* markets can range from atomistic (many nondominant competitors) to oligopolistic (a few dominant competitors) or monopolistic (a single firm). Atomistic markets are usually more favorable to export entry than oligopolistic or monopolistic markets, which

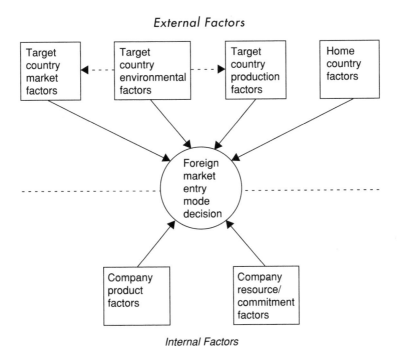

External Factors

| Target country market factors | Target country environmental factors | Target country production factors | Home country factors |

Foreign market entry mode decision

| Company product factors | Company resource/ commitment factors |

Internal Factors

FIGURE 3

Factors in the Entry Mode Decision

often require entry via equity investment in production to enable the company to compete against the power of dominant firms. In target countries where competition is judged too strong for both export and equity modes, a company may turn to licensing or other contractual modes.

Another dimension of the target country market that deserves mention is the availability and quality of the local *marketing infrastructure*. For instance, when good local agents or distributors are tied to other firms or are simply nonexistent, an exporting company may decide that the market can be reached only through a branch/subsidiary entry mode.

Target Country Production Factors. The quality, quantity, and cost of raw materials, labor, energy, and other productive agents in the target country, as well as the quality and cost of the economic infrastructure (transportation, communications, port facilities, and similar considerations) have an evident bearing on entry mode decisions. Low production costs in the target country encourage some form of local production as opposed to exporting. Obviously, high costs would militate against local manufacturing.

Target Country Environmental Factors. The political, economic, and sociocultural character of the target country can have a decisive influence on the choice of entry mode. Perhaps most noteworthy are *government policies and regulations* pertaining to international business. Restrictive import policies (high tariffs, tight quotas, and other barriers) obviously discourage an export entry mode in favor of other modes. The decision of several Japanese automobile companies to manufacture vehicles in the United States instead of exporting them from Japan was largely a response to actual and potential U.S. import restrictions. Similarly, a restrictive foreign investment policy generally discourages equity investment in favor of other primary modes, and may discourage sole ventures in favor of joint ventures or acquisitions in favor of new establishments. In contrast, a target country may encourage foreign investment by offering such incentives as tax holidays.

Another environmental factor is *geographical distance*. When the distance is great, transportation costs can make it impossible for some export goods to compete against local goods in the target country. Thus high transportation costs discourage export entry in favor of other modes that do not incur such costs. When "knock-down" shipments substantially reduce transportation costs, it may be possible for an exporting company to compete by establishing an assembly operation in the target country, representing only a modest shift to an investment entry mode.

Many features of the target country's economy can influence the choice of entry mode. The *size* of the economy (as measured by gross domestic product), its *absolute level of performance* (gross domestic product per capita), and the relative importance of its economic sectors (as a percentage of gross domestic product) relate closely to the market size for a company's product in the target country. Still other features pertain to the *dynamics* of the target country's economy: the rate of investment, the growth rate of gross domestic product and personal income, changes in employment, and the like. Dynamic economies may justify entry modes with a high break-even point even when the current market size is below the break-even point.

International managers should also examine the target country's *external economic relations:* the direction, composition, and value of exports and imports, the balance of payments, the debt service burden, exchange rate behavior, and so on. Substantial one-way changes in external economic relations are indicators of probable future changes in government policies on trade and international payments. For example, a persistent weakening of a country's balance of payments commonly leads to import and/or payment restrictions (particularly in developing countries) and/or devaluation of the exchange rate. Each of these prospective changes will have a different influence on entry modes. Although import restrictions discourage export entry, exchange controls that limit the repatriation of income and capital tend to discourage equity entry more than other modes. When the exchange rate is allowed to depreciate, the effect is to discourage export entry and, at the same time, encourage equity investment entry.

Sociocultural factors also influence a company's choice of entry mode. Of general significance is the *cultural distance* between the home country and target country societies. When the cultural values, language, social structure, and ways of life of the target country differ strikingly from those of the home country, international managers are more inclined to feel ignorant about the target country and fearful of their capacity to manage production operations there. Furthermore, great cultural distance usually makes for high costs of information acquisition. Thus a substantial cultural distance favors nonequity entry modes that limit a company's commitment in the target country.

Cultural distance also influences the time sequence in the choice of target countries, because companies tend to enter first those foreign countries that are culturally close to the home country. For that reason (as well as because of physical proximity) Canada is a favorite first-entry country for equity investment by U.S. companies. Because managers are much more confident about their capacity to run operations in a target country that is culturally close to the home country, they are more willing to choose high-commitment entry modes than would otherwise be the case.

In closing this brief overview of environmental factors, we should mention the influence of political risk on entry modes, a subject treated in Chapter 6. When international managers perceive high political risks in a target country, such as general political instability or the threat of expropriation, they favor entry modes that limit the commitment of company resources. Conversely, low political risks encourage equity investment in a target country.

Home Country Factors. Market, production, and environmental factors in the home country also influence a company's choice of entry mode to penetrate a target country. A big domestic market allows a company to grow to a large size before it turns to foreign markets. As the reader will see later, when large companies go abroad, they are more inclined than small companies to use equity modes of entry. (Another effect of a large domestic market is to make companies more domestically oriented and less interested in *all* forms of international business than firms in small-market countries.) Conversely, companies in small-market countries are attracted to exporting as the way to reach optimum size with economies of scale.

The competitive structure of the home market also affects the entry mode. Firms in oligopolistic industries tend to imitate the actions of rival domestic firms that threaten to upset competitive equilibrium. Hence, when one firm invests abroad, rival firms commonly follow its lead. Because oligopolists are unlikely to view a rival's exporting or licensing activities as a competitive threat, oligopolistic reaction is biased toward investment in production. Indeed, the bulk of U.S. investment abroad has been made by companies in oligopolistic industries. In contrast, companies in atomistic industries are more inclined to enter foreign markets as exporters or licensors.

Two other home country factors deserve mention. High production costs in the home country relative to the foreign target country encourage entry modes involving local production, such as licensing, contract manufacture, and investment. The second factor is the policy of the home government toward exporting and foreign investment by domestic firms. When the home government offers tax and other incentives for exporting but at the same time is neutral or even restrictive on foreign investment, then its policy is biased in favor of exporting and licensing or other contractual modes of foreign market entry.

Internal Factors

How a company responds to external factors in choosing an entry mode depends on internal factors.

Product Factors. International product policies are taken up in Chapter 3. For the moment we are concerned only with how product factors influence the entry mode.

Highly *differentiated* products with distinct advantages over competitive products give sellers a significant degree of pricing discretion. Consequently such products can absorb high unit transportation costs and high import duties and still remain competitive in a foreign target country. In contrast, weakly differentiated products must compete on a price basis in a target market, which may be possible only through some form of local production. Hence high product differentiation favors export entry, while low differentiation pushes a company toward local production (contract manufacture or equity investment). The great majority of U.S. exports of manufactures consists of highly differentiated products.

A product that requires an array of *pre- and postpurchase services* (as is true of many industrial products) makes it more difficult for a company to market the product at a distance. Ordinarily the performance of product services demands proximity to customers; thus service-intensive manufactured products are biased toward branch/subsidiary exporting and local production modes of entry.

If a company's product is itself a *service,* such as engineering, advertising, computer services, tourism, management consulting, banking, retailing, fast-food services, or construction, then the company must find a way to perform the service in the foreign target country, because services cannot be produced in one country for export to another. Local service production can be arranged by training local companies to provide the service (as in franchising), by setting up branches and subsidiaries (such as an advertising agency or branch bank), or by directly selling the service under contract with the foreign customer (as in technical agreements and construction contracts).

Technology-intensive products give companies an option to license technology in the foreign target country rather than use alternative entry modes. Since technology intensity is generally higher for industrial products than for consumer products, industrial-products companies are more inclined to enter licensing arrangements than consumer-products companies. The latter can, of course, license their trademarks, but only after they have achieved an international reputation.

Products that require considerable *adaptation* to be marketed abroad favor entry modes that bring a company into close proximity with the foreign market (branch/subsidiary exporting) or into local production. The latter is indicated when adaptation would require new production facilities and/or the adapted product could not be sold in the domestic market. Until the 1980s, for example, Ford and General Motors manufactured vehicles in Europe that were fundamentally different from the vehicles they manufactured at home.

Resource/Commitment Factors. The more abundant a company's resources in management, capital, technology, production skills, and marketing skills, the more numerous its entry mode options.

Conversely, a company with limited resources is constrained to use entry modes that call for only a small resource commitment. Hence company size is frequently a critical factor in the choice of an entry mode.

Although resources are an influencing factor, they are not sufficient to explain a company's choice of entry mode. Resources must be joined with a willingness to *commit* them to foreign market development. A high degree of commitment means that managers will select the entry mode for a target country from a wider range of alternative modes than managers with low commitment. Hence a high-commitment company, regardless of its size, is more likely to choose equity entry modes.

The degree of a company's commitment to international business is revealed by the role accorded to foreign markets in corporate strategy, the status of the international unit, and the attitudes of managers. For most companies, international commitment has grown along with international experience over a lengthy period of time. Success in foreign markets has encouraged more international commitment, which in turn has led to more success. Conversely, failure early in a company's international experience can reverse or limit its commitment.

Table 2 summarizes the influence of external and internal factors on the choice of entry mode. It reaffirms the earlier statement that a company's selection of its entry mode for a target/product country is the net result of several often conflicting forces.

Dynamics of Entry Mode Decisions

Once started in international business, a company will gradually change its entry mode decisions in a fairly predictable fashion. Increasingly, it will choose entry modes that provide greater control over foreign marketing operations. But to gain greater control, the company will have to commit more resources to foreign markets and thereby assume greater market and political risks. Growing confidence in its ability to compete abroad generates progressive shifts in the company's trade-off between control and risk in favor of control. Consequently the evolving international company becomes more willing to enter foreign target countries as an equity investor.

TABLE 2
External and Internal Factors Influencing the Entry Mode Decision

	Generally Favors:				
	Indirect and Agent/ Distributor Exporting	Licensing	Branch/ Subsidiary Exporting	Equity Investment/ Production	Service Contracts
External Factors (Foreign Country):					
Low sales potential	X	X			
High sales potential			X	X	
Atomistic competition	X		X		
Oligopolistic competition				X	
Poor marketing infrastructure			X		
Good marketing infrastructure	X				
Low production cost				X	
High production cost	X		X		
Restrictive import policies		X		X	X
Liberal import policies	X		X		
Restrictive investment policies	X	X	X		X
Liberal investment policies				X	
Small geographical distance	X		X		
Great geographical distance		X		X	X
Dynamic economy				X	
Stagnant economy	X	X			X

TABLE 2 (continued)

	Generally Favors:				
	Indirect and Agent/ Distributor Exporting	Licensing	Branch/ Subsidiary Exporting	Equity Investment/ Production	Service Contracts
Restrictive exchange controls	X	X			X
Liberal exchange controls				X	
Exchange rate depreciation				X	
Exchange rate appreciation	X		X		
Small cultural distance			X	X	
Great cultural distance	X	X			X
Low political risk			X	X	
High political risk	X	X			X
External Factors (Home Country):					
Large market				X	
Small market	X		X		
Atomistic competition	X		X		
Oligopolistic competition				X	
Low production cost	X		X		
High production cost		X		X	X
Strong export promotion	X		X		
Restrictions on investment abroad	X	X			X
Internal Factors:					
Differentiated products	X		X		

TABLE 2 (continued)

	Generally Favors:				
	Indirect and Agent/ Distributor Exporting	Licensing	Branch/ Subsidiary Exporting	Equity Investment/ Production	Service Contracts
Standard products				X	
Service-intensive products			X	X	
Service products		X		X	X
Technology-intensive products		X			
Low product adaptation	X				
High product adaptation		X	X	X	
Limited resources	X	X			
Substantial resources			X	X	
Low commitment	X	X			X
High commitment			X	X	

The evolution of a manufacturing firm's entry mode decisions is depicted in Figure 4. Because of constraints imposed by size, some companies may not evolve beyond branch/subsidiary export, while other companies move on to joint and sole ventures in local production. Since the export mode is not available to them, service companies will follow a different evolutionary path, but the direction will also be toward greater management control (and greater risk).

Table 3 offers a verbal description of four stages in the international evolution of a manufacturing company. Stage 4 denotes the multinational company, which designs its foreign market entry strategies from a global perspective rather than a single-country perspective, a subject taken up in Chapter 10. For the present discussion, the key distinction between stage 1 and stage 4 is the willingness of managers to choose an entry mode for a given prod-

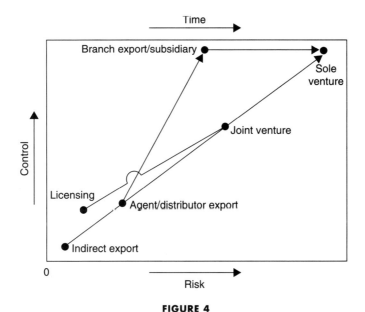

FIGURE 4

Evolution of a Manufacturer's Decision on Entry Mode

uct/target country from the full range of entry modes. Stage 1 managers are constrained to one or two entry modes; stage 4 managers are able to evaluate all possible entry modes to select the most appropriate one.

Changes in internal factors, particularly a growing commitment to foreign markets, are the principal forces shaping a company's international evolution. But external factors, as described earlier, are the most influential forces shaping a company's entry mode decision for a *specific* product or target country. That is why a stage 4 company may use all the primary entry modes (exporting, contractual arrangements, and investment in production) to penetrate country markets throughout the world. The multinational company has taken to heart the injunction that there are many ways to skin the international business cat.

Changes in external factors in the foreign target country may encourage or force a company to revise its entry mode. It is vital, therefore, that a company continually monitor external factors in the target country and be prepared to revise its entry mode in order to sustain or strengthen its market position.

TABLE 3

Stages in the International Evolution of an Enterprise

Stage 1: Indirect/ad hoc exporting	Indirect exporting or the servicing of occasional, unsolicited export orders. May also include unsolicited licensing arrangements. Weak commitment to foreign markets.
Stage 2: Active exporting and/or licensing	Efforts to penetrate foreign markets through agent/distributor or branch/subsidiary exporting. May include active solicitation of licensing arrangements. International business viewed as separate and distinct from domestic business.
Stage 3: Active exporting, licensing, and equity investment in foreign manufacture	Efforts to penetrate foreign markets involve manufacture in some countries, combined with exporting and/or licensing in other countries. An international division with authority over all forms of international business replaces the export department. But international business is not integrated across countries and regions, nor is international business strategy integrated with domestic business strategy.
Stage 4: Full-scale multinational marketing and production	Multiple national markets are served from multiple national sources. Some companies replace the international division with a companywide production organization based on geographical area. Other companies replace it with a companywide organization based on product. Hence the home country is treated as the one of many national markets in which the company "happens" to have its corporate headquarters.

The International Marketing Plan

The design of a company's market entry strategy for a given product/target country requires the formulation of a marketing plan as well as the choice of an entry mode. The entry mode is intended to penetrate the foreign target *country;* the marketing plan is intended to penetrate the foreign target *market.*

The foreign marketing plan is an action program that specifies marketing objectives and goals; policies and resource allocations to achieve the objectives and goals; and a time schedule. The plan

TABLE 4
The International Marketing Plan: Instruments of Action

Product	A combination of tangible and intangible attributes that confer benefits on users. These attributes form three subsets: physical, package (including trademark), and service (pre- and postpurchase). A given product may have one, two, or all three dimensions.
Price	Price is the exchange ratio between a product and money. A company's pricing discretion is dependent on the degree of product differentiation achieved in the market. Together with sales volume, price determines sales revenue.
Channel	A chain of marketing agencies that links the producer to its final buyers. The distinctive channel flow is a series of transactions that ultimately transfer ownership to final buyers. The producer may own none, some, or all of its channel agencies.
Logistics	A chain of agencies that accomplishes the physical movement of a product from the producer to the final buyers. Logistic activities include transportation, handling, and storage, as well as the choice of production location.
Promotion	All communications initiated by a seller that are addressed to final buyers, channel members, or the general public and are intended to create immediate sales or a positive image for the seller's product and/or company. Promotion includes personal selling, advertising, sales promotion, and publicity.

also includes an analysis of the target market, a description of the market environment, a competitive audit, a financial analysis, and a control system. The foreign marketing plan is examined in Chapter 8, and only some preliminary comments are offered here.

Plan objectives may include objectives for sales volume, market share, profits, and return on investment, for marketing effort as well as (setting up a distribution network, reaching an advertising goal, positioning the product, and so on).

To design a marketing plan, managers must make decisions on the product, pricing, channels, logistics, and promotion. Taken together, these decisions compose the "marketing mix" of the plan. These five policy areas are described in Table 4.

The foreign marketing plan is intimately related to the entry mode. Most significantly, the entry mode determines the degree of

Entry Strategies for International Markets

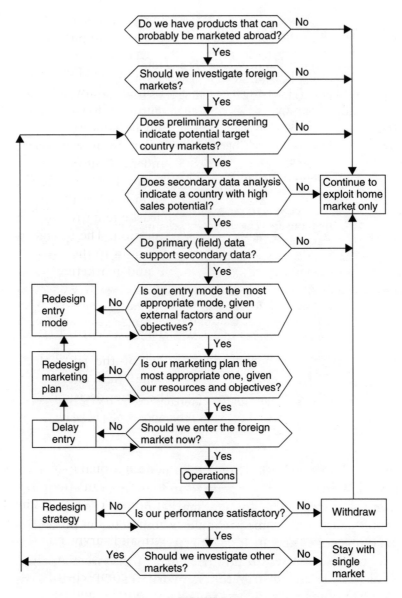

FIGURE 5

A Logical Flow Model of the Entry Decision Process

a company's *control* over the marketing program in the target country. Some entry modes (indirect exporting and pure licensing) allow a company little or no control over the marketing program. Other modes afford limited control (agency/distributor exporting and joint ventures), while still others allow full control (branch/subsidiary exporting and sole ventures). Regardless of the entry mode, however, a company should be concerned with the marketing of its product in a target country. Even when its product is marketed under the direction of independent outside firms, a company's profits will depend on the market performance of those firms. Furthermore, a company cannot select the most appropriate entry mode unless it makes at least a tentative marketing plan for the product/target market in question. The foreign marketing plan becomes, therefore, a critical input to the entry mode decision. Decisions on the entry mode and marketing plan are truly *joint* decisions.

A Logical Flow Model of the Entry Decision Process

Figure 5 presents a logical flow model of the entry decision process. In the remainder of this text we shall flesh out this model, with the intent of helping managers make better decisions.

Summary

1. Companies become committed to international markets only when they no longer believe that they can attain their strategic objectives by remaining at home. The point is not that all companies should go international, but rather that all companies should plan for growth and survival in a world of global competition.

2. International market entry strategy is a comprehensive plan setting forth the objectives, goals, resources, and policies that will guide a company's international business operations over a future period long enough to achieve sustainable growth in world markets. For most companies the entry strategy's time horizon is from three to five years.

3. Product/market entry strategies require decisions on (1) the choice of a target product/market, (2) the objectives and

goals in the target market, (3) the choice of an entry mode to penetrate the target country, (4) the marketing plan to penetrate the target market, and (5) the control system to monitor performance in the target market.

4. International market entry modes may be classified as export, contractual, and investment entry modes. A company's choice of its entry mode for a given target country is the net result of several often conflicting forces.

5. Once started in international business, a company will gradually change its entry mode decisions in a fairly predictable fashion. Increasingly, it will choose entry modes that provide greater control over international marketing operations. But to gain greater control, the company will have to commit more resources to foreign markets and thereby assume greater market and political risks.

6. The foreign marketing plan is an action program that specifies marketing objectives and goals; policies and resource allocations to achieve the objectives and goals; and a time schedule. To design a marketing plan, managers must make decisions on the product, pricing, channels, logistics, and promotion.

7. Decisions on entry mode and the marketing plan are truly joint decisions.

CHAPTER 3

Deciding on the International Product Candidate and Target Market

I n planning international market entry strategies, managers are striving to match products against markets. Which products shall we market abroad? To which countries? These are the two key questions at the start of the planning process. It follows that decisions on international products and markets involve the simultaneous determination of a candidate product and a target market.

This chapter elaborates the first box in Figure 2 (p. 23). To simplify that elaboration, we assume that the company is considering international market entry for the first time. We also focus on the choice of a *single* target product/market; entry strategies for multiple products in multiple country markets are treated in Chapter 10. We begin by examining the choice of a candidate product for foreign market entry and then turn to the choice of a target market. The latter step involves an overview of country markets, screening country markets, and estimating industry market potentials and company sales potentials.

Choosing the Candidate Product

The most critical element in planning international market entry strategies is the choice of the product. A company with a single product needs only to decide whether that product is a suitable candidate for international market entry, that is, one with good enough prospects to warrant an investigation of foreign markets. But the majority of companies with two or more products must decide which of these products is the best candidate for expansion abroad.

Product Screening

Product screening is intended to save time and money by indicating which of a company's products, if any, justifies a systematic appraisal of international markets. The profile of an ideal product candidate drawn up by a company's managers would probably include the following features: ready market acceptance, high profit potential, availability from existing production facilities, and suitability for marketing abroad in much the same way as at home. Only some companies will have a product that rates highly on all these features, but a candidate product must possess certain advantages that will allow it to obtain a competitive niche in foreign markets. These advantages may be low price or distinctive features (quality, design, technical superiority, and the like) that differentiate the candidate product from rival products.

For the most part, U.S. manufacturers must rely on product differentiation rather than price to achieve a competitive position in foreign markets, although price can seldom be ignored as an influence on buying decisions. Hence a good candidate product is almost always found among a company's most competitive products in the home market. Conversely, a product not competitive at home is a poor candidate for foreign markets. A good candidate product may face a mature or declining market at home, however, if its life cycle is more advanced at home than abroad.

Company managers need to appraise each product by getting answers to the following questions:

- Is this product competitive at home? What are its competitive strengths and weaknesses?
- What need (or needs) does this product serve in the domestic market? Do these same needs exist in foreign markets? If they do, which products currently meet those needs in foreign markets? If they do not, can this product serve other needs that do exist in foreign markets?

- How new is this product to foreign markets? How much competition is it likely to encounter? What competitive advantages and disadvantages does this product have in foreign markets?
- Does this product have the same use conditions in foreign markets as in the home market?
- Does this product require after-sales services or complementary products for its use? Are they available in foreign markets?
- Does this product have to be adapted to foreign markets in one or more of its physical, package, and service attributes?
- Can this product be marketed abroad the same way as at home?

Answers to these questions relating to foreign markets are seldom specific at this early planning stage prior to a systematic investigation of international markets. But even answers based on general knowledge should help managers choose a candidate product.

The Global Product Life Cycle

The concept of a product life cycle can also assist managers in choosing a candidate product for foreign markets. All generic products experience a life cycle whose shape and duration varies from one product to another and from one country market to another for the same generic product. The conventional product life cycle is depicted in Figure 6.

In the *introduction* phase, the product is new to the market and the innovating company strives to develop an awareness of the product's benefits and to obtain a trial use by early adopters. In the *growth* phase, sales of the product move up rapidly due to the cumulative effects of promotion and distribution efforts by the innovating company and by rival companies that now enter the market with their own versions of the product. In the *maturity* phase, sales growth continues but at a diminishing rate while competition intensifies as rival sellers try to maintain market shares. In the *saturation* phase, sales reach a plateau determined by the level of replacement demand, and rival sellers defend their brands against other brands and against other (newer) substitute prod-

American movies, music, TV programs, and home video account for an annual U.S. trade surplus of $8 billion. Only aircraft exceeds popular culture as a U.S. export. In a few years, the foreign revenues of Hollywood studios should be more than their domestic revenues. The American music business (mainly rock and roll) gets more than 70 percent of its sales, which total $20 billion a year, outside the United States. Sales of U.S. television programs in Europe are estimated at $600 million a year. Of course, not all pop culture is American; about one-fifth of the world's rock and roll is British, and about three-quarters of the music sold in Japan is by Japanese artists. But fascination with U.S. pop culture drives the global market.

It has become apparent that there is now a single global youth culture. Only three years old, MTV Europe has attracted 20 million viewers, becoming a powerful international advertising medium. European and Japanese firms have invested heavily in the U.S. pop culture business. Of five global record companies, only Warner is an American corporation. Of the eight major Hollywood film studios, only Disney, Orion, Paramount, and Warner have U.S. owners. Matsushita (Japan) acquired MCA in 1990 for $7 billion, and Sony (Japan) bought CBS Records in 1988 for $2 billion.

Adapted from "America's Hottest Export: Pop Culture," *Fortune*, December 31, 1990, pp. 50–60.

ucts. As individual company products lose their differentiation and price competition becomes more intense, sellers direct their efforts at cutting production and marketing costs. Competition becomes relatively stable unless a seller makes substantial improvements in the generic product. In the *decline* phase, sales start to drop as the product is progressively replaced by a new generic product. Several competitors abandon the product while others try to "milk" the product of all possible profits.

The life cycle concept is ordinarily used by managers to analyze the dynamics of a given target country market over time, but it can also be used to identify the relative positions of a generic product in several country markets at the same time. This *global* product life cycle is shown in Figure 7.

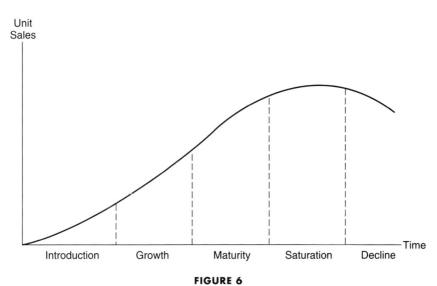

FIGURE 6

Life Cycle of a Generic Product in a Target Market Over Time

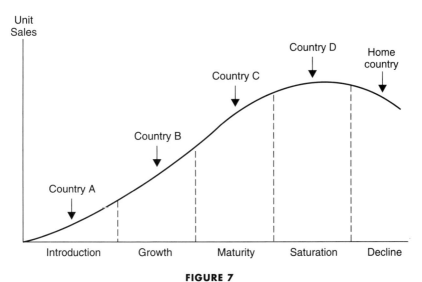

FIGURE 7

Global Life Cycle of a Generic Product at a Given Time

Firms in the United States and a small number of other advanced countries introduce most of the new consumer and industrial products. Generally, new products are first commercialized in the home market and then spread to other country markets at varying speeds. At any one time, therefore, a product occupies different phases of the global life cycle in different countries. It is at the most advanced phase in the home country and the next most advanced phase in other industrial countries, while it is at earlier phases in developing countries. Indeed, it may not have been introduced at all in the least developed countries. At some time in the future, the global life cycle will run its course as the generic product in question experiences saturation and decline in all country markets.

The global product life cycle has important implications for companies contemplating international market entry. A company that faces a saturated or declining home market for its product may be able to exploit growth opportunities in foreign markets in earlier phases of the product cycle. To put the matter another way, managers should look for a candidate product that occupies early phases of the life cycle abroad. Also, since different national markets have different *imitation lags* with respect to the home (innovating) country, the global product life cycle can help managers in the selection of foreign target markets.

As communication among national markets improves and as more countries come closer to matching the affluence and sophistication of the United States and other advanced countries, product imitation lags become ever shorter. This speedup in global product life cycles means that companies must respond more quickly than in the past to foreign market opportunities. If a company delays foreign market entry, it is likely to find that its product type has already reached advanced phases of the life cycle in other industrial countries. Multinational firms are now introducing new products simultaneously in several national markets, and by so doing they are not only responding to the speedup of the global product life cycle but also adding to it.[1]

Adapting Products for International Markets

Manufacturers may need to adapt their products to foreign markets to gain a desired level of buyer acceptance. Adaptation may be called for in the physical product, the way in which the physical product is identified and presented to final buyers (product package), or the way in which the use of the physical product is facilitated and made effective (product services). Whether—and how—the several dimensions of a product should be adapted to the requirements of international markets should be decided only after answering many questions relating to potential consumers and users, environmental conditions, government regulations, competition, and the expected profit contributions of specific adaptation. Some issues to be addressed are as follows:

The Target Market
    Who buys the product?
    Who uses the product?
    How is the product used?
    Where is the product bought?
    How is the product bought?
    Why is the product bought?
    When is the product bought?

The Macroenvironment
    Geography
    Climate
    Economic
    Sociocultural
    Political/legal

Government Regulations
    Tariffs
    Labeling
    Patents/trademarks
    Taxes
    Other

Competition
    Price
    Performance
    Design or style
    Patent protection
    Brand name
    Package
    Services

Company's Product
   What should be its physical attributes (size, design, materi-
      als, weight, color, other)?
   What should be its package attributes (protection, color, de-
      sign, brand name, other)?
   What should be its service attributes (use instructions, instal-
      lation, warranties, repair/maintenance, spare parts, other)?
   What is the expected profit contribution of each product
      adaptation?

Although some product adaptation may be mandated by legal/
technical requirements or by climate, it is seldom an either-or proposition in all of the product's different dimensions. Ordinarily managers have considerable discretion in deciding how far to carry
product adaptation; how they use that discretion depends on the
other elements of their international market entry strategy. That is
why two companies with the same generic product may follow
different product strategies in the same target market.

   A product policy that limits adaptation to foreign markets may
be called a *product standardization* strategy. This strategy conceives a global market for the product. Although national differences may be recognized, managers assume that they can be overcome with a promotional effort that adapts consumers and users
to the company's product rather than the other way around. With
this strategy, products are the same across national markets. Standardization keeps down the costs of adaptation, but it incurs
higher costs of promotion intended to bring about a convergence
of disparate national demands on the company's product. At the
other extreme, a *product adaptation* strategy conceives multiple
national markets, taking account of differences that distinguish
those markets from one another and from the home market. With
this strategy, managers adapt a product to the preferences of each
national market or national submarkets. As compared to standardization, this strategy carries higher costs of adaptation but incurs lower costs of promotion that is intended to inform buyers
how well the product matches their preferences rather than to
change those preferences.

   Few companies can profitably follow a pure version of either of
these strategies. Some adaptation is nearly always desirable in one
or more product dimensions. Complete product adaptation implies

Ikea, a Swedish furniture retailer, was unknown outside Scandinavia two decades ago, but now it has become a global company with retail outlets in Europe, North America, and Asia. From 10 stores in five countries in 1974, Ikea had grown to 119 stores in twenty-four countries by mid-1993; 12 of these stores are in the United States. Starting in Sweden, Ikea expanded into Denmark and Norway in the 1960s, moved into other Western European countries in the 1970s, and entered the United States and other non-European countries in the 1980s. Ikea's sales in 1992 were $3.2 billion.

Ikea stores are distinctive in design and operation. Usually situated just outside a big city, these stores are large showrooms (about six times the size of the average supermarket) located next to huge self-service warehouses. To keep costs down and prices low, they sell unassembled furniture of simple Scandinavian design, offering a large selection of colors, styles, and materials. Customers are met at the door not by salespersons but with catalogs, tape measures, pens, and notepaper. Then they move through a store layout allowing them to look at merchandise, get information, and make purchase decisions without sales help. The key selling tool is a catalog with prices and specifications of all items on sale. Also, each furniture piece is graded on an A-B-C scale. Appealing to young householders, Ikea staff take care of young children in a playroom and even warm a baby's bottle. Each store has a restaurant and snack bar, featuring Swedish specialties at low prices. These services encourage browsing by customers. One service that Ikea does *not* provide is home delivery: customers pick up purchased items in the warehouses. Does this approach work? When Ikea opened a store in New Jersey in 1990, the response was phenomenal: the New Jersey turnpike was backed up for nine miles as twenty-six thousand shoppers crowded the store on the first day of business.

Ikea does little manufacturing: to keep prices down, it designs its furniture for low-cost manufacturing and distribution, contracting out production to eighteen hundred suppliers located in some fifty countries. It works closely with suppliers on material sourcing and production efficiency. Because orders for the global market are very large, suppliers are able to cut costs through economies of scale. Ikea follows certain principles in its global marketing plans. First, it tries to address universal needs with a core product assortment that consumers want around the world. Second, it tries to act locally by allowing store managers to add local products to the core product assortment and to adapt store operations to make shoppers feel comfortable. Third, Ikea believes in starting small and expanding gradually. All in all, Ikea has demonstrated that it is possible to differentiate even such a mature business as furniture retailing and to achieve global success with that differentiation.

Adapted from "Ikea's New Realities: Recession and Aging Consumers," *New York Times,* April 25, 1993, p. F4; "Ikea's Got 'Em Lining Up," *Fortune,* March 11, 1991, p. 72; and "A Swedish Company Corners the Business: Worldwide," *Management Review,* April 1991, pp. 10–13.

a different product for each individual buyer, a strategy that is out of the question for the vast majority of products. Generally, therefore, companies end up with a *hybrid* product strategy, whether or not they started that way. Because user needs and preferences are more similar across national markets for industrial products than for consumer products, strategies biased toward standardization are more common for the former, while the latter favor strategies based on adaptation. But industrial products can benefit from discretionary adaptation (particularly in after-sales services), and consumer products can benefit from standardization. The issue of adaptation versus standardization is examined in a multiple product/market context in Chapter 10.

Decisions on product adaptation should be made in reference to a specific target market. At the early planning stage of choosing a candidate product, therefore, managers can make only preliminary judgments on adaptation, drawn from a general knowledge of foreign markets. But this knowledge must be precise enough to indicate whether adaptation is necessary (or desirable) with respect to the physical, package, or service dimensions of the product. At times, mandatory adaptation may be so costly as to disqualify a product, but for most candidate products adaptation is seldom a black-and-white proposition. Some adaptations are nearly always desirable—for instance, the printing of package materials (and sales literature) in a language understood by foreign buyers. The language need not be a buyer's native tongue: English is satisfactory for former British colonies, French for former French colonies, and so on. Hence a label printed in three major languages can be understood in most country markets.

Preliminary Screening of Country Markets

After choosing the candidate product, company managers can turn to the identification of the country market with the highest sales potential. We discuss the process of deciding on the foreign target market according to the model presented in Figure 8. In this section we consider the first phase of the model: preliminary screening.

The purpose of preliminary screening is to identify country markets whose size warrants further investigation. Preliminary screening tries to minimize two errors: (1) ignoring countries that offer good prospects for a company's generic product, and (2) spending too much time investigating countries that are poor prospects. To minimize the first error, which is by far the more common, preliminary screening should be applied to *all* countries. Too often, managers start with assumptions or prejudices that rule out certain countries (or even regions) as possible target markets. Self-imposed constraints, such as "We will consider only markets in Europe," can lead to the choice of an inferior target market. To minimize the second error, preliminary screening should be quick and economical, using quantitative data that are readily available from public sources. At the same time, the data used as screening variables should discriminate among countries with respect to market size.[2]

In screening foreign markets for first-time entry, managers are most probably looking for an *export* target market. For the most part, countries are screened for investment entry only after a company has exported to them. Investment screening, which requires the assessment of many nonmarket factors, is treated in Chapter 6. Nonetheless, it is a mistake to make a first time screening solely for export markets. To do so could mean the rejection of a country that offers a good market for nonexport entry. Instead, preliminary screening should identify prospective target countries without regard to entry mode. Prospects can later be screened for export entry.

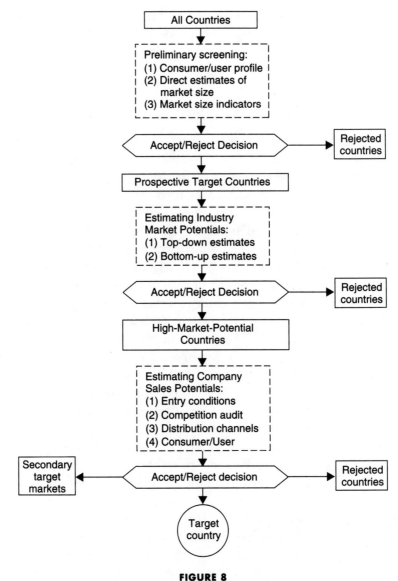

FIGURE 8

Model for Selecting a Target Country

Consumer/User Profile

Before undertaking preliminary screening, managers should first construct the *consumer/user profile* of the generic candidate product: the attributes of the individuals and/or organizations that are actual or potential customers. The profile embodies answers to the first group of questions listed in the preceding section—answers that managers have presumably already arrived at in choosing the candidate product. In drawing up the consumer/user profile, managers in companies just entering international business must rely mainly on their experience in the home market. For consumer products, the profile describes the typical consumer in one or more market segments in terms of characteristics such as income, social class, life style, age, and sex; for industrial products, it describes the size, input-output relationships, organization, and other features of typical customers in industries or government agencies that use or can use the candidate product.

The consumer/user profile guides managers in the selection of multicountry statistics that are most useful as indicators of market size.

Direct Estimates of Market Size

Preliminary screening requires a quick assessment of the market potential facing the candidate product in scores of countries. Estimates of market potential need to be only good enough to identify prospective target countries. Consider the market-potential equation $S_i = f(X_1, X_2, \ldots, X_n)$, where S_i is the potential sales of generic product i in a given country over the planning period and X_i through X_n are economic and social factors that collectively determine S_i. S_i may be estimated directly by projecting actual sales data (time series analysis) or by projecting the apparent consumption or imports of the product. Or S_i may be estimated indirectly by using projections of one or more of the X factors.

For most generic products, multicountry sales statistics are simply not available from published sources. Nor are managers likely to have access to the statistics needed to calculate the apparent consumption of the candidate generic product in the many countries undergoing preliminary screening, namely, local production *plus* imports *minus* exports. Even in the comparatively few instances when they are available, sales and apparent consumption figures may not be good indicators of market potential, because they are historical in nature. As observed earlier, a product is usually in different phases of its life cycle in different countries, and it may not even be present in some countries. When using sales or apparent consumption data, therefore, managers also need to estimate their likely values in the future. To do so, they can project sales or apparent consumption trends (based, say, on figures for the last three years) and check on their agreement with economic and social indicators.

Import/export data may also be used for direct estimates of market size. Ideally, managers would have easy access to statistics on imports of the candidate generic product for all countries, as well as on their country origins. They could then construct a global export/import matrix that would identify key import markets and key competitors. International managers, however, are seldom blessed with such data. International trade statistics, such as those appearing in *Commodity Trade Statistics* (published by the United Nations), use broad product categories that conceal many candidate products. Given a lack of multicountry data, managers can fall back on U.S. government statistics that show the country destinations of U.S. exports by 3,500 product categories.[3] These statistics can identify the leading country markets for U.S. exports of the candidate product, but they overlook any major importing countries that obtain the product mainly from exporters other than the United States.

To conclude, international trade statistics are at best only a partial measure of market potential; their usefulness is limited by a historical bias, distortions created by trade barriers, and broad product categories. Low imports do not necessarily imply a small market potential: import restrictions or local production may be the explanation. In preliminary screening, trade statistics are most useful when combined with economic and social indicators.

Indirect Estimates of Market Size

Because of the general paucity of multicountry data on product sales, and because of their historical bias, a manager must rely on quantitative economic/social statistics as indicators of market potential. For preliminary screening, these market indicators should be readily available for all countries and be comparable across countries. Many such multicountry indicators appear in publications of the United Nations, the International Monetary Fund, the World Bank, and other international agencies. A partial list of economic and social statistics available from only a few United Nations sources follows.[4] The most commonly used general indicators of market size are GDP (or GNP), GDP per capita, average growth rates of GDP, and imports.

National Account Statistics
1. National income, gross domestic product, and net material product
2. Expenditure on gross domestic product, and net material product by use
3. National income and national disposable income
4. Gross domestic product and net material product by kind of economic activity
5. Gross domestic product and net material product at constant prices

Population and Manpower
1. Population by sex, rate of increase, surface area, and density
2. Employment/hours of work in manufacturing
3. Unemployment
4. Scientific and technical manpower and expenditure for research and development

Production
1. Agriculture/forestry/fishing/mining
2. Index numbers of industrial production
3. Manufacturing production (food, textiles, paper, rubber products, chemicals, building materials, metals, transportation equipment)
4. Construction (output and employment, activity)
5. Energy (output and employment in electricity, gas, and water supply)

International Trade
1. Imports by end use
2. Exports by industrial origin
3. Source/destination of imports and exports
4. Imports/exports by commodity

Other Economic Statistics
1. Transportation (railways, international seaborne shipping, civil aviation traffic, motor vehicles in use, international tourist travel)
2. Wages and prices (earnings in manufacturing, index numbers of wholesale prices, consumer price index numbers)
3. Consumption (total and per capita consumption of steel, fertilizers, newsprint, and other commodities)
4. Finance (balance of payments, exchange rates, money supply, international reserves)

Social Statistics
1. Health (hospital establishments and health personnel)
2. Education (number of teachers and school enrollment, public expenditures on education)
3. Culture (number of books produced by subject and language, number of radio and television receivers—total and per capita)

Managers should choose as indicators those economic/social statistics that most closely match the consumer/user profile of the candidate product. If, for example, the product is a household appliance, then private consumption expenditure on durable goods is a better indicator than gross domestic product. If the product is a machine, then industrial production in the appropriate sector is superior to manufacturing as a percentage of gross domestic product. Ordinarily, several indicators do a better screening job than only one.

Accept/Reject Decisions

The fundamental accept/reject decision rule used in preliminary screening may be expressed as follows: If $S_{i,j} \geq a$ (where $S_{i,j}$ is the market size for product i in country j and a is a threshold value in dollars, units, rank order, or an index), then accept the country as a prospective target country for further investigation. But since $S_{i,j}$ is estimated by using several indicators, managers can interpret this rule in more than one way.

One interpretation is to establish minimum values for *all* the selected market indicators, rejecting those countries whose indicators fall below them. This interpretation assumes that a country's market size is critically dependent on each indicator and that a high value for one indicator cannot offset a low value for another one. If this assumption is false, then faulty screening is a likely consequence.

A second interpretation is to consider one or a few indicators as decisive and reject all countries whose decisive indicators fall below minimum values, regardless of the values of their other indicators. If the indicator or indicators are truly decisive measures of market size, then this approach is defensible, but then there is no need for managers to collect information on any other indicators in screening for market size.

In most instances, the most satisfactory interpretation of the accept/reject rule is a weighted average of the selected indicators. The weights assigned to the individual indicators reflect the judgment of managers as to the relative influence of those indicators on market size. To calculate a weighted average, managers need to express the values of the indicators in a common unit (say, as percentages). One approach is the construction of a multiple-factor index. Accept/reject decisions are then made in terms of a minimum index value or in terms of a country's rank order.

In applying their accept/reject rule, managers identify a group of prospective target countries that represent only a small fraction of the 150 or so countries in the world. They may then decide to narrow down the list of accepted countries by applying criteria other than market size. This practice is not recommended for preliminary screening, but it is more defensible when employed *after* countries have been screened for market size, for then managers can better appraise the opportunity cost of rejecting a country. Political instability is probably the most common reason to reject a country that offers good market potential for a candidate product.

Estimating Industry Market Potentials

After preliminary screening, the next stage of the target market selection model depicted in Figure 8 is a more refined estimate of the market potentials for the candidate generic product in the comparatively small number (say, fifteen) of prospective target countries.

Industry market potential (IMP) is defined as the most probable total sales of a product by all sellers in a designated country over a strategic planning period.[5] IMP, then, is total industry sales projected over a lengthy future period, say, three to five years. It is management's judgment of how big the industry market is now and how it is likely to grow in the future.

Two fundamental approaches may be used by managers to estimate industry market potentials. The *top-down* approach can be depicted as follows: IMP $= f(X_1, X_2, \ldots, X_n)$, where X_1 through X_n are a set of predictor variables that have an established relationship to industry sales. A common technique to determine those relationships is a regression analysis of historical data. As seen earlier, this approach is well suited to preliminary screening where economic/social statistics are used as predictor variables (indicators). It is also well suited to making IMP estimates for consumer products that are sold to very large numbers of final buyers. To illustrate, one might estimate the IMP for television sets by using the following predictor variables: number of households, percentage of population literate, percentage of population living in urban areas, percentage of population in nonagricultural activities, per capita income, index of standard of living, price per unit, and price per unit/per capita income. The coefficients of these variables could be obtained from a regression analysis of historical sales of television sets.

The *bottom-up* approach can be expressed as follows: IMP $= S_1Q_1 + S_2Q_2 + \ldots + S_nQ_n$, where S represents the number of final users in each segment comprising the total industry market and Q represents the average quantity of the candidate product type purchased by users in each segment. If actual purchase data are available for these segments, then IMP may be estimated with time series analysis. Other sources of estimation include surveys of buyer intentions and expert opinion. Since purchase data are rarely available and buyer surveys and expert opinion polls are likely to be costly and time-consuming when many countries are being investigated, it is usually desirable for managers to estimate the Q values indirectly by relating sales to some characteristic of the actual or potential users making up each segment. Conceptually, this involves a reformulation of the preceding equation: IMP $= a_1U_1 + a_2U_2 + \ldots + a_nU_n$, where the U variables represent the output, employment, or other characteristics of the different user groups (market segments) and the *a* variables represent the use coefficients that relate the amount of product used to the *U* variables. Thus a_1 might represent the amount of component materials, the number of component parts, or the amount of operating supplies per unit of output, and U_1 the output (actual or potential) of users in that segment.

The bottom-up approach is best suited to industrial products or, more generally, products that have a limited number of identifiable end users. It requires managers to (1) identify the actual and potential uses of the candidate product (the basis of the consumer/user profile), (2) identify the actual and potential users (S_1 through S_n) for each use in the prospective target country, and (3) estimate the actual and potential use of the product by each user segment. The latter requires information on industrial category, size, output, and other characteristics of user firms, on the current use of substitute products, on the ability of firms to buy the candidate product, and on other factors that influence purchase decisions.

The top-down and bottom-up approaches are complementary. Whenever feasible, managers should use both. Divergent top-down and bottom-up estimates call for a reconsideration of both estimates; convergent estimates justify confidence in their accuracy.

Managers are concerned with two dimensions of an industry market potential: (1) the absolute size of the current market, and (2) the projected growth of the market over the strategic planning period. The accept/reject decision, therefore, involves a trade-off between size and growth. This trade-off is illustrated by the nine-cell matrix in Figure 9.

In practice, company managers would assign specific percentages to the three growth categories in Figure 9 and specific dollar or quantity amounts to the three size categories. If a country were to fall in cell 3, it would be clearly acceptable as a high market potential country, because it offers a large, high-growth market. Conversely, if a country were to fall in cell 7, it would be clearly unacceptable as a high market potential country. But what about countries falling in the other cells? The accept/reject designation of these cells would depend on the growth/size trade-off established by company managers, a conditionality indicated by ques-

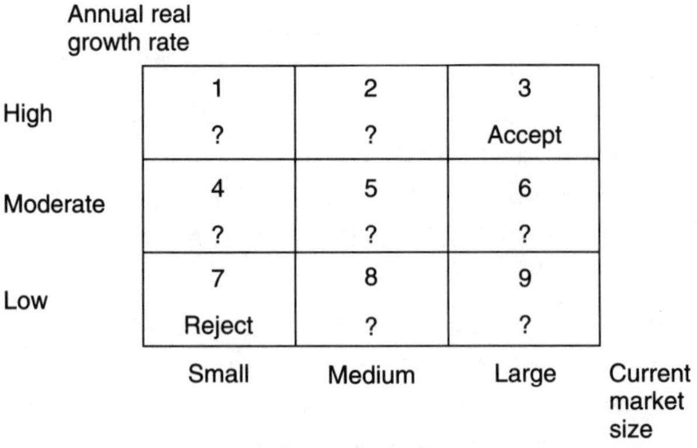

Annual real
growth rate

	Small	Medium	Large
High	1 ?	2 ?	3 Accept
Moderate	4 ?	5 ?	6 ?
Low	7 Reject	8 ?	9 ?

Small   Medium   Large   Current
market
size

FIGURE 9

Accept/Reject Matrix for Selection of Countries with High Market Potential

tion marks. If, for example, large market size were deemed very important, then managers might accept a country falling in cell 9, despite its low growth. Conversely, if high growth were deemed critical, managers would reject a country falling in cell 9 but accept a country falling in cell 1, despite its small market size. In short, there are no absolute accept/reject standards; the accept/reject rule is itself a management decision. Whatever the rule used by managers, we assume in this exposition that certain countries are accepted as high market potential countries (say, five in number). The next stage in the selection of a foreign target market is to estimate the sales potentials for the company's own product in those countries.

Estimating Company Sales Potentials

We define *company sales potential* (CSP) as the most probable sales of a company's product in a designated country over a strategic planning period, given assumptions with respect to entry mode and marketing effort.[6] Company sales potential may also be viewed as a company's most probable share of a country's industry market potential. CSP depends not only on external market factors but also on a company's international market entry strategy. Different strategies will generate different CSPs. Specifically,

CSP depends on the entry mode (export, investment, licensing, and other contractual arrangements) and on the level of marketing effort in the marketing plan (resources committed to product, pricing, distribution, and promotion policies).

To estimate company sales potential, therefore, managers need to make assumptions about their company's entry mode and international marketing plan. As we shall stress in later chapters, managers should make systematic comparisons of alternative entry modes in searching for the right mode. An input in those comparisons is the CSP of each entry mode—that is, the cash inflow (revenues) projected over the strategic planning period. It follows that decisions on the target country, the entry mode, and the marketing plan are joint decisions.

In this discussion of company sales potential, we assume that the company is entering foreign markets for the first time. A derivative assumption is that company managers prefer export entry. We must stress, however, that the target selection model offered in Figure 8 is *not* linked to a given entry mode. Rather, its purpose is to identify the country with the highest CSP. Once the identification is made, it is up to company managers to decide on the entry mode that can best exploit that potential. For that reason the managers of our representative company should not immediately reject a high-IMP country because it cannot be entered via exports. Instead, they should go on to complete the CSP profile of that country by estimating sales potential based on local production of the company's product. In short, it is important for managers to identify countries with high CSP, regardless of the feasibility of export entry or any other single entry mode. The starting point is market opportunity for the company's candidate product; how that opportunity is best exploited comes later. Although company resources and other factors may constrain a company to some form of export entry now, international managers should consider the entry mode, as well as the marketing plan, as decision variables over the longer run.

Figure 10 is presented as an aid in making CSP estimates for high-IMP countries and in comparing them across countries. For our representative company, the first area of investigation is an appraisal of *export entry conditions:* (1) import regulations and (2) transportation and other logistical costs to move the product

High-IMP Countries

	1	2	3	4 - - - - n	
Industry market potential					
Export entry conditions					
Nonexport entry conditions					
Competitive audit					
Availability of distribution channels					
Consumers/ Users					
Required marketing effort					
Company sales potential					
Overall rating as target country					

FIGURE 10

Company Sales Potential Matrix for Selecting the Target Country/Market

from the home country to the foreign country in question. Import regulations, which are mainly restrictive, include import duties and nontariff trade barriers, such as border taxes, health regulations, quotas, industrial standards, and antidumping laws. In most instances, import regulations add to the cost of export entry; at the extreme, they render export entry unprofitable or impossible. Managers need to ascertain export entry conditions and the attendant costs for their candidate product for each high-IMP country. For the reason mentioned earlier, managers should also review nonexport entry conditions, but at this stage only to a degree sufficient to establish the feasibility (as contrasted to the desirability) of nonexport entry.

The significance of export entry costs for CSP depends mainly on the capacity of the candidate product to absorb those costs and still remain competitive in the foreign market. This brings us to a second area of investigation: a *competitive audit* of each high-IMP country audit. The following questions need to be answered in such an audit:

Basic Information
1. Which competitive products are sold in country X?
2. What are the market shares of competitive products?
3. How do competitive products compare with our own in reputation, features, and other attributes?
4. Which support facilities (production, warehousing, sales branches, and so on) do competitors have in country X?
5. Which problems do competitors face?
6. Which relationships do competitors have with the local government? Do they enjoy special preferences?

Marketing Information
1. Which distribution channels are used by competitors?
2. How do competitors' prices compare with our own?
3. What credit terms, commissions, and other compensation are extended by competitors to their channel members?
4. What promotion programs are used by competitors? How successful are they?
5. How good are competitors' postsales services?

Market Supply Information
1. How do competitive products get into the market?
(If they are imported:)
2. Who are the importers?
3. How do importers operate?
4. What credit, pricing, and other terms are extended to importers by foreign suppliers?
5. How long has each importer worked with its foreign supplier? Is it satisfied with its supplier?
(If they are produced locally:)
6. Who are the producers?
7. Are the producers entirely locally owned, or is there foreign participation?
8. What advantages do local manufacturers have over importing competitors?

Comparisons between the company's product and those of competitors should go beyond price to encompass quality, design, and other features of product differentiation. Nor should comparisons be confined to the physical product; they should also be made for package and service dimensions. Again, comparisons should be made among all products that satisfy the same function or need. In the final analysis, the company is competing not against other products but for the favor of potential customers.

Managers should also assess other aspects of the marketing effort of potential competitors—namely, their pricing, channel, and promotion policies. It is wise to focus on the market leaders, who can be expected to offer the stiffest competition. What are the sources of each leader's strength? Low prices? Product quality? Distribution? Service? Something else?

Another element of the competitive audit is an appraisal of *market structure*. What is the degree of monopoly in the market? Is competition rigorous or loose? Market structure bears directly on ease of entry for a newcomer. Some country markets have strong associations of local producers who bend their collective efforts to keep out foreign intruders. Other country markets are dominated by a few big firms with a host of small followers. Still other country markets may have no dominant firms and a loose competitive structure that facilitates entry.

A third area of investigation is the *availability of distribution channels* for the company's product. CSP analysis of channel structure is limited to questions of channel availability: Can we obtain adequate distribution of our product in this country? Can we match the distribution of the market leaders? Are there any distribution bottlenecks that would require extraordinary marketing effort (and time) to overcome? As we shall observe in discussing export entry, good distribution is vital to an effective marketing plan.

A fourth area of investigation is the ultimate *consumer/user* of the company's product in high-IMP countries. Evidently, the more managers know about the final consumers or users of their product in these countries, the better they can estimate company sales potentials. Answers to the questions under "The Target Market" on page 51 indicate the key attributes of potential customers. Although a thorough assessment of consumers or users may not be cost-effective when management is undertaking comparative CSP evaluation, managers should try to get enough information to make confident judgments on the probable responses of consumers or users in each country to the company's product and other elements of its marketing plan. As observed earlier, it may be possible to improve consumer/user responses through product adaptations of one sort or another. Once a target country is chosen, the design of the marketing plan will call for a fuller investigation of final consumers or users. Hence we shall return to this subject in Chapter 8.

The end result of these investigations is a *sales potential profile* for each high-IMP country. Managers now know whether their company can compete in each country and what marketing effort will be needed to do so. They are also able to project the sales of the company's product over the strategic planning period. In most instances, they should select the country with the highest sales potential as the target country. But managers committed to export entry will reject the country with the highest sales potential if it has negative entry conditions. More generally, sales potential estimates may not fully capture all the factors of interest to managers, such as risk. Hence the overall rating of a country is not necessarily identical with its CSP. Sales potential profiles are informed judgments by managers rather than the outcome of routine calculations. It is seldom possible to quantify all the many market factors, and it is even more difficult to relate them to sales potential. In this respect, we should also recall that the *highest* sales potential in a given country is conditional on the choice of an optimum entry mode, which is the subject of the next four chapters.

Summary

1. The most critical element in planning international market entry strategies is the choice of the product. A candidate product must possess certain advantages that will allow it to obtain a competitive niche in foreign markets. Managers need to decide which of their products justifies a systematic appraisal of foreign markets.
2. The concept of a product life cycle can assist managers in choosing a candidate product for foreign markets. Managers should look for a candidate product that occupies early phases of the life cycle abroad.

3. A product policy that limits adaptation to foreign markets may be called a product standardization strategy. At the other extreme, a product adaptation strategy takes account of differences among country markets in decisions on the physical, package, and service attributes of a candidate product. Few companies can profitably follow a pure version of either strategy.

4. After choosing the candidate product, company managers can turn to the identification of the country market with the highest sales potential. The first phase of the target selection model is preliminary screening, which is applied to all countries. Preliminary screening should be quick and economical but also comprehensive. Before undertaking preliminary screening, managers should construct the consumer/user profile of the candidate product type: the attributes of the individuals and/or organizations that are actual or potential customers.

5. Because of the general paucity of multicountry data on product sales, and because of the historical bias of such data, managers must rely on quantitative economic and social statistics as indicators of market potential. In applying their accept/reject rule, managers identify a group of prospective target countries that represent only a small fraction of the 175 or so countries in the world.

6. After preliminary screening, the next stage of analysis is a more refined estimate of the market potentials for the generic candidate product in the comparatively small number of prospective target countries. Industry market potential (IMP) is defined as the most probable total sales of a product by all sellers in a designated country over a strategic planning period. Top-down or bottom-up approaches may be used to estimate IMPs. The accept/reject decision involves a trade-off between size and growth.

7. The third stage of the target selection model is estimating company sales potentials (CSPs) for high-IMP countries. Company sales potential is defined as the most probable sales of a company's product in a designated country over a strategic planning period, given assumptions with respect to entry mode and marketing effort. A CSP matrix may be used by managers as an aid in drawing up CSP profiles for

individual countries and making comparisons among them. In most instances, managers should select the country with the highest sales potential as the target country, but the overall rating of a country is not necessarily identical with its CSP.

Annotated Bibliography of International Statistical Information

United States Department of Commerce

Foreign Trade Reports, FT 410. Monthly. U.S. exports by product and country of destination. Uses five-digit Schedule B classification for products.

Guide to Foreign Trade Statistics. Latest edition. Identifies and describes the coverage of all foreign trade reports and tabulations prepared by Census.

Index to Foreign Market Reports. Monthly. Lists all the *Foreign Market Reports* prepared by Department of Commerce by country and SIC product code.

Statistical Classification of Domestic and Foreign Commodities Exported from the United States (Schedule B Manual). Latest edition. Describes Schedule B product classifications used in all official U.S. export statistics.

United Nations

Commodity Trade Statistics, Series D. Annual. Imports and exports of member countries by SITC product classifications.

Current Economic Indicators. Quarterly. Lists about five hundred economic indicators for the world's countries.

Monthly Bulletin of Statistics. Monthly supplement to *Statistical Yearbook.*

Statistical Yearbook. Data for more than 150 countries on broad range of economic and social subjects, including population, manpower, mining, agriculture, construction, manufacturing, trade, and national accounts.

Yearbook of National Account Statistics. Per capita gross domestic product, national income, disposable income, expenditure on gross domestic product, annual growth rates, and other aspects of national accounts.

Yearbook of International Trade Statistics. Imports and exports by unit and value for 132 countries.

Organization for Economic Cooperation and Development

Foreign Trade Bulletins, Series C. Semiannual. For the twenty-one OECD countries, this publication gives in two volumes (imports and exports) the quantity and value of international trade for 272 commodity categories.

Main Economic Indicators. Monthly. Indicators include national accounts; industrial production; deliveries, stocks, and orders; construction; retail sales; and other data for the twenty-one OECD countries.

Statistics of Foreign Trade, Series A. Monthly. Shows total trade statistics for each OECD country, including the composition of trade by SITC categories.

Other International Organizations

International Monetary Fund. *International Financial Statistics.* Monthly. Data for 104 countries on exchange rates, balance of payments, international reserves, money supply, prices, interest rates, and other subjects.

World Bank (International Bank for Reconstruction and Development). *World Bank Atlas.* Annual. Population, gross domestic product, and average growth rates for every country in the world.

World Bank. *World Bank Catalogue of Publications.* Latest edition. Listing of all World Bank publications, free and for sale.

Private Sources

Exporters Directory/U.S. Buying Guide. Phillipsburg, New Jersey: The Journal of Commerce. Latest edition. Includes a nationwide directory of 40,000 U.S. exporters, and an SITC product index listing 1,300 products together with their U.S. exporters.

Exporters Encyclopedia. Parsippany, New Jersey: Dun's Marketing Services. Updated annually, this publication covers in-depth shipping and marketing information on more than 220 world markets.

Inter-Trade Center File of Information Services. New York: World Trade Center. Computer storage of sources of all types of information related to international trade, according to function, subject matter, institution, country or region, and commodity.

Sources of European Economic Information. New York: Unipub. Latest edition. Describes nearly two thousand statistical bulletins, yearbooks, general publications, directories, and reports for seventeen European countries.

World Data Bank. New York: Marketing Control, Inc. Stores forty-six commercial descriptors, forty-eight socioeconomic descriptors, and forty-four geopolitical descriptors for forty-five major countries.

CHAPTER 4

Entering International Markets Through Exports

A fter deciding on its target country market and product, a company must decide on the most appropriate entry mode. In this chapter we examine the advantages and disadvantages of alternative export entry modes and the requirements of direct export: selecting foreign agents and distributors, establishing sales branches or subsidiaries, learning about export procedures and documentation, making payments arrangements, and organizing for export. We open with a discussion of the reasons exporting is the most common way for a manufacturer to enter international business for the first time.

Exporting as a Learning Experience

To go international for the first time, a company must overcome anxieties about its ability to compete in foreign markets. The neophyte international firm therefore is more concerned with minimizing international market and political risks that with maximizing control over international marketing operations. Given this situation, exporting will usually appear to the manufacturer as the best entry mode.

By using indirect channels, a firm can start exporting with no incremental investment in fixed capital, low startup costs, few risks, and profits on current sales. Furthermore, the firm can gradually increase its export effort by building on prior success in foreign markets: adding products to the export line, entering new target markets, and shifting to direct exporting. Thus exporting enables a firm to adopt an exploratory, experimental behavior to obtain knowledge about foreign markets and its ability to compete in them. In other words, exporting can become an *international learning experience,* a development process that takes the firm toward more and more international sophistication and commitment.[1]

Figure 11 depicts the effect of this learning experience on risk perception. At the start, the company has no experiential knowledge of foreign countries and markets, and this felt ignorance generates uncertainties that cause managers to perceive foreign business risks as far higher than domestic business risks. But as the company gains knowledge and confidence from actual export experience, perceived foreign risks decline to approach the level of perceived domestic risks. At the same time, rational decision making displaces or limits the behavioral factors (fears, anxieties, ethnocentric biases, and so on) that dominated earlier decision making. Managers now consider direct export modes that allow greater control over the foreign marketing effort; risk is balanced against opportunity. Thus the firm moves along the path of entry mode dynamics as described in Chapter 2.[2]

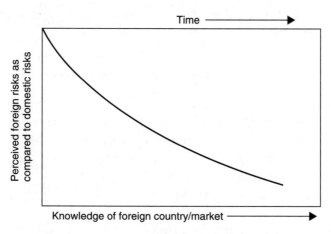

FIGURE 11

Exporting as a Learning Experience

Licensing and equity investment in foreign production do not offer the advantages of exporting as a first learning experience. Although licensing is also easy to initiate with low startup costs, it is available only to manufacturers that have technology or trademarks desired by foreign firms. Moreover, the return on licensing is ordinarily limited in both size and duration. Apart from these constraints, licensing simply does not afford managers a learning experience comparable to exporting, because the marketing of licensed products is controlled by the foreign licensees. Nonetheless, in some instances licensing can be the most attractive entry mode for a neophyte firm. Licensing can also provide an export entry for intermediate products, and a licensing arrangement later may be transformed into a joint or even sole manufacturing venture.

Equity investment in foreign production is seldom used by manufacturers new to international business. Direct investment should be made only after a company has an intimate understanding of the investment climate, the market, competition, and production in the target country. This formidable knowledge requirement can seldom be met by a neophyte international company. Furthermore, equity investment often demands a substantial capital investment and, at the same time, exposes the investor to political risks that are largely absent in exporting. Although a joint venture can facilitate an early entry into equity foreign production, it too requires knowledge and skills unlikely to be possessed by a company without prior international experience. In short, for a manufacturing firm to start its international learning experience with equity foreign production is akin to a person learning to swim by jumping into deep water: learning would be intense, but the cost of failure would be very high.

Direct Exporting

To get its product into a foreign target market, a company can use any one of several export modes or channels. The principal export channels are depicted in Figure 12. The key distinction among these alternative channels is the presence or absence of independent export agencies located in the home country. When a manufacturing firm uses domestic agencies, it does not undertake ex-

Most U.S. exporters are small companies. One survey of fifty-one thousand exporters found that more than forty-four thousand employed fewer than five hundred workers. Most of these companies are closely held or family enterprises. Small companies are now using fax machines, toll-free telephone numbers, and overnight delivery services to cut export costs. Life Corporation (U.S.), a manufacturer of emergency oxygen kits with $5 million in sales, ships its products mostly by air to forty-three countries. The company tries to answer fax inquiries on the day they are received, and then sends videotapes of its kits by air express. Exporters are finding that toll-free numbers can bring frequent calls from foreign customers. AT & T, MCI and Sprint offer phone hookups that allow small exporters to send electronic-mail messages to their distributors' computers. In this way, Sharper Finish (U.S.), a manufacturer of commercial laundry equipment with $3 million in sales, keeps in close contact with three hundred distributors in thirty countries. Bigger companies use satellite computer hookups. Royal Appliance Manufacturing (U.S.), maker of the Dirt Devil hand-held vacuum with sales of $273 million, links its computers to its European subsidiaries by satellite. Each day's sales figures are sent back to U.S. headquarters in Cleveland. These and other innovations, such as credit cards and satellite TV channels, have greatly lowered barriers to export by small companies.

Adapted from "Little Companies, Big Exports," *Business Week,* April 13, 1992, pp. 70–72.

porting on its own and has at most a marginal role in the foreign marketing of its product. That is why exporting through domestic intermediaries is called indirect exporting.

Indirect exporting may be a good way for a firm to enter foreign markets for the first time. But with the qualified exception of export management companies, indirect exporting does not allow a manufacturing firm to have its own international market entry strategy. Indirect exporting demands little if any foreign country/market knowledge on the part of the manufacturer, but for the same reason, it insulates the manufacturer from foreign markets. Thus a company that wants active penetration of international

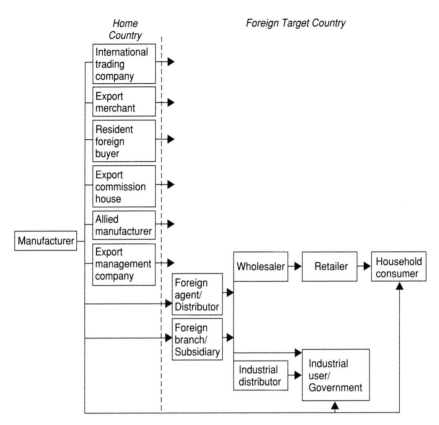

FIGURE 12

Principal Indirect and Direct Export Channels

markets will look to direct export channels. Since this book deals with international market entry strategies, we shall consider indirect exporting only in the final section of this chapter, where we address companies that have not yet entered international business.

Direct exporting offers several advantages to the manufacturer: (1) partial or full control over the foreign marketing plan (distribution, pricing, promotion, product services, and so on); (2) concentration of marketing effort on the manufacturer's product line; (3) more and quicker information feedback from the target market, which can improve the marketing effort with, say, closer product adaptation or more responsive pricing; and (4) better protection of trademarks, patents, goodwill, and other intangible property.

But these advantages can be realized only when the exporting firm assumes responsibility for the international marketing effort in carrying out its entry strategy.

Direct exporting also requires that the manufacturer learn the procedures and documentation of export shipments and international payments arrangements. Thus direct exporting has higher startup costs, greater information requirements, and higher risks than indirect exporting.

Direct exporting relies on two principal channels: the foreign agent/distributor channel and the foreign branch/subsidiary channel.[3] A third and less common channel is direct contact between the manufacturer and final buyers in the target market, such as mail-order exporting and the use of company representatives working out of the home country. As Figure 12 indicates, a direct export channel is an element of the full marketing channel, and its selection therefore is both an entry mode decision and a marketing plan decision.

It is reasonable to regard the marketing channel in a foreign target country as an extension of a direct export channel. Accordingly, we define a direct export channel as the chain of marketing agencies that links a domestic manufacturing company to the *final* buyers (or users) of its product in the foreign target market. These agencies negotiate sales transactions, direct the physical movement and storage of the product, and provide other services in order to place the product ultimately in the ownership and possession of final buyers where, when, and in the quantities they want it. The foreign agencies participating in a direct export channel may be independent middlemen or owned by the manufacturer; they may be many or few in number. Since the first and last links in the direct export channel are the manufacturer and final buyers, respectively, it is logical to consider them also as channel elements. It is important for manufacturers to conceive the export channel as the full marketing channel rather than as a channel that stops with the foreign distributor or agent.

Foreign marketing agencies—agents, distributors, sales branches, sales subsidiaries, wholesalers, and retailers—are distinguished from *facilitating* agencies such as transportation companies, public warehouses, forwarders, customs brokers, banks, advertising agencies, consultants, and government agencies. Facilitating agencies provide services to the manufacturer that are necessary or

Recent innovations—inexpensive fax machines, international toll-free calling, the spread of credit cards, and faster air courier delivery—have promoted mail-order exporting from the United States. Efficient service, coupled with a variety of products not offered by local merchants (or offered only at high prices), is persuading foreign shoppers to phone, fax, or mail orders for all sorts of products, including electronic equipment, clothing, and golf clubs. For example, Express Technology, a computer software company located in Arizona, sells its products *only* to overseas buyers. It has order takers who speak Spanish, German, French, and Japanese on duty mostly from 2:00 A.M. to 9:00 A.M. Express Technology has worked out mail delivery arrangements with Airborne Express, United Parcel Service, and DHL Worldwide. Running advertisements in computer magazines in Western Europe and Latin America, the company emphasizes its guarantee of satisfaction, including a refund of postage costs to return any defective merchandise. In 1991 Express Technology's sales reached $4.5 million.

Not until 1990 did L. L. Bean, located in Maine, set up an international department to push foreign sales. After only one year, the department grossed $38 million, 6 percent of Bean's total sales. Sharper Image, located in San Francisco, markets electronic gear to some seven thousand overseas customers annually from its regular catalogue. Its average overseas order is $400, compared to $150 for an average domestic order. Austad's, a golfing equipment company in North Dakota, responds to fax orders coming from countries all over the world. Its sales to Japan almost doubled between 1991 and 1992. Dell Computer, located in Texas, entered Europe in 1987 with mail-order marketing even though its managers knew that European customers had never bought big-ticket items such as computers through the mail. In every country, Dell managers were told that mail order would not work. But by the start of 1992 European sales (mainly to business customers) had reached $240 million a year, nearly 30 percent of Dell's total corporate sales. Advertising in computer magazines and direct mailings, Dell stressed its reputation for quality, service, and price. It backed up that reputation with deliveries in about two days and with monthly calls to customers to make sure everything was satisfactory. Dell was also helped by European computer prices that were twice those in the United States.

Adapted from "The Latest in Buzzwords: Mailed from America," *New York Times*, August 16, 1992, p. F4; and "Dell: Mail Order Was Supposed to Fail," *Business Week*, January 20, 1992, p. 89.

helpful to the export process, but they do not engage in export sales transactions or control the marketing effort as channel members do.

Determining the Direct Export Channel

To make a rational determination of a direct export channel for a target country/market, managers need to make decisions on three levels. First, they must decide what the channel is intended to accomplish (determining *performance specifications*). Second, they need to decide which channel (or channel mix) is optimum by matching their performance specifications against alternative channel systems, with due regard paid to costs (determining *channel type*). Finally, having determined the most appropriate channel type (or types), managers need to develop criteria to guide the selection of individual channel members (determining *channel members*).

Determining Performance Specifications

To determine their performance specifications for a direct export channel, managers should answer the following questions:

- What geographical market coverage do we want in the target country?
- How intensive should our market coverage be?
- What specific selling and promotion efforts do we want from channel agencies?
- What physical supply services (for example, volume and location of inventories and delivery systems) do we want from channel agencies?
- What pre- and postpurchase services (for instance, credit, installation, maintenance, and repair) do we want from channel agencies?

Answers to these and similar questions, which depend on a company's objectives in the target country (reflecting the nature of the market and competition), its product, and its marketing plan, constitute the performance specifications of the channel.

The desired intensity of market coverage deserves special comment because it has implications for channel control, pricing policy, promotion, and other elements of the export marketing plan. If a company wants *intensive* or blanket coverage of a dispersed market, then it will need many channel members, especially at the final-buyer level. It will be inclined to use multiple channels with little or no interest in protecting any one channel. Intensive coverage encourages heavier reliance on advertising and less direct promotional support of channel members. Intensive coverage also limits channel control, because intermediaries have no particular allegiance to the manufacturer and can easily resist its efforts to influence their behavior.

More commonly, a company adopts a policy of *selective* market coverage. At the extreme, a selective policy uses a single agent or distributor (or sales branch/subsidiary) who is given exclusive selling rights in a designated territory that may embrace the entire target country. Exclusive distribution arrangements offer the exporting company more control over channel performance, but in turn they demand protection and active support. A policy of selective distribution may fall short of exclusive distribution by using a limited number of agents or distributors to cover the market.

Determining the Channel Type

Even with the guidance of performance specifications, the determination of the most appropriate channel type is a difficult task. For one thing, managers will be trying to satisfy several channel objectives—sales volume, low costs, control, the cooperation of channel members, and so on—that can seldom be met fully by any given channel system. Furthermore, their ability to estimate the sales potentials and costs of alternative channels is commonly limited by insufficient and/or unreliable information. Inevitably, therefore, the determination of the most appropriate channel becomes a screening process that leans heavily on qualitative assessments and judgment. Even so, managers should endeavor to estimate the profit contributions (incremental revenues minus incremental costs) of alternative channels over the entry planning period.

The first screening step for most companies is to compare the branch/subsidiary channel against the agency/distributor channel. The principal appeal of the former is control. When the salesmen of a branch call directly on final buyers (as is common for many industrial products but not for consumer products), then the manufacturer controls the full marketing channel. When branch salesmen call on wholesalers and retailers, the manufacturer has only partial control over the full marketing channel, but it is still greater than with a channel using foreign agents or distributors. Channel control is significant because with control a company can more nearly develop a channel that meets its specifications. The importance of channel control depends, therefore, on how closely alternative channels meet performance specifications. Only when alternative channels are inadequate in this respect will the branch/subsidiary channel afford higher sales over the entry planning period, and then only if the manufacturer makes the necessary commitment of resources.

The possibly superior performance of the branch/subsidiary channel is acquired at the cost of a higher break-even sales volume. Agency/distributor costs are mostly *variable* costs (commissions and markups) tied to sales volume, but a substantial fraction of branch/subsidiary costs are *fixed* costs that represent office and storage facilities and permanent working capital needed to finance administrative/marketing overheads, minimum inventories, minimum accounts receivable, a minimum sales force, and so on.[4] The key question, then, becomes at which level of sales (if any) in the target market, branch/subsidiary unit sales costs will fall below agent/distributor unit sales costs. Next comes the question of whether the manufacturer can reasonably plan to reach that sales level over the entry planning period.

To sum up, the choice between a branch/subsidiary channel and an agency/distributor channel depends on both expected performance (how closely the channel matches specifications) and costs. Managers should try to estimate the profitability of alternative channels through contribution analysis over the planning period. But they may reject the most profitable channel because it fails to meet a critical specification. For example, manufacturers of technical products who are proud of their quality image will not use agents or distributors who cannot offer proper service backup to customers, even if that channel is the most profitable. As a consequence, they may refuse to sell to small country markets that cannot justify a branch/subsidiary channel. More generally, manufacturers are inclined to use an agent/distributor channel for initial market entry because of the higher risks associated with a branch/sub-sidiary channel.

If a manufacturer decides to use an agent/distributor channel, then a second screening step compares foreign agents against foreign distributors in the target country. A *foreign agent* is an independent middleman who represents the manufacturer in the target country. The agent does *not* take title to the manufacturer's goods, and he or she seldom holds any inventory (beyond samples) or extends credit to customers.[5] The agent's primary task is to make sales to other middlemen (wholesalers, retailers, and so on) or to final buyers, and he or she may also provide some technical services. Thus the agent is essentially a salesperson, and his or her compensation is ordinarily a commission based on sales. When the manufacturer receives an order from the foreign agent, it bills the buyer and ships the goods directly to him or her.

A *foreign distributor* is an independent merchant who takes title to the manufacturer's goods for resale to other middlemen or final

Gamble Brothers (U.S.), a manufacturer of cabinet doors and drawers with five hundred employees, started its export business by appointing an agent in the United Kingdom. It then extended export sales to Ireland, Spain, France, the Benelux countries, and Greece. In the first two years, export sales reached $3 million. The company's export manager emphasizes the importance of "old-fashioned" homework to gain a knowledge of all aspects of exporting, including finance, freight, currency differences, buying methods, and local customs. Pure Water (U.S.), a maker of water purification systems, is another story of export success. For much of its quarter-century history, its exports were minimal. But now they have grown to 70 percent of company sales, as Pure Water responds immediately to foreign customers by faxing a reply on the same day as the inquiry is received. Senior management is fully committed to exporting, extending an open invitation to overseas distributors to visit the company's plant in the United States.

Adapted from "Exporting Pays Off," *Business America*, June 1, 1992, p. 12, and November 2, 1992, p. 24.

buyers. In addition to assuming ownership risks, the distributor performs more functions than the agent, including stocking inventories, promotion, extending customer credit, order processing, physical delivery, and product maintenance and repair. The distributor's compensation is his or her profit margin.

The analytical approach to choosing between an agent channel and a distributor channel is the same as that used to choose between the primary branch/subsidiary and agency/distributor channels. Managers need to evaluate how closely each alternative channel matches their channel specifications and how alternative channel costs compare over the entry planning period. In general, the distributor assumes a fuller range of functions but is more difficult to control than the agent. When comparing costs, it is necessary to consider *all* incremental channel costs—not only agent commissions and distributor functional discounts, but also the cost of all channel functions assumed by the manufacturer (in-channel promotion, stocking, handling, shipping, order processing, final-buyer services, credit, and so on). Although agent commissions may be substantially below the functional discounts granted to distributors, the cost of an agent channel may be greater when account is taken of all the channel costs.

With expected sales figures and incremental cost estimates in hand, managers can calculate the respective profit contributions of the agent and distributor channels over the entry planning period. But not all channel performance specifications are captured by expected sales. If a critical specification can be met by only one of the channels (say, customer services), then it will be chosen even when it has a lower profit contribution. Considerations of control, risk, and legal factors may lead to a similar result.

Up to this point we have assumed that the manufacturer will use only one channel type in the target country. But if the manufacturer seeks to penetrate two or more distinctive market segments in the target country, it may find that multiple channels are more appropriate than any single channel. For example, the manufacturer might decide on a distributor channel to cover the replacement market, but an agent channel (or its own salesmen) to sell to the original-equipment market. Or again, the manufacturer might use an agent for sales to local (or small) customers, but sell directly to multinational firms doing business in the target country or to large customers. When a company uses multiple channel types in a target country, it should take care to define the "jurisdiction" of each channel in its contractual arrangements.

Summing up, the determination of the channel type calls for a two-step screening process that involves trade-offs among control, profitability, performance specifications, and risks. In general, the shorter the channel used by the manufacturer, the greater the latter's control, but also the greater its resource commitment and risk. Over time these trade-offs may shift with changes in the company's resources, products, and marketing plan or with changes in the market, competition, channel systems, and government laws and regulations. Hence the most attractive direct export channel may become obsolete in the future. For this reason manufacturers should avoid getting locked into a given channel system beyond the entry planning period.

Choosing a Foreign Agent/Distributor

When a company decides that its most attractive export channel is an agent or distributor channel, it must then initiate a screening process to choose individual agents or distributors.[6] Finding good foreign distributors and agents is a major problem for manufacturers, and it demands considerable attention and effort. In this section we shall focus on choosing a distributor, but what we have to say is fully applicable to choosing an agent.

The screening process to choose a foreign distributor has four phases: (1) drawing up the distributor profile, (2) locating distributor prospects, (3) evaluating distributor prospects, and (4) choosing the distributor.

The Distributor Profile

The distributor profile lists all the attributes that a company would like to get in its distributor for a foreign target market. In effect, the profile is an adaptation of the company's channel performance specifications, and it therefore reflects the product, marketing ob-

Medical Graphics (U.S.), a maker of diagnostic systems to detect lung and heart disease with sales of $11 million, went international in 1987. Three years later, its international sales had grown to 30 percent of total company sales. As of 1993 Medical Graphics has twenty-one distributors in Western European and Pacific Rim countries. In 1990 the company set up its first sales subsidiary in Germany, replacing a poorly performing distributor. This entry decision was also influenced by the large sales potential in Germany and the commitment to the European market that the subsidiary would demonstrate to Medical Graphics' distributors and customers in the region. The German subsidiary also provides marketing and technical support for the company's distributors in nine other European countries. Medical Graphics, however, does *not* plan to establish any other subsidiaries. It favors distributors because they are less expensive and less risky than sales subsidiaries. Start-up costs for its German subsidiary were three times the typical start-up costs for a distributor system ($50,000 compared to $15,000). Also, distributors know the local market. Medical Graphics undertakes a thorough market research before choosing a distributor.

Adapted from "Balancing Overseas Sales Costs," *North American International Business,* August 1990, pp. 44–46.

jectives, and the marketing plan. It includes the following specifications, as well as any others of concern to the manufacturer:

- Trading areas covered
- Lines handled
- Size of firm
- Experience with manufacturer's or similar product line
- Sales organization and quality of sales force
- Physical facilities
- Willingness to carry inventories
- After-sales servicing capability
- Knowledge/use of promotion
- Reputation with suppliers, customers, and banks
- Record of sales performance

- Cost of operations
- Financial strength/credit rating
- Overall experience
- Relations with local government
- Knowledge of English or other relevant languages
- Knowledge of business methods in manufacturer's country
- Willingness to cooperate with manufacturer

Screening Distributor Prospects

Information on prospective distributors in a target country may be obtained from numerous sources: government agencies, banks, manufacturers exporting complementary lines, trade associations, trade publications, transportation agencies, freight forwarders, trade fairs, advertising agencies, directories, chambers of commerce, unsolicited inquiries, personal visits, and others. When using these sources to identify prospective distributors, the manufacturer should look for prospects who appear to match its profile.

After the manufacturer has developed a prospect list, it needs to obtain more information for a second screening. The most direct way to do this is by writing a letter to each prospective distributor, asking about the latter's interest in handling the manufacturer's product line and for information relating to the items in the distributor profile developed in the preceding step. Bank references and names of the distributor's suppliers in the manufacturer's own country are particularly helpful information items, because they can be checked personally by the manufacturer.

Several of the letters will probably go unanswered either because a distributor is not interested in the manufacturer's product line or because he or she already handles a competitive product line. To lower the proportion of nonresponses, the manufacturer's first letter to prospective distributors should be a *sales* letter that promotes the product line by citing its competitive advantages and sales potential in the distributor's country, important customers in the home country, and the manufacturer's reputation. It is a good idea, therefore, for the manufacturer to send sales literature along with the letter.

Evaluation of the responses to the first letter, checks with bank and supplier references, and other information provide the basis for a second screening. Next, a follow-on letter can be sent to the remaining prospects, asking each distributor to outline the marketing plan he or she would use for the manufacturer's product line (the manufacturer can design a special form for this purpose), the support he or she would want from the manufacturer (including functional discounts), expected sales volume, and any other information pertinent to the manufacturer's profile. Given this information from responses to the second letter, as well as information from other sources, the manufacturer is able to determine a limited number of "best" prospects.

It is strongly advised that the manufacturer make a final choice only after a round of personal interviews with all the best prospects. Apart from providing answers to specific questions and laying the ground for contract negotiation, personal interviews are the best way for the manufacturer to judge whether it can work with the distributor in carrying out the marketing plan. There is simply no substitute for face-to-face meetings to gain a "feel" for the distributor and his or her organization. The final choice of a distributor is well worth the time and money for personal visits, because the success of the marketing plan will depend mainly on his or her efforts. Furthermore, if the manufacturer makes a bad choice, it will be time-consuming and sometimes costly to undo the arrangement. There is an old saying in the export business: "Your line is only as good as your distributor or agent."

Negotiating the Distributor Contract

The ultimate choice of a distributor is the outcome of a negotiation in which the distributor chooses the manufacturer, as well as the other way around. This is particularly true of good distributors who already handle the lines of several reputable manufacturers and are frequently asked to take on new lines. Consequently, the more precisely the manufacturer knows what the distributor wants, the more prepared he or she is to negotiate a viable agreement. This most certainly does not mean that the manufacturer should give in to all the demands of the distributor, but rather that the manufacturer should anticipate what is most important to the distributor in an agreement.

The *distributor's* profile of an ideal supplier will contain the following points:

- Differentiated, well-known, prestige product with good sales potential
- Functional discounts that allow high markups
- Exclusive distribution rights protected by the manufacturer
- Contractual obligations assumed by the manufacturer for a lengthy period, with indemnities paid for any cancellation by the manufacturer
- Right of the distributor to terminate the agreement without indemnities
- Right to design and implement the marketing plan without interference or control by the manufacturer
- Generous credit terms
- Full support by the manufacturer—inventory backup, quick order servicing, technical and sales training, advertising, allowances, special discounts, and so on
- Product warranties
- Freedom to handle other lines, whether competitive or complementary to the manufacturer's line
- Paid visits to the manufacturer's headquarters or to regional meetings
- Obligation to provide only minimum information to the manufacturer

Even if the manufacturer could meet all these conditions, it would be foolish to do so: it would have only a marginal influence on the marketing plan, and it would assume costs that would make the channel unprofitable or less profitable than an alternative channel. Hence the need for the give-and-take of negotiations in face-to-face meetings.

The negotiation process may be viewed as a reconciliation of the manufacturer's and the distributor's respective profiles. In most negotiations, both sides will compromise on some issues. The manufacturer should be prepared for failure by leaving open its options to negotiate with other distributor prospects. Unless it has dominant bargaining power in all target markets, the manufacturer should not insist on a standard agreement in every particular. Good distributors in one target market may refuse to agree to a standard contract, whereas that contract may be overly generous in a distributor-abundant target market. Flexibility is the hallmark of the effective negotiator.

The Distributor Contract

Notwithstanding examples of successful oral agreements, the manufacturer's agreement with a distributor should take the form of a written contract. The written contract is particularly important when things go wrong. Moreover, it can lay the foundation for cooperation in designing and carrying out the marketing plan. Although it should be adaptable to circumstances, every distributor contract should clearly define all rights and obligations so that both parties fully understand them. The key elements in a distributor contract are as follows:

General Provisions
    Identification of parties to the contract
    Duration of the contract
    Conditions of cancellation
    Definition of covered goods
    Definition of territory or territories
    Sole and exclusive rights
    Arbitration of disputes

Rights and Obligations of Manufacturer
    Conditions of termination
    Protection of sole and exclusive rights
    Sales and technical support
    Tax liabilities
    Conditions of sale
    Delivery of goods
    Prices
    Order refusal
    Inspection of distributor's books
    Trademarks/patents

Information to be supplied the distributor
Advertising/promotion
Responsibility for claims/warranties
Inventory requirements

Rights and Obligations of Distributor
Safeguarding manufacturer's interests
Payments arrangements
Contract assignment
Competitive lines
Customs clearance
Observance of conditions of sale
After-sales service
Information to be supplied to the manufacturer

For most manufacturers, the three most important points in the contract are (1) sole and exclusive rights, (2) competitive lines, and (3) termination and cancellation.

Apart from the question of exclusive distribution rights from the marketing standpoint, there may also be a question of their legality in some countries. In the European Community, for example, the antitrust authorities have generally outlawed exclusive arrangements that restrict sales from one member country to another. As for lines handled, few manufacturers want their distributors to sell lines competitive with their own, although they may urge distributors to take on complementary lines.

The cancellation/termination provisions are probably the single most critical element in the distributor contract. On the one hand, the manufacturer wants a contract that is easy to terminate in the event a distributor does poorly with the line and also as a basis of control over the marketing program. On the other hand, it is in the manufacturer's interest that the distributor feel secure enough to justify a commitment to the manufacturer's product line. Many manufacturers make this trade-off by having a trial period, such as six months or a year, before entering a more permanent arrangement. When the contract is for an indefinite period, it is common to allow either party to terminate it sixty days after proper notice. A cancellation clause usually allows termination without notice for specific reasons, such as the distributor's bankruptcy, reorganization, death (if an individual), or prolonged failure to pay bills. In some countries, poor sales performance cannot be used to cancel a contract without notice.

This last point brings up the question of the local laws that govern the contract. The manufacturer should not sign a distributor contract until it has been fully checked by legal counsel to ensure that its provisions conform to the laws of the target country. Several countries have special laws that protect distributors and agents by making it very difficult or costly for the manufacturer to terminate an agreement. In those instances, termination/cancellation clauses must be carefully worded to guard the interests of the manufacturer.

A final point: a contract is the legal basis for cooperation between the manufacturer and the distributor, but it cannot guarantee cooperation. Cooperation will require the attention of managers who know how to build a smooth-working channel team with shared expectations and values. Much of a good export manager's job is taken up with the care and feeding of foreign representatives.[7] This task is magnified by the many pitfalls of cross-cultural communication, a subject examined in Chapter 9.

Export Operations

It is beyond the scope of this text to describe export operations in any detail. Instead, this section highlights three key aspects of the export transaction: (1) documentary requirements, (2) terms of sale, and (3) payment arrangements. The section closes with some observations on organizing for export.

Documentary Requirements

The documentary requirements of international commercial transactions have been described as a major nontariff trade barrier. It is estimated that nearly one-half of all shipments are delayed by documents that arrived late. Some progress has been made in recent years in simplifying, eliminating, and standardizing documents in the United States and abroad. Moreover, computerized documentation is being adopted by ocean and air carriers. Nonetheless,

Harley Davidson (U.S.), manufacturer of super-heavyweight motorcycles with an engine capacity of more than 850 cubic centimeters, launched an aggressive marketing strategy at the end of the 1980s that exploited Harley's American image. In 1993 its sales abroad reached 24 percent of total company sales of $1.2 billion, up from 14 percent in 1989. This global success story stands in stark contrast to Harley's situation in the early 1980s, when poor quality and Japanese imports were driving the company to the brink of bankruptcy. But instead of giving up, Harley fought back by raising product quality and creating an aggressive marketing strategy, comprising Harley Owners Groups (HOGs), magazines, clothing, and bike rallies, that packaged an American life-style. The key shift in thinking was the decision taken to stress customer satisfaction regardless of its effect on short-term profits.

After its comeback in the U.S. market (raising its share of the super-heavyweight market from 23 percent in 1983 to 63 percent in 1989), Harley turned to the international market even though it could sell all it produced at home. Up to that time, Harley's exports had been modest: little effort was made to build up a dealer network abroad, and the company's conception of international marketing was limited to translating U.S. ads word-for-word into a foreign language. Harley recruited more dealers in Japan and Europe and adapted its U.S. marketing package to foreign countries by creating HOGs overseas, publishing its magazines in foreign languages, and sponsoring beer and band rallies. It also started creating ads for particular countries. In 1993, for instance, Harley's Japanese unit was granted permission to run a separate advertising campaign mixing American and Japanese images, such as American riders passing a geisha in a rickshaw. Also, in Tokyo, Harley has two stores that exclusively sell Harley clothing and accessories. Harley's big bikes, known affectionately as "hogs", have become as much a symbol of Americana as hamburgers, cokes and Levi's. As one Harley executive says, "You have to understand, we are not selling transportation. We are selling a life-style, an experience, fun."

Adapted from "The Rumble Heard Round the World," *Business Week,* May 24, 1993, pp. 58–60; and "How Harley Outfoxed Japan with Exports," *New York Times,* August 12, 1990, p. F5.

documentation requirements will continue to burden export/import operations for the indefinite future.

Fortunately, exporters can use specialists to prepare most documents: international freight forwarders to handle documents on the physical shipment side and banks to handle them on the payments side. Exporters must still prepare certain documents (notably, the pro forma invoice), however, and they must understand and check the accuracy of other documents even when they are prepared by others. Other than from forwarders and banks, information on documentation may be obtained from the U.S. government, foreign embassies and consuls, the International Chamber of Commerce, carriers, accounting firms, professional associations, and trade publications. Taken singly, the preparation and function of export documents can be learned by export managers and their assistants in a short time.

Here is a list of the principal documents used in exporting, followed by a brief description of each.

Required by Foreign Customer
1. Pro forma invoice
2. Acceptance of purchase order
3. Ocean (airway) bill of lading
4. Certificate (or policy) of insurance
5. Packing list

Required by Exporter
1. Purchase order
2. Letter of credit or draft (trade) acceptance

Required by Freight Forwarder
1. Shipper's letter of instructions
2. Domestic (inland) bill of lading
3. Packing list
4. Commercial invoice (incomplete)
5. Letter of credit (original copy)

Required by U.S. Government
1. Export declaration
2. Export license (strategic goods having military significance)

Required by Foreign Governments
1. Certificate of origin
2. Customs invoice
3. Consular invoice

Required by Exporter's Bank
1. Exporter's draft
2. Commercial invoice
3. Consular invoice
4. Insurance certificate
5. Ocean (airway) bill of lading

Several documents are needed by the foreign customer. The *pro forma invoice* is the exporter's response to a sales inquiry; it is the proposed terms of sale expressed in invoice form. The exporter's *acceptance of a purchase order* sent to the foreign customer evidences the exporter's obligation to make the shipment and the exporter's claim to receive payment as specified in the purchase order, possibly with later modifications. The *commercial invoice,* addressed to the customer, indicates the quantities and prices of the goods sold, freight and insurance costs, the country of origin, identifying marks, packing, weight, and any other information relevant to the shipment. The *ocean (or airway) bill of lading,* issued by the international carrier, is a very important document serving three functions: (1) it is a receipt for goods delivered to the carrier, (2) it is a contract for services to be rendered by the carrier, and (3) when made out to the exporter's own order, it is a document of title necessary to possess the goods at the point of destination. Most exporters carry an open insurance policy covering marine and war risks that allows them to insure a specific shipment by issuing a *certificate of insurance* against the policy. As the name implies, a *packing list* shows the quantity and type of merchandise shipped to the importer; it enables him or her to locate a particular item when there are several packages with different contents.

The exporter needs documents evidencing the export order and the means of payment. The *purchase order* received from the foreign customer specifies the items, quantity, price, shipping date, packing, shipping marks, export routing, insurance, and payment terms. One form of payment is the *letter of credit* issued by the importer's bank, which obligates that bank to pay the exporter upon the latter's presentation of documents as specified in the letter. A second form of payment is the documentary draft drawn by the exporter on the importer. When the exporter extends credit, the importer must "accept" the draft to obtain the bill of lading, which is needed to gain possession of the merchandise. The resulting draft (trade) acceptance evidences the exporter's claim for payment.

When employed by an exporter, the freight forwarder requires several documents. The *shipper's letter of instruction,* sent by the exporter to the forwarder once the shipment has left the factory for the exit port, asks the forwarder to arrange international shipment and to submit the necessary documents to a named bank. Accompanying the letter are the commercial invoice (to be completed by the forwarder), packing list, original letter of credit, domestic (inland) bill of lading, and a power of attorney allowing the forwarder to complete the export declaration and present documents to the exporter's bank.

For most export shipments, the U.S. government requires only an *export declaration* listing the consignee, destination, carrier, merchandise, and other features of the shipment. For exports of strategic goods of military significance, however, the exporter must also obtain a validated export license from the U.S. Department of Commerce.

Foreign governments require certain documents before allowing entry of the merchandise. The *certificate of origin,* prepared by the exporter, certifies the country of origin of the merchandise in the shipment. The *customs invoice* is a copy of the commercial invoice (with some modifications) used to clear the merchandise through customs. The *consular invoice* is essentially the commercial invoice certified by a consul of the destination country. Not all governments require these documents, but some governments require additional documents, such as an inspection certificate.

The exporter's bank needs several documents to arrange payment by letter of credit or draft, including the exporter's draft on a bank or on the importer.

Terms of Sale

Before he or she can receive an export order, the exporter must determine the terms of sale. The most widely recognized codification of export terms of sale are *International Commercial Terms* (Incoterms) adopted by the International Chamber of Commerce. Exporters should specify this code when quoting terms of sale to buyers.[8] A standard quotation specifies when ownership passes from the exporter to the importer and which party pays the shipment costs (transportation, port charges, documentation, import tariffs, and so on).

The most common terms of sale are Ex factory, FAS (Free Along Side), and CIF (Cost, Insurance, Freight). Under Ex factory, the exporter quotes a price that applies only at his factory location. The importer pays all the costs and assumes all the responsibilities to move the goods to the foreign destination. Very similar is the quotation FOB (Free on Board), named inland carrier at named inland point of departure, where the price applies only at an inland shipping point but the exporter arranges for loading on a specified carrier.

Under FAS, the exporter quotes a price including delivery of the goods alongside a designated overseas vessel and within reach of its loading tackle. The importer handles all subsequent movement of the goods. Under CIF, the exporter quotes a price that includes the cost of goods, the marine insurance, and all transportation charges to a foreign port of entry. The importer is responsible for taking delivery of the goods from the vessel and paying all costs at the point of destination, such as landing costs and customs duties.

Ex factory (or FOB at an inland point) is the easiest quotation for the manufacturer to prepare, but it places a burden on the importer, who must calculate all the subsequent shipment and documentation costs to arrive at his or her landed cost. For that reason, importers prefer a CIF quotation. A good compromise is the FAS quotation, because it is comparatively easy for the exporter to prepare and for the importer to calculate the landed cost. Exporters should be flexible in their terms of sale and respond in some measure to the interests of importers. It is inexcusable for a manufacturer to lose an export sale because a refusal to quote FAS or CIF terms. The form of the terms of sale is a technical, procedural question that need not affect profits or risk.

Methods of Payment

Two risks are involved in international payments: (1) nonpayment, and (2) variations in the foreign exchange rate. The risk of nonpayment itself is actually two risks: default by the importer, and the imposition of exchange controls by the target country's government, prohibiting the importer from buying foreign exchange. The foreign exchange risk is assumed by the exporter when payment is specified in a foreign currency, the importer's currency, or a third-country currency. In these cases, a depreciation of the foreign currency in terms of the exporter's currency between the time of the order and the time of payment will result in a smaller home-currency payment to the exporter. Because the dollar is the principal international currency, U.S. manufacturers are usually able to quote in dollars and thereby pass on the exchange risk to the importer. When an exporter is compelled to quote in a foreign currency to obtain a sale, then he or she can hedge on the forward exchange market if he or she does not want to assume the exchange risk. In general, exporters should avoid speculating on the foreign exchange rate by assuming the exchange risk—it is not their métier.

Ranked by an ascending risk of nonpayment, the alternative methods of payment for an export shipment are (1) cash in advance, (2) irrevocable, confirmed letter of credit, (3) documentary draft, (4) open account, and (5) consignment. *Cash in advance* requires the importer to finance the entire export transaction with little or no risk to the exporter. But insistence on cash in advance may lose sales for an exporter in a competitive target market.

An *irrevocable, confirmed letter of credit,* issued by the importer's bank and confirmed by a bank in the exporter's country, allows the exporter to get paid on the presentation of the required documents to the domestic, confirming bank. Thus the exporter does not rely on the importer for payment, and payment is not jeopardized by foreign exchange restrictions. Letter-of-credit payment is very favorable to the exporter because it amounts to payment at the time of shipment. But once again, insistence on this payment term may cost the exporter sales if competitors are willing to offer easier terms.

A common method of export payment is for the exporter to draw a draft (bill of exchange) on the importer and send it for collection through the exporter's bank, accompanied by the negotiable bill of lading and other documents that control the shipment. Documentary drafts may be sight or time drafts. With a sight draft, the documents are delivered to the buyer only against his or her payment. The exporter is subject to the risks of nonacceptance of the shipment by the importer, and to foreign exchange restrictions. With a time draft payable a certain number of days after sight (the date of presentation) or on a certain date, the exporter extends credit to the importer. The importer gets the documents against his or her "acceptance" of the draft, by which he or she promises to pay on the draft's maturity date. Thus, in addition to taking the risks of a sight draft, the exporter assumes the risk of default by the importer. But in that event, the exporter does have clear documentary proof of his or her claim on the importer, namely, the draft (or trade) acceptance.

Exporters may also bill export sales on an *open-account* basis, usually offering more generous terms than they offer domestic customers. With this method, the exporter provides complete financing of the transaction, and in the event of default or foreign exchange restrictions, he or she has only weak evidence of claim for payment. Because of its risky nature, open-account payment should be confined to the exporter's own branches or subsidiaries or to importers in convertible-currency countries whom the exporter fully trusts.

By far the riskiest method of payment is *consignment:* the importer is not obligated to pay until he or she has sold the exporter's merchandise. Understandably, consignment should be restricted to branches, subsidiaries, and trusted foreign representatives.

As with terms of sale, exporters should be flexible in their payment arrangements. Export credit is often necessary for sales in competitive markets and for capital-equipment sales in all target markets. When extending credit through documentary time drafts, the exporter can lower the risk of nonpayment by making credit checks on importers and exchange control checks on target countries. U.S. exports can obtain export credit insurance (protecting against the risks of nonpayment for both commercial and political reasons) from the Foreign Credit Insurance Association (FCIA), an association of insurance companies. Credit insurance allows the exporter to extend more liberal credit terms to importers and in turn to obtain more liberal financing from his or her own bank, with the insured export receivables offered as collateral.

Organizing for Export

Organizing for export starts with a consideration of the target markets that a company presently serves and expects to serve in the future. The goal should be an export organization that can conceive and carry out aggressive foreign market entry strategies and, at the same time, fully meet the pressing demands of day-to-day operations.

Companies newly entering into direct export are likely to establish an export department staffed by only an export manager and a few assistants. This department is usually subordinate to the domestic sales department and depends on other departments for order filling, accounting, credit approval, and the like. Known as a "built-in export department," this arrangement is a good way to gain export experience with only a limited commitment of the company's resources. But it does place the export manager in a weak position unless he or she is demonstrably supported by higher management. Once successful experience is gained in export markets, therefore, the built-in department should be transformed into a full-function department, division, or subsidiary that has the authority and resources to plan, operate, and control export marketing activities. It is unwise to postpone this transformation until the built-in department becomes obviously inadequate to do the export job. Export sales may be small today, but organization should point to the future. Too often, company organizations—shaped by long experience in domestic markets—fail to adjust, or adjust too slowly, to market opportunities opening up abroad.

Export managers should have the authority to formulate, execute, and control export strategy. In specific terms, they should be authorized to select international target markets and design the international marketing plan, as well as manage export operations. It is most unfair for higher management to demand export success and, at the same time, deny export executives any voice in, say, export pricing. At the very least, export managers should be allowed to participate in decisions that have a direct bearing on the export effort. Not to give them that authority is to ignore foreign markets that may become as important to a company's future as markets at home. Manufacturers that want to go after international markets cannot afford to hamstring export managers by keeping them subordinate to domestic sales or any other domestic function.

Getting Started in Export

This section is addressed to the U.S. company that wants to enter export markets but has no prior experience in international business. To obtain information on foreign markets and how to go about exporting, the company can contact many sources, but three sources deserve special mention: (1) the U.S. Department of Commerce and its regional offices, (2) the international department of the manufacturer's bank, and (3) export management companies.

U.S. Department of Commerce

The International Trade Administration (ITA) of the U.S. Department of Commerce is the principal U.S. government agency engaged in export promotion.[9] Its Trade Information Center in Washington, D.C., provides information on *all* U.S. government programs supporting the exporting activities of firms: export counseling, seminars and conferences, overseas buyers and representatives, overseas events, export financing, and technical assistance.

In addition to supplying information to help exporters screen potential market opportunities, the ITA locates potential buyers (as well as distributors, joint venture partners, and licensees) through an extensive network of commercial officers in foreign countries. Its Export Contact List Service provides mailing lists of prospective foreign buyers from an automated worldwide file of companies; the Trade Opportunities Program (*TOP*) offers sales leads on foreign firms wanting to buy or represent U.S. products and services; the Agent/Distributor Service searches for foreign representatives on behalf of U.S. exporters; the *World Traders Data Reports* offer background reports on specific foreign firms, including size, reputation, area covered, preferred language, product lines, financial references, and trade references; *Commercial News USA* provides exposure for U.S. products and services through an illustrated catalog distributed in 140 countries and through electronic bulletin boards;

and Trade Event Programs enable a firm to present its products to an overseas market via international trade fairs, U.S.-sponsored trade shows, trade delegations, and missions.

Banks

The international departments of banks can provide information to manufacturers on export financing, payment, and documentary requirements. Banks can also obtain information on foreign firms and countries through their extensive links with other banks throughout the world. Frequently, banks can obtain this information more quickly than the U.S. Department of Commerce.

Export Management Companies (EMCs)

An EMC is an international marketing specialist that functions as the export department of several manufacturers in noncompetitive lines. But it is difficult to generalize about EMC's beyond that statement, because their services are adapted to individual clients, product lines, market, and their own resources. In a word, the population of EMCs is extremely heterogeneous. No one knows the exact size of that population, but it probably runs about twelve hundred firms, which represent some ten thousand manufacturers and account for about 10 percent of U.S. manufactured exports.

The wide diversity among EMCs makes it difficult for the manufacturer to find an EMC that best suits its purposes. A rational search process resembles that for finding foreign agents and distributors. The first step is drawing up a list of EMCs that appear to have experience with the manufacturer's product line and target markets. To do this, the manufacturer can obtain information from EMC regional associations, trade publications, and the U.S. Department of Commerce.[10] The second step is for the manufacturer to narrow the list down to, say, the five best prospects. The third step is to contact directly these key prospects. The fourth step is to choose the most appropriate EMC. Since few EMCs can do a good job in all foreign markets or for all product lines, the manufacturer that wants worldwide distribution or has two or more product lines may find that two or three EMCs can do a better job than a single one.

About three hundred thousand companies with fewer than five hundred employees produce two-thirds of Germany's gross domestic product, train nine out of ten apprentices, and employ four out of five workers. Known collectively as the *Mittelstand*, these companies (mostly run by owner-managers) are also powerful exporters, overcoming high labor costs and a strong exchange rate that make their products expensive. How do they do it? Mainly by targeting small but highly profitable niches in world markets. Because of their intensive R & D, these firms commonly beat big firms to the market with new products. Collectively, the *Mittelstand* companies generate about 30 percent of Germany's exports. Of course, not all of them are direct exporters, with many acting as suppliers to big firms. (For instance, BMW, the auto manufacturer, uses one thousand suppliers; Mercedes-Benz, the auto and truck manufacturer, buys more than $15 billion of supplies from fifty thousand companies inside Germany.) A survey of *Mittelstand* companies reveals that they focus narrowly on a particular market segment, usually one requiring technical expertise. They leverage this specialization across broad geographical markets, obtaining scale economies to recover R & D costs and keep down unit costs.

Despite their small size, *Mittelstand* firms want control over their foreign operations, partly to support close relations with customers. They are willing to make a strong commitment to export markets with high up-front investments and by keeping the same managers in charge of foreign units for a decade or more. *Mittelstand* companies work hard to create service networks in export markets that match those in Germany. They compete on product quality, closeness to customers, and service. Part of the *Mittelstand's* competitive strength comes from German business culture: managers focus on quality, profits, worker training, and family ownership. And some of their export success is attributable to an infrastructure that greatly assists small firms. Embassies, banks, trade associations, and chambers of commerce identify export opportunities and quickly relay the details back to Germany. Trade associations, trading companies, and banks enable firms to exploit export opportunities with assistance in documentation, translation, legal services, and shipping arrangements. Also, specialized banks and *Mittelstand* departments of big banks provide export financing and arrange credit and political risk insurance through Hermes, a government-sponsored export credit agency.

Adapted from "Think Small: The Export Lessons To Be Learned from Germany's Midsize Companies," *Business Week,* November 4, 1991, pp. 58–65; and "Lessons from Germany's Midsize Giants," *Harvard Business Review,* March-April 1992, pp. 115–123.

In using EMCs, manufacturers should try to maximize the advantages and minimize the disadvantages of this indirect export channel. The principal advantage is access to foreign markets by "plugging in" to the EMC's foreign marketing network. The manufacturer can strengthen this advantage by carefully selecting the EMC in the first place and then supporting it. The latter step involves working with the EMC to design a foreign marketing plan for the manufacturer's product line; contributing product information, sales literature, sales training, samples, and advertising and technical assistance; and backing up the EMC's export operations with the prompt servicing of orders.

The principal disadvantage of the EMC channel is the manufacturer's loss of control over foreign sales. But this loss can be moderated by (1) specifying in the EMC contract key decisions requiring the exporter's approval (for example, prices and credit, (2) requiring periodic sales reports by product and market, (3) including a termination clause enabling the exporter to break the EMC contract without cause (say, with sixty days' notice), and most important, (4) working intimately with the EMC.

Summary

1. To go international for the first time, a company must overcome anxieties about its ability to compete in foreign markets. Given this situation, exporting will usually appear to the manufacturer as the best entry mode. In other words, exporting can become an international learning experience.
2. To get its product into a foreign target market, a company can use any one of several export modes or channels. Exporting through domestic intermediaries is called indirect exporting. But a company that wants active penetration of foreign markets will look to direct export channels.
3. Direct exporting relies on two principal channels: the foreign agent/distributor channel and the foreign branch/subsidiary channel. A direct export channel is the chain of marketing agencies that links a domestic manufacturing company to the final buyers (or users) of its product in the foreign target market.

4. To make a rational determination of a direct export channel for a target foreign country/market, managers need to make decisions on three levels: channel performance specifications, the channel type, and the channel members.

5. If a manufacturer decides to use an agent/distributor channel, then a second screening step compares foreign agents against foreign distributors in the target country. Thus the determination of the channel type calls for a two-step screening process involving trade-offs among control, profitability, performance specifications, and risks.

6. When a company decides that its most attractive export channel is an agent or distributor channel, then it must initiate a screening process to choose individual agents or distributors. This involves drawing up the distributor (agent) profile, locating prospects, evaluating prospects, and choosing the distributor or agent. The ultimate choice of a distributor (agent) is the outcome of a negotiation in which the distributor (agent) is choosing the manufacturer, as well as the other way around.

7. Notwithstanding examples of successful oral agreements, the manufacturer's agreement with a distributor (agent) should take the form of a written contract. For most manufacturers, the three most important points in the contract are sole and exclusive rights, competitive lines, and termination. A contract is the legal basis for cooperation between the manufacturer and the distributor (agent), but it cannot guarantee cooperation.

8. Three key aspects of export operations are documentary requirements, price quotations, and payments arrangements.

9. Fortunately, manufacturers can use specialists to prepare most documents: international freight forwarders to handle documents pertaining to physical shipment and banks to handle those relating to payments.

10. It is inexcusable for a manufacturer to lose an export sale because the company refuses to quote FAS or CIF terms. The form of the export price quotation is a technical, procedural question that need not affect profits or risk.

11. As with terms of sale, the manufacturer should be flexible in payment arrangements. Export credit is often necessary

for sales in competitive markets and for capital-equipment sales in all target markets.

12. An export organization should be able to conceive and carry out aggressive foreign market entry strategies and, at the same time, fully meet the pressing demands of day-to-day operations. Manufacturers that want to go after foreign markets cannot afford to hamstring export managers by keeping them subordinate to domestic sales or any other domestic function.

13. To obtain information on foreign markets and how to go about exporting, the U.S. manufacturer can contact many sources, but three deserve special mention: the U.S. Department of Commerce and its regional offices, the international department of the manufacturer's bank, and export management companies.

CHAPTER 5

Entering International Markets Through Licensing and Other Contractual Arrangements

B roadly defined, international licensing includes a variety of contractual arrangements whereby domestic companies (licensors) make available their intangible assets (patents, trade secrets, know-how, trademarks, and company name) to foreign companies (licensees) in return for royalties and/or other forms of payment. Commonly, the transfer of these intangible assets or property rights is accompanied by technical services to ensure the proper use of the assets. In the case of franchising, the service element is particularly prominent, because it includes general management and marketing assistance as well as technical assistance in operations. But the core of a licensing agreement is the transfer of intangible property rights, and it is this transfer that distinguishes licensing from other contractual arrangements (such as management and technical-assistance agreements) that provide only professional services to the recipient firm.

A company may license abroad for several different reasons. One reason is simply to get incremental income on technology that has already been written off against domestic sales. Licensing may also be used to acquire the research output of a foreign company in return for that of the domestic company (a practice known as cross-licensing). Some companies have negotiated licensing contracts to protect their patents and trademarks in a foreign country against loss for nonuse or against possible infringement. And many companies have entered into formal licensing agreements with their own controlled foreign subsidiaries to establish their legal ownership of patents and trademarks (rather than ownership by the subsidiaries), to facilitate the repatriation of income when exchange controls restrict dividend payments, or to meet home or foreign government requirements. When a company licenses an independent foreign company, however, the purpose ordinarily is to penetrate a foreign market. It is this use of licensing as a *primary* entry mode that is the focus of this chapter.

Licensing as a Primary Entry Mode

As is true of any entry mode, licensing offers both advantages and disadvantages to international companies.

Advantages of Licensing

The most obvious advantage of licensing as an entry mode is the circumvention of import barriers that increase the cost (tariffs) or limit the quantity (quotas) of exports to the target market. Instead of transferring a physical product, the manufacturer transfers intangible assets and services that are not subject to import restrictions. Commonly, manufacturers have used licensing when exports were no longer possible to a target market (with the sudden imposition of tariffs or quotas) or when exports were no longer profitable (with the appearance of more intense competition). A prolonged depreciation of a target country's currency may also swing a manufacturer from export to licensing. In some instances, licensing may enable a manufacturer to continue exporting to a restricted target market by replacing shipments of final products with shipments of intermediate products to a licensee firm. Licensing also overcomes the problem of high transportation costs, which make the export of some products noncompetitive in target markets.

Another advantage of licensing is lower political risks than with equity investment. For one thing, many host governments prefer licensing over foreign investment as a way to get technology. For another, licensing is immune to expropriation, because the licensor does not own physical assets in the target country. If the worst happens, the most that a manufacturer can lose is the licensing income. This may not be inconsequential, but the loss is far below what would be sustained with a manufacturing subsidiary.

In some situations, a company may be kept out of a target country by both import and investment restrictions, and licensing becomes the *only* viable entry mode. Manufacturers of military equipment or of other products deemed critical to the national interest (such as communications equipment) may be compelled to enter licensing agreements because the host government requires at least some of the product to be manufactured in its own country by indigenous companies.

Apart from these external factors, several factors *internal* to a company may favor licensing over alternative entry modes. For companies whose end product is a service (which cannot be exported), licensing or franchising may be a more attractive way to provide the service than through a branch or subsidiary. Again, if a manufacturer's product requires substantial physical adaptation to meet the needs of a target market, licensing may be advantageous because it can transfer much of the adaptation cost to the foreign licensee and, at the same time, avoid the higher resource costs and risks of equity investment.

This last remark brings up another internal factor, namely, the resources (managerial, technical, and financial) that a company is able and willing to commit to a foreign target market. As a low-commitment entry mode, licensing is especially attractive to small manufacturers. A low or uncertain sales potential in the target market adds to the attractiveness of licensing compared to that of equity investment or even direct export.

Disadvantages of Licensing

Clearly, a company cannot use licensing as an entry mode unless it possesses technology, trademarks, or a company name that is attractive to potential foreign users. For companies lacking these assets, licensing is simply not an entry option. Apart from this limitation, licensing may have several disadvantages for manufacturers.

The foremost disadvantage of licensing from an entry strategy perspective is the licensor's lack of control over the marketing plan and program in the target country. Even when the licensor makes a good selection of its licensee, it remains dependent on the licensee's market performance, and it can do little to compel a better performance short of terminating the license if the contract permits. This disadvantage can be alleviated by developing a close working relationship with the licensee, but it can only rarely be eliminated even in franchising. In this respect, a foreign licensee resembles a foreign distributor.

Another disadvantage is the absolute size of income from a licensing arrangement as compared to that from exporting to, or investing in, the target country. Royalty rates are generally limited by rates in a company's prior licensing agreements, by industry practice, by competition, and sometimes by host governments. Royalty rates seldom exceed 5 percent. Furthermore, unlike export or investment income, licensing income is limited to the duration of the licensing agreement, which is usually five to ten years.

The absolute size of licensing income is not small in all circumstances, and it must be weighed against the lower direct risks of licensing. Moreover, licensing income is not confined to royalties (a matter taken up later), and the duration of a licensing contract may be extended with product improvements and a continuing need by the licensee for technical assistance. A final qualification of this income disadvantage is that the profitability of a licensing arrangement can be high even when the absolute income size is small.

A disadvantage of licensing that is commonly ignored, to the licensor's subsequent regret, is the risk of creating a competitor in third markets or even in the licensor's home market. Although the political risk of licensing is low, the ultimate commercial risk can be very high. Armed with the licensor's technology, the licensee may become a formidable competitor in world markets. Manufacturers can try to minimize this risk by restricting the licensee to sales in the latter's own country and/or by contractually binding the licensee to discontinue the use of the licensed technology after termination of the contract. But these efforts may be prohibited by the host government and may even be illegal under U.S. antitrust laws. Apart from these obstacles, legal action taken against a foreign licensee for contract violation is costly, time-consuming, and uncertain of success. Before licensing a foreign company, therefore, a company needs to assess the risk of creating a future competitor. In particular, the notion that licensing can be used to explore or test a new market with the prospect of later entry by the licensor as an investor deserves careful scrutiny. Finally, the competitive risk that arises from divulging trade secrets to a licensee may be compounded by the licensee's inadvertent or purposive disclosure of those secrets to third parties. In some instances, the host government may not allow the licensor to bind the licensee to an "oath of secrecy."

Another drawback of a licensing arrangement is its exclusiveness. The licensing agreement usually gives the licensee the exclusive rights to use the licensed technology and trademark in the production and sale of designated products in the licensee's country. Hence with respect to those products, the licensor cannot use an alternative entry mode over the agreement's life. This *opportunity cost* of licensing (the cost of not being able to enter the market in another way) may be moderated, but not eliminated, by contract provisions that allow the licensor to terminate the contract for inadequate performance or to acquire equity in the licensee firm and thereby transform a licensing arrangement into a joint venture.

Protecting Industrial Property Rights Abroad

A company can use licensing to enter a foreign target market only if it can secure legal protection of its industrial property rights in the target country. Unfortunately, patents, trademarks, service marks, and trade names registered in the home country do not afford protection in foreign countries. Nor is there a single international authority that confers industrial property rights on a global basis; such rights can be obtained for a particular country only by applying for them in that country. The country-by-country quest for industrial property rights faces so many legal pitfalls that every company is strongly advised to rely on legal counsel for advice and assistance. The following observations are intended only to alert managers to the general situation.

Obtaining Patent Protection

A patent is a public document issued by a government that grants to its owner for a limited period of time the right to exclude others

FlowMole Corporation (U.S.) installs underground utility cables and pipes without digging a trench. A FlowMole crew uses electromagnetic guidance to track a hydraulically powered drill head (the "mole") as it moves underground. Next, a reaming device widens the tunnel to the desired size and threads in the utility cable. This operation disturbs the surface with only two small holes at the start and end of the tunnel, avoiding excavation costs, backfilling, and site restoration. FlowMole decided from the start that it wanted to go international. Just one year after it began in 1985, the company demonstrated its equipment in Great Britain and then in the Netherlands and Germany. These demonstrations stimulated business in those countries and led to demonstrations in other European nations.

FlowMole explored two entry modes: (1) licensing local companies to provide installation, and (2) direct contracting with installation done by FlowMole crews (as in the United States). It chose licensing in Belgium, the Netherlands, and Germany, and direct contracting in Britain. But the effort in Britain to transfer a service technology and also act as contractor for its application proved very costly due to FlowMole's ignorance of local regulations and ways of doing business. The company, which had total sales of only $13 million, lost more than $1 million in Britain. This loss persuaded FlowMole to switch to licensing in that country. With licensing, FlowMole leases its equipment to licensees and trains them to use the system to provide a high-quality customer service. FlowMole gets revenue from equipment rentals, royalties, and the sales of spare parts.

In 1990 FlowMole had thirty-three systems operating in Europe. These operations have benefited the company with more than revenues. For instance, the technology developed to ream larger-diameter tunnels in Europe and the knowledge gained in licensing and leasing may now be used in some parts of the United States. Currently, about 10 percent of the company's revenue comes from Canada and Europe.

Adapted from "The $1 Million Lesson," *North American International Business*, August 1990, pp. 30–34.

from making, using, or selling an invention described in the patent. It cannot be assumed that a patent issued by a company's home country will ensure the issuance of a patent covering the same invention by a foreign country. Indeed, in some instances, a patent application may be turned down because the invention has become "public knowledge" through the prior issuance of a patent by the home government! Furthermore, national patent systems differ widely around the world with respect to criteria of "novelty," patent duration (ranging from five to twenty years), patentability (some countries allow only process patents or exclude patents for certain types of products, such as pharmaceuticals), renewability, "working" requirements (some countries require that a patent be commercially utilized within a certain time or be lost), taxation, and many other features.

Although multiple-country patent protection requires multiple-country patent applications, international agreements facilitate patent filings. Under the International Convention for the Protection of Industrial Property (the "Paris Union"), a company that files an original patent claim in one member country has a "right of priority" in filing claims in other member countries for a period of one year following the original filing.[1] About ninety countries belong to the convention, including all the industrial countries. The message of the convention is clear for a U.S. company that wants to obtain foreign patent rights: it should apply for those rights within one year after applying for a U.S. patent. Failure to do so may mean a permanent loss of patent rights in other countries. A company must decide within one year where it wants patent protection, even though it may not know the commercial value of that protection. The prospects for a less arduous passage through the jungle of international patent protection have become somewhat brighter in recent years with two new treaties.[2] But most developing countries still remain outside any international agreement.

The legal complexities in obtaining, maintaining, and enforcing patents make it all the more urgent for companies to have an international patent strategy. Consider only two questions, listed below, that need to be answered with respect to obtaining patents.

First, should a company keep patentable knowledge as a trade secret or seek international protection? A patent makes a trade secret public knowledge in return for statutory protection of the owner's exclusive use. A patent owner has exclusive rights, however, only in countries where he or she holds valid patents. In all other countries his or her invention is in the public domain, because it is no longer a trade secret. (When a patent is issued by the home government, a copy is routinely sent to foreign patent offices.) Given the uncertainties pertaining to the acquisition, maintenance, and enforcement of patents, a company may well conclude that it can control the use of its technology more effectively by keeping it a trade secret than by patenting it. Another consideration is the high cost of securing a patent, which can run to $50,000 or more in some countries.

The trade-secrets approach can work only if a company maintains secrecy. If a trade secret can be fairly easily copied by outsiders, then it is advisable to get patent protection. Furthermore, technology patented abroad can usually command higher royalties, because the licensee also benefits from the patent. Sometimes it may not be possible to license a product in the absence of a patent. Given the many trade-offs, the choice between trade secrets and patents is a difficult one for many companies.

Second, if a company decides to obtain patent protection, where should it seek that protection? In other words, in which countries are the benefits of patent protection likely to outweigh its costs? This question can be answered rationally only through a close examination of a company's current and prospective foreign market entry strategies over a lengthy planning period. Advanced planning is critical, because a company must be prepared to move quickly to obtain international patent protection on new technology. Also, premature disclosure (such as describing the invention anywhere in the world before the first patent application or, in some instances, placing an invention in public use or on sale anywhere in the world) can jeopardize patent rights in many countries.

Obtaining Trademark Protection

A trademark is a name, device, or symbol used by a producer or seller to identify its products and distinguish them from others. As is true of patents, trademarks must be registered in each country for protection. Protection can run anywhere from seven to twenty-five years and is ordinarily renewable. Outside the United States, there are more than 150 separate jurisdictions in which a company can register a trademark.

In the majority of countries, the one who first registers a trademark is considered its legal owner. A company may find, therefore, that its trademark is already registered in a foreign target country by someone who has no intention to manufacture or market a product using that trademark. In that event, the company must buy its own trademark from the legal owner, use a new trademark, or stay out of the country. To forestall this situation, companies should register their trademarks in all foreign countries they are likely to enter in, say, the next five years, whether as a licensor, an exporter, or an investor.

In the United States and several other countries whose legal systems derive from England, trademark protection can be obtained only by demonstrating prior commercial use. In this country, the Lanham Act specifies the kinds of symbols and names that can be protected by law and sets up registration procedures. But registration is not compulsory and does not establish ownership of the trademark. Instead, a company must prove it first used the trademark in the United States, and the usual proof is actual sale of the products carrying the trademark.[3] Moreover, the use of the trademark must be continued to maintain protection. Trademarks may also be lost if they move into popular usage as generic terms, as has happened in the United States to linoleum, cellophane, kerosene, lanolin, shredded wheat, aspirin, nylon, and many other names. It is the responsibility of the owner to prevent his or her trademark from slipping into generic use.

Even when their trademarks are properly registered, it may be difficult for companies to protect them against infringement in many countries because of loose administration of trademark laws, cumbersome legal processes, and inadequate penalties. Counterfeiters in Italy, Taiwan, Hong Kong, South Korea, and other Southeast Asian countries market their own Hennessey brandy, Dior and Cardin fashion apparel, Puma sport shoes, Dunlop tennis racquets, Samsonite luggage, and even Coca-Cola. Although most pirate brands are high-priced consumer items, medical vaccines, heart pacemakers, and helicopter parts have also turned up with false trademarks.[4]

Under the Paris Union, the owner of a trademark is given six months for priority filing after the filing date in his or her home country.[5] Hence a company must act fast to be sure of having the right to use its trademark in target countries. Gaining protection outside the Paris Union countries can be time-consuming and difficult. Trade names, as distinct from trademarks, are protected in all Paris Union countries without the need to register them; however, it is common to register a trade name in a local commercial register maintained by a court or government office in the target country.

Maintaining Trade Secrets

A trade secret is know-how that it kept secret within an enterprise, offers a competitive advantage, and is not generally known to the industry. Trade secrets cover manufacturing processes; methods and techniques; plans, designs, and patterns; formulas; business information; and products. Trade secrets do not have statutory protection like patents and trademarks, but the laws of many countries protect ownership rights in trade secrets, conditional on the maintenance of secrecy. The latter is not always possible. It is legal, for example, for a competitor to buy a company's product and then attempt to copy it by reverse engineering. Once a trade secret becomes public knowledge, anyone can use it freely. The possession of trade secrets does not create any right to prevent others from independently creating and using the same know-how.

Under the laws of some countries it may be possible for a company to prevent employees from communicating trade secrets without permission or to prevent a competitor from disclosing or using a trade secret acquired illegally. But the general absence of special legislation in national systems and of special provisions in international treaties, together with the costs and uncertain outcome of legal action, make it very important that a licensor take contractual safeguard measures to prevent the disclosure or un-

The violation of patents, trademarks and copyrights—known as piracy—may be the world's fastest-growing and most profitable business. It is costing U.S. companies billions of dollars each year: $4 billion in pharmaceuticals, $9 billion in software, $2 billion in sound recordings, $1 billion in movies, and $1 billion in books. European companies also suffer from piracy; indeed, the most pirated single product is Zantac, the antiulcer drug of the British firm Glaxo Holdings. Most likely, losses are far higher than these estimates indicate, because piracy deters entry into foreign markets. In Brazil, India, and Hungary, local companies can copy pharmaceuticals legally because laws of these countries do not recognize pharmaceutical patents. Other nations, notably Thailand and Taiwan, do not enforce their laws on patents and copyrights.

Spokesmen of developing countries commonly argue that their countries have a right to copy products. In 1991 JC Penney (U.S.) lost the exclusive right to its own name in Singapore although it was the first to register the trademark "Penney's." A Singapore national later registered the business name "JC Penney Collections." Penney brought suit, but the high court of Singapore supported the national on the grounds that Penney had not actually used its trademark in Singapore and had no reputation in that country. In contrast, some developing countries are now strengthening protection for industrial (or intellectual) property. In 1991 Mexico adopted a law that offers twenty-year patents and fifty-year copyrights. After an investigation by Microsoft Corporation (U.S.) uncovered a copyright violation in Taiwan, local police seized five thousand counterfeit packages of Microsoft's Windows software and MS-DOS programs. (It is estimated that nine-tenths of all software sold in Taiwan is counterfeit.) Software piracy also occurs in the European countries, Japan and the United States itself. Russia has become a counterfeiter's heaven: almost all music sales in that country are pirated releases. Weak protection of intellectual property has kept Western firm producers, record companies, computer software companies, and publishers out of Russia. Ironically, Melodiya, a state-owned recording company in Russia, is being hurt by pirates who copy its Russian classical recordings and then export the copies under their own labels.

As the world's greatest producer of intellectual property, no country has more to lose from piracy than the United States.

Nonetheless, in the past this country has been reluctant to enter international treaties protecting industrial property rights. This posture has now changed: the United States has acted to broaden the coverage of the General Agreement on Tariffs and Trade (GATT) to include industrial property rights, and in 1989 it joined the Berne Convention. Multilateral and bilateral agreement among countries on the recognition and enforcement of intellectual property rights can do much to restrain piracy by making it less profitable. Also, individual firms need to register patents, trademarks, and copyrights wherever they do business and aggressively protect their rights.

Adapted from "The Patent Pirates Finally Walking the Plank," *Business Week,* February 17, 1992, pp. 125–127; "Fake Windows, Ersatz DOS, Angry Uncle Sam," *Business Week,* May 18, 1992, p. 130; "In Russia's Free Market, Cultural Privacy Thrives," *New York Times,* July 2, 1993, p. A4; "Trademark Piracy at Home and Abroad," *Wall Street Journal,* May 7, 1991, p. A22; "Are Pirates Cutting into Your Sales?" *International Business,* July 1991, pp. 30–31.

warranted use of trade secrets by a licensee before, during, and after a licensing agreement.

Profitability Analysis of a Proposed Licensing Venture

Many manufacturers regard licensing as an entry mode to be used only when they cannot use exporting or equity investment to penetrate a foreign target country. As a consequence, they treat licensing as a marginal activity undeserving of any careful evaluation of its benefits and costs. This casual approach encourages bad decisions of two sorts. On the one hand, manufacturers may ignore licensing when it is a more profitable way to gain entry into a target market than alternative entry modes. On the other hand, they may enter licensing agreements without assessing all relevant revenues and costs over the duration of those agreements. Thus the neglect of systematic analysis heightens the risk of both underlicensing (not licensing when one should) and overlicensing (licensing when one should not).

Managers can rationally choose licensing as a primary entry mode only when they compare the expected profitability of a proposed licensing venture with the expected profitability of alternative entry modes, notably export and equity investment. Moreover, they can do a good job of negotiating licensing agreements only when they are aware of all prospective revenues and costs. Not to undertake profitability analysis is to treat licensing as a tactical, ad hoc decision when it is truly a strategic decision that will determine a company's long-run position in a target market and possibly in third markets as well. In this section we suggest how managers can apply profitability analysis to a proposed licensing venture, but a fuller treatment of profitability analysis in the context of all entry modes is postponed until Chapter 7.

Projecting Incremental Revenues

Profitability analysis requires that managers make estimates of both incremental revenues and incremental costs projected over the life of a proposed licensing venture. The *profit contribution* of the venture is then calculated by subtracting all incremental costs from all incremental revenues.

Licensing revenues are dependent mainly on the ability of a prospective licensee to manufacture and market the licensed product over time. Hence the licensor first needs to research the foreign target market to ascertain the *market potential* for his kind of product. Next, he or she needs to estimate the *sales potential* (market share potential) of the prospective licensee by evaluating his or her capacity to manufacture the licensed product at a competitive cost and quality and to sell it in the target market. The licensor's estimate of the licensee's sales potential is the basis for the former's projection of royalty revenues calculated as a percentage of sales at an expected royalty rate.

After projecting running royalty revenues, the licensor needs to identify and estimate other kinds of licensing revenues, including the following:

- Lump-sum royalties (including disclosure fees)
- Technical-assistance fees
- Engineering or construction fees

- Equity shares in licensee firm
- Dividends on equity shares
- Profits from sales to licensee (machinery, equipment, raw materials, components, or nonlicensed products)
- Profits from purchase and resale of goods manufactured by licensee
- Savings from use of licensed products in licensor's own operation
- Commissions on purchases or sales made for licensee
- Rental payments on licensor-owned machinery or equipment
- Management fees
- Patents, trademarks, and know-how received from licensee (grant-backs)

Since the licensing venture is prospective, these revenues are based on the agreement that the licensor *plans* to negotiate in view of its knowledge of the target market and the prospective licensee, its licensing experience, and other factors. After estimating all revenues, the licensor projects the aggregate cash inflows that are anticipated over the life of the proposed licensing venture.

Projecting Incremental Costs

The next step in profitability analysis is an estimation of all costs incurred by the licensor in transferring technology and related services to the prospective licensee over the agreement's life. The possible costs are classified as opportunity, start-up, and ongoing costs:

Opportunity Costs
    Loss of current export or other net revenues
    Loss of prospective revenues

Start-Up Costs
    Investigation of target market
    Selection of prospective licensee
    Acquisition of local patent/trademark protection
    Negotiation of licensing agreement
    Preparation and transfer of blueprints, drawings, and other
        documents
    Adaptation of technology for licensee

Training licensee's employees

Engineering, construction, and plant installation services

Contribution of machinery, equipment, and inventory to
  licensee

Ongoing Costs

Periodic training and updating of licensee

Maintaining local patent/trademark protection (including
  policing and litigation costs)

Quality supervision and tests

Auditing and inspection

Marketing, purchasing, and other nontechnical services

Management assistance

Correspondence with licensee

Resolution of disputes

Maintenance of licensor staff

The licensor's *opportunity costs* are the revenues that are forsaken if it enters the prospective licensing venture. The licensor may give up actual and future net revenues from exports or other operations in the target country that are ruled out by the licensing agreement. Furthermore, the licensor may lose net revenues in third markets if the licensee enters those markets. The most obvious opportunity cost is incurred when the licensor must discontinue export sales of the licensed product to the target market. *Prospective* opportunity costs can be assessed only by reference to the manufacturer's international business strategies over the planning period. At one extreme, a manufacturer may have no plans to enter the target market in any other way and is not concerned with possible licensee competition in third markets. In that event, it will assess prospective opportunity costs of a licensing venture as zero. At the other extreme, a manufacturer may want to keep its options to enter the target market as an exporter or investor or may be fearful of licensee competition in third markets. Such a manufacturer may assess prospective opportunity costs as so high as to prohibit a pure licensing agreement, rejecting licensing altogether or combining it with equity investment in the licensee firm. Admittedly, it is difficult for managers to place a dollar value on prospective opportunity costs, but an appraisal of those costs is nonetheless important, as testified by the unfortunate experiences of many manufacturers that entered licensing agreements without considering such costs.

Start-up costs include all transfer costs incurred by the licensor to establish the licensing venture and to get the licensee into volume production and marketing of the licensed product. Start-up *time* depends mainly on the complexity of the technology package and the ability of the licensee to assimilate it. Start-up time probably runs from one to two years for the majority of licensing ventures. It is common for licensors to demand lump-sum payments to cover all or part of their start-up costs.

Ongoing costs include all costs incurred by the licensor to maintain the licensing agreement as a profitable venture over its duration, which is ordinarily five to ten years.

The licensor is now ready to calculate the *profit contribution* of the proposed licensing venture by subtracting aggregate costs from aggregate revenues. Since the time paths of revenues and costs will differ, it is desirable to use net present values in calculating the profit contribution.[6] The resulting figure should then be compared with the estimated profit contributions of alternative entry modes to help managers decide which is the most appropriate entry mode for the company. Assuming that the company chooses a licensing venture, its managers can use the profitability analysis as a framework for negotiations with the prospective licensee.

The reader may note that we have not included the "cost" of the licensor's industrial property rights in this discussion of licensing costs. Treated as an overhead cost, R & D has usually been charged off against domestic sales by the time the technology is licensed to a foreign company. Moreover, the same technology may be licensed again and again to different licensees. Thus any assignment of R & D cost to the technology package of a specific licensing venture would be arbitrary and bear no relationship to its value. As the reader shall see, the economic value of a technology package is determined by negotiations between the licensor and the prospective licensee. Since industrial property rights are not capitalized in the ordinary licensing agreement, the value of these rights is implicitly expressed in the licensor's profit contribution.[7]

Negotiating the Licensing Agreement

If the licensor decides to go ahead with a licensing venture, the profitability analysis will also provide guidelines for negotiating the licensing agreement. The first task is to select the prospective licensee in the target country.

Selecting the Prospective Licensee

The screening process used to select a licensee candidate resembles that used to select a foreign distributor, as described in Chapter 4. The process has four steps: (1) determining the licensor's licensee profile, (2) sourcing licensee prospects, (3) evaluating and comparing licensee prospects, and (4) selecting the most appropriate licensee candidate.

The *licensee profile* lists all the attributes that the licensor would like to get in its licensee for a given target market. The profile, therefore, is an ideal construct that reflects the licensor's objectives and its profitability analysis of the prospective licensing venture. It specifies the desired licensee qualifications relating to product line, technical competence, production facilities, quality control, distribution system, general management, business reputation and honesty, financial strength, size, ownership, compatibility as a working partner, and any other attributes that the licensor considers important to the success of the venture. The licensor should go beyond a simple listing of qualifications by rating them in importance, because it will almost certainly be impossible to find a live license candidate who matches the profile on all points.

The licensor can obtain the names of prospective licensees from several sources. Probably the most common source is the unsolicited inquiry from a foreign company. Indeed, many licensors have responded *only* to unsolicited inquiries in establishing licensing arrangements. Given the nonselective character of unsolicited inquiries, however, the licensor should also undertake an active search for licensing prospects who will satisfy its licensee profile. If the licensor is currently exporting to the target country, its agents, distributors, or customers may be good licensing prospects or may supply leads to prospects. Names may also be obtained from the advertisements of foreign companies in trade publications; representatives of industry, banks, and governments in both the home and target countries; promotion by the licensor in trade publications and other media; and international trade fairs and other gatherings of businesspeople.

To evaluate licensee prospects, the licensor needs to get information on them. As in the case of distributor prospects, the most direct way is to write a letter to each prospect asking about his or her interest in a licensing agreement and about his or her qualifications. Evaluation of the responses to this letter, checks with banks and other references, and additional information obtained from private and government sources may then be supplemented by a second letter to the most promising candidates. The licensor is well advised, however, to make the final selection only after personal visits to the best prospects. If the licensor has done a systematic screening job, it can be reasonably confident that it has found

---

In 1992, the United States and China reached an agreement providing more protection against illegal copying in China of U.S. pharmaceuticals, computer software, books, and music recordings. China agreed to adopt international standards on industrial property rights and to enact laws extending the duration and scope of patent, copyright, and trade-secret protection. For instance, the duration of patents will increase from fifteen to twenty years. China also agreed to join the Berne Convention and the Geneva Phonograms Convention, which uphold high standards for copyright protection. American trade associations estimate that illegal copying in China causes $400 million of annual losses in pharmaceuticals and $419 million in computer software, books, and music recordings. The United States had threatened to impose prohibitive tariffs on $1.5 billion worth of imports from China in retaliation for losses of royalties to American companies caused by illegal copying unless the Chinese government provided greater protection.

Adapted from "U.S. and China Reach Accord on Copying," *New York Times,* January 17, 1992, p. D1.

a good candidate who will justify the time and expense of negotiating a licensing agreement.

The Negotiation Process

Although international licensing negotiations sometimes have been conducted entirely by correspondence, it is always advisable to have face-to-face negotiations. Several negotiating sessions are the rule rather than the exception, and the average negotiations (including the preparation of legal documents) last six months to one year. Since the negotiations are between nationals of different countries, they are exposed to all the perils of cross-cultural communication. Even when both parties can obviously benefit each other, negotiations may collapse because of misunderstanding and distrust engendered by cultural pitfalls.[8]

So many individual points must be settled in licensing negotiations that the ensuing agreement will most probably be unique. Several of these points are identified in the next subsection. In this subsection we describe the negotiating process in terms of a normative model (Figure 13) that focuses on the determination of the

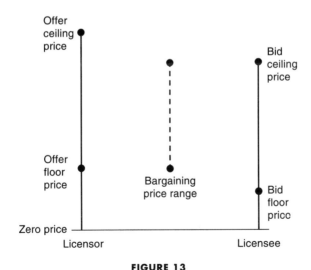

FIGURE 13

Determination of the Bargaining Price Range in Licensing Negotiations

price of the manufacturer's technology package. (The term *technology package* embraces all industrial property rights, technical assistance, and any other assets or services supplied to the licensee by the licensor under an agreement.)

The model postulates that the prospective licensor enters negotiations with a range of possible offer prices for a given technology package, while the prospective licensee enters negotiations with a range of possible bid prices. The overlapping of these two ranges determines the *bargaining price range*.

The licensor's offer price range is established by its floor and ceiling prices. The *offer floor price* is the sum of the licensor's opportunity costs and the costs of transferring the technology package to the licensee. Clearly, the licensor will not accept a price below this floor, because to do so would cause actual or prospective cash loss. The *offer ceiling price* is the licensor's estimation of the value of the technology package to the licensee, that is, how much the use of the technology package would increase the licensee's net cash flow (profit contribution) over the agreement. Although the licensor, like any seller, would like to get as much as possible for the technology package, he or she cannot rationally expect to get more than its value to the licensee. To make a good estimate of this value, the licensor needs to know the sales potential of the licensed product in the target market.

On the other side, the licensee's bid price range is also determined by floor and ceiling prices. The *bid floor price* is the licensee's estimate of the licensor's transfer costs. (The licensee ignores the licensor's opportunity costs and, in any event, does not have the information to estimate them.) The licensee cannot rationally expect to get the technology package for less than its transfer costs. The *bid ceiling price* is the lowest of three values: (1) the incremental cash flow the licensee would obtain from the use of the technology package, (2) the cost of the same or a similar technology package from another supplier, and (3) the cost of developing the technology package independently.[9] Under no circumstances would the licensee be willing to pay more than the expected incremental cash flow. It is almost certain that the licensee's full cost of duplicating the technology package would exceed the other two values. (Duplication would also take much more time than acquiring the package under license.) When the licensee can obtain the technology package from more than one source, the bid ceiling price will usually be determined, therefore, by the lowest alternative offer price. The licensor must at least meet this price in order to negotiate an agreement.

The licensor's floor price and the licensee's ceiling price together determine the bargaining range in the negotiations, as shown in Figure 13. The negotiated price will be at a point on this range.[10]

The price or compensation to be received for the technology package is not the only issue to be resolved in licensing negotiations. Two other key issues are the *content* of the technology package itself (the mix of patents, trademarks, know-how, and services), and the *use conditions* of the package. During the course of negotiations, therefore, the opening bargaining price range will shift with negotiated changes in the technology package and use conditions. (New information and new circumstances that affect the behavior of either party can also cause shifts in the bargaining range.) The negotiation process therefore is likely to encompass a sequence of bargaining price ranges over time as well as bargaining within each range at a particular time.

Licensing negotiations can become very complex, because the many elements that make up the three groups of issues may be combined in any number of ways. This flexibility generates many trade-offs that facilitate a final agreement. The technology price, for instance, may be raised or lowered by changes in the technology package or its use conditions. Moreover, the compensation mix is also variable, so that, say, a lower royalty rate may be traded off against lump-sum payments, minimum annual royalties, service fees, equity, and other forms of compensation. Flexibility in the compensation mix may be critical to the success of negotiations when a royalty rate ceiling is imposed by the host government or when the licensee insists on a "conventional rate." In sum, licensing negotiations are open-ended in several directions.

This discussion of the negotiating process indicates that licensors can negotiate more effectively when they have made a profitability analysis of the proposed licensing venture. For then they will better know their objectives, the value of the technology package to the licensee, and the trade-offs among the many elements of a licensing agreement. The stronger the licensor's bargaining leverage, the closer the final negotiated price will be to the licensee's bid ceiling price. Conversely, the weaker the licensor's bargaining leverage, the closer the final price will be to his or her offer floor price. But the *actual* compensation from a licensing agreement will be completely determinable only at the conclusion of the agreement, some years into the future.

This last observation points to the risks assumed by both parties to a licensing agreement. Terms must be negotiated before the value of the technology package to the recipient can be ascertained.

Over the past quarter century, the beer brewing industry has been undergoing a process of internationalization. Ranked by volume, the largest exporters of beer are the Netherlands, Germany, the former Czechoslovakia, Belgium, and Canada; the largest importers are the United States, the United Kingdom, France, Italy, and Germany. But most countries that export beer also import it (and vice versa), reflecting the appeal of individual brands to different local tastes and preferences. In addition to exporting, licensing agreements are also a common entry mode in this industry. For instance, Anheuser-Busch (U.S.) licenses Labatt (Canada) to brew and market Budweiser and Michelob in Canada, and Miller is licensed to brew and market Lowenbrau beer in the United States. In the late 1980s there were at least thirty licensing agreements between brewers throughout the world. Compared to exporting, licensing offers several advantages to the brewer entering foreign markets: circumvention of trade barriers, reduction in transportation costs (beer is about 90 percent water, with a shelf life of only three to four months), and avoidance of investment in production and distribution systems. It is estimated that the volume of licensed production of U.S. beers in Canada is more than seventeen times the volume of beer exported from the United States, and the dominance of licensed production over exports is true elsewhere. The beer industry is also marked by investment entry into foreign markets. Hence the volume of international trade in beer greatly underestimates the internationalization of the industry.

Despite the rapid pace of the industry's internationalization, it is not always easy for brewers to penetrate foreign markets. For instance, North American brewers are having a hard time in building sales in Western Europe in face of prejudice against American beers, European taste preferences, the exclusive ties between European brewers and pubs, and the resistance of supermarkets to foreign newcomers. Cultural resistance, as well as high costs, poses obstacles to the acquisition of European breweries by North American beer companies. Heineken (the Netherlands) is the most global beer company, brewing its beer in fifty countries; it is the leading imported beer in the United States. In 1990 its foreign sales were 85 percent of its total sales. In contrast, only 3 percent of Anheuser-Busch's sales were foreign in the same year.

Adapted from Jeffrey D. Karrenbrock, "The Internationalization of the Beer Brewing Industry," *Review* (Federal Reserve Bank of St. Louis), November-December 1990, pp. 3–19; "Wooing Jacques and Fritz Six-Pack, *Business Week,* February 4, 1991, pp. 92–93; and "Cheers to Heineken," *Fortune,* November 19, 1990, p. 172.

The costs and income of the two parties are contingent on the other's performance over the agreement's life, as well as on the market and other external factors. The licensor, therefore, must assess both the business risks and the political risks of a proposed licensing venture.

The Licensing Contract

The successful conclusion of negotiations is marked by the signing of a licensing contract.[11] A licensing contract has the following elements:

Technology Package
 Definition/description of the licensed industrial property
  (patents, trademarks, know-how)
 Know-how to be supplied and its method of transfer
 Supply of raw materials, equipment, and intermediate goods

Use Conditions
 Field of use of licensed technology
 Territorial rights for manufacture and sale
 Sublicensing rights
 Safeguarding trade secrets
 Responsibility for defense/infringement action on patents
  and trademarks

Exclusion of competitive products
Exclusion of competitive technology
Maintenance of product standards
Performance requirements
Rights of licensee to new products and technology
Reporting requirements
Auditing/inspection rights of licensor
Reporting requirements of licensee

Compensation
Currency of payment
Responsibilities for payment of local taxes
Disclosure fee
Running royalties
Minimum royalties
Lump-sum royalties
Technical-assistance fees
Sales to and/or purchases from licensee
Fees for additional new products
Grantback of product improvements by licensee
Other compensation

Other Provisions
Contract law to be followed
Duration and renewal of contract
Cancellation/termination provisions
Procedures for the settlement of disputes
Responsibility for government approval of the license
   agreement

Three of these elements deserve some comment, namely, territorial rights, performance requirements, and the settlement of disputes.

Territorial Rights. The licensor's ownership of patent and trademark rights in the target country is the legal basis for an exclusive license that gives manufacturing and sales rights only to the licensee in that country. Under an exclusive license, the licensor agrees not to allow the use of the technology package by itself or another company in the same territory and field. Whether a licensor should grant an exclusive license depends on its market entry strategy and on its bargaining power with a prospective licensee. To illustrate, a licensor may want to grant a *nonexclusive* license in order to be free to license other companies or use the rights and know-how on its own in the target country at a later time. In contrast, the licensee usually presses for an exclusive license that will keep out the licensor or other licensees. Quite commonly, a good licensing candidate may refuse to assume the responsibilities of an agreement unless he or she is granted exclusive rights.

An exclusive license by itself does not prevent the licensee from selling outside the exclusive territory. As observed earlier, patent and trademark rights are limited to a given national jurisdiction. Consequently, whether a licensor can limit a licensee's rights to sell outside the target country depends on government policy and laws in that country as well as on laws governing restrictive business practices in the home country. If a licensee in country A wants to export licensed products to country B, where the licensor also holds industrial property rights, then the import of that product would infringe on the licensor's rights in country B. Hence there would be no need to include a provision in the licensing contract prohibiting the export of the licensed product from country A to country B.

Suppose the licensor does not have industrial property rights in country B, as is always true with trade secrets. In that case it can control the export of the licensed product from country A to country B only through contractual arrangements with its licensee in country A. But now comes the rub. In many countries, export limitations are not allowed in licensing agreements, because the host government wants to increase exports of industrial products. Furthermore, American manufacturers have to worry about U.S. antitrust laws that question export limitations because the latter may restrain competition in U.S. trade. Inability to control a licensee's exports may carry such great opportunity costs for the licensor as to doom any licensing venture. The obvious way to avoid legal complications is to grant only nonexclusive licenses, but this policy can cut the value of the licensor's technology to prospective licensees, as well as create unacceptable opportunity costs.

Performance Requirements. The success of a licensing venture depends on the licensee's ability and willingness to manufacture the licensed product to agreed quality standards and to exploit fully its sales potential in the target market. This dependence is particularly acute with an exclusive licensing agreement. To protect its interests, therefore, the licensor needs to include performance provisions in the contract with respect to both production and sales. Penalties for the licensee's failure to meet the stipulated performance requirements can include fees, liquidated damages, or termination of the contract.

As for production, quality control may be exercised by the licensor in several ways: an agreed standard of quality; the right of the licensor to inspect the licensee's operations and make product tests; the use of the licensor's own engineers to supervise the licensee's production; the use of specified raw materials, equipment, and components; and so on. Apart from suffering damage to its reputation, the licensor may lose its trademark rights in the target country if the licensee fails to meet the usual quality standards.

As for sales, the licensor may specify a minimum volume of sales or minimum promotion and other marketing expenditures. But the most common way to motivate the licensee's selling efforts is the requirement of minimum royalty payments. In this way, the licensor is assured of a certain royalty income regardless of the sales of the licensed product. Minimum royalty payments are especially desirable in exclusive licensing ventures.

Settlement of Disputes. The terms of a licensing contract should be explicit, but at the same time they should be flexible enough that both parties can execute them. Nonetheless, disputes will arise from time to time. In most instances, they can be settled by reference to the written contract and by talking over differences. But with some disputes, settlement may require use of external procedures, which should be spelled out in the contract.

In general, litigation should be avoided by the licensor, not only because it is costly and time-consuming, but also because jurisdiction may be established in the foreign country even though the contract specifies that the governing law is that of the licensor's country. The best way to avoid litigation of disputes is to provide for arbitration that is binding on both parties. The arbitration clause in the contract should state the applicable arbitration rules (the most common are those of the American Arbitration Association and the International Chamber of Commerce) or name the arbitration tribunal.

Working with the Licensee

The licensing contract marks the conclusion of formal negotiations, but it is only the start of the licensing venture. Both parties must now cooperate in building that venture so that it can meet their shared expectations. In most instances, the licensee will need continuing technical assistance from the licensor, who in turn has an obvious interest in helping the licensee exploit the sales potential of the licensed product in the target market. A licensing venture, therefore, should be regarded as a *nonequity joint venture* that combines the strengths of the two parties in the pursuit of common goals. When a licensor views its obligations to the licensee as ending with an initial transfer of industrial property rights and know-how, it is using licensing as a source of income, not as an instrument to build a market position in the target country.

This chapter has focused on licensing as a *primary* entry mode, that is, the use of licensing as a full alternative to exporting or equity investment. But licensing is an extremely flexible vehicle that may be easily combined with other entry modes to form *mixed* entry modes. Indeed, licensing is used most frequently in association with equity joint or sole manufacturing ventures. For instance, in recent years more than three-quarters of the royalties and licensing fees received by U.S. companies have been from affiliated foreign firms. In fact, the line dividing licensing from direct investment is sometimes hard to distinguish. A licensing contract that arranges for compensation in the form of equity in the licensee company or gives the licensor an option to invest in that company can transform a licensing venture into an equity joint venture. Also, as has been noted, licensing agreements may involve the sale of intermediate and other products by the licensor to the licensee or, conversely, the sale of finished products by the licensee to the licensor.

To conclude, licensing may be combined with other entry modes to create a mixed entry mode that is superior to any of its constituents. And a pure licensing venture can grow in time into an equity joint venture or stimulate other international business arrangements. These two features alone ensure that licensing will always be an important element in the foreign market entry strategies of many companies.

International Franchising

Franchising is a form of licensing in which a company (franchisor) licenses a business system as well as other property rights to an independent company or person (franchisee). The franchisee does business under the franchisor's trade name and follows the policies and procedures laid down by the franchisor. Essentially, therefore, the franchisor licenses a way of organizing and carrying on a business under its trade name. In return the franchisor receives fees, running royalties, and other compensation from the franchisee.

Franchising has grown explosively in the United States and is now common in diverse business fields: fast-food restaurants, car rentals, construction, soft drinks, hotels and motels, and several services ranging from real estate brokerage to the preparation of tax forms. After establishing franchise systems at home, many U.S. franchisors expanded into foreign countries. Holiday Inn, McDonald's, Kentucky Fried Chicken, and Avis (to name only a few) have become household names in scores of countries. Much earlier, Singer Sewing Machine, Coca-Cola, Pepsi-Cola, and Hilton Hotels showed the way. Although non-U.S. companies have also become international franchisors (such as Wimpy's, Bake 'n' Take, and Benihana), U.S. companies have dominated this form of enterprise in both numbers and sales volume, so much so that franchising has a distinctly American flavor.

As with any other mode of foreign market entry, franchising offers both advantages and disadvantages to a company. The principal advantages are (1) rapid expansion into a foreign market with low capital outlays, (2) a standardized method of marketing with a distinctive image, (3) highly motivated franchisees, and (4) low political risks. Key disadvantages of franchising resemble those of traditional licensing: (1) limitations on the franchisor's profit, (2) lack of full control over the franchisee's operations, (3) the possible creation of competitors, and (4) restrictions imposed by governments on the terms of franchise agreements.

International franchising is particularly attractive to a company when it has a product that cannot be exported to a foreign target country, it does not want to invest in that country as a producer, and its production process (business system) can be easily transferred to an independent party in the target country. Thus physical products whose manufacture requires substantial capital investment and/or high levels of managerial or technical competence are poor candidates for franchising. The same is true of service products (which *must* be produced at the foreign point of sale) that involve sophisticated skills, such as advertising, accounting, banking, insurance, and management consulting. That is why international

---

Bandag (U.S.), a tire retreading company, has been in Europe since the 1950s, with an affiliate in Belgium that marketed through exclusive distributors throughout the region. Although these distributors built a reputation for quality, they charged high prices and were content with low sales volumes. In the early 1980s, as Bandag's last patents were running out, management decided to abandon its distribution network in Europe and replace it with a more aggressive franchise network. This shift in entry strategy worked; Bandag's share of Europe's retread market rose from 5 percent to 20 percent, with a corresponding jump in revenues.

The success of the franchise system owes a great deal to Bandag's unique approach to sales and service. Instead of making customers come to the franchise outlets, the franchisees go to the customers with specially designed Mercedes trucks loaded with tires and equipment. In this way, worn tires are replaced with retreads on the spot. Also, the trucks are sent out after hours so that customers can keep their trucks on the road during the day. With 336 outlets in Western Europe, Bandag is poised to take advantage of the single regional market for trucking that is now in place in the European Community. By intensifying cross-national competition, it is anticipated that single market will induce truckers to use more retreads (which sell for about half the price of new tires). In addition to adding franchisees in Western Europe, Bandag plans to enter the cost-conscious markets of Eastern Europe in the year ahead.

Adapted from "Bandag: Retreading the Tire Business," *Business Week,* January 20, 1992, pp. 88–89.

franchising is most popular in consumer service products that can be created with comparatively low levels of capital and skills.

For companies with franchisable products, therefore, the critical choice is between franchising and equity investment in a joint or sole venture. This choice is another illustration of the trade-off between control and risk, which was discussed in Chapter 2. When a company is starting its penetration of a foreign market, it may choose franchising as an entry mode because of its lower risks. But as the company gains experience in that market, it may replace its franchisees with joint or sole ventures, which give it more control. Thus for many companies franchising may prove to be a transitional entry mode that takes them into joint or sole ventures at a later time. This transition will occur, of course, only when it is the most profitable way to exploit the target market. For that reason, it is least likely to occur in developing countries that place constraints on foreign ownership. Also, for internal reasons some firms will choose to stay with franchising, just as many companies have chosen to stay with exporting.

The steps to establish franchising systems abroad resemble those of traditional licensing: (1) assessing sales potential in the target market, (2) finding suitable franchisee candidates, (3) negotiating the franchise agreement, and (4) building a working partnership with the franchisee. Franchising differs from ordinary licensing mainly in a greater emphasis on control over the franchisee's operations. The franchise contract usually stipulates that the franchisor can terminate the contract after a one- or two-year trial period, and later for the franchisee's failure to perform to agreed standards and sales volume. Other provisions cover the franchisor's right to inspect all aspects of the franchisee's operations, to prohibit any activities of the franchisee that harm the product/service image, and so on. The contract may also include an operating manual, to which the franchisee must conform if he or she is not to lose the franchise. As in licensing, some governments may not allow certain provisions intended to protect the franchisor's interests, such as territorial limitations or fixing the prices at which the franchisee must sell. Especially in developing countries, it may be difficult or impossible to terminate a franchise agreement for poor performance or to buy out a franchise.

Franchising will not work unless the franchisor offers continuing support to the franchisee. One kind of support is logistical:

supplying equipment, signs, promotional materials, products, and other physical inputs needed by the franchisee. Other support—such as training, financing, and technical, accounting, merchandising, and general management assistance—is necessary to achieve a desired level of franchisee performance. A third kind of support is promotional, particularly mass advertising to spread the company name and presell franchised products and services. The franchisor may also need to adapt its franchise package to the political, economic, and sociocultural environment of the target country. For example, Kentucky Fried Chicken in Germany was not allowed to import cooking oil used in the United States because it contained antifoaming agents prohibited by German health authorities. The agents were required because the oil had to be used in special pressure-frying equipment, and a substitute additive approved by the authorities drastically changed the taste of the product. To cite another example, when the fast-food chain Beef-A-Roo went into Australia, it was forced to change its trade name to Beef Ranch because "roo" means kangaroo meat, which is disdained by urban Australians.

Franchising has become a powerful entry mode for products and services that can be reproduced by independent franchisees. For U.S. companies that can overcome new management and political problems, international franchising bids fair to rival the franchising boom in the United States.

Other Contractual Entry Modes

In addition to licensing, technical assistance, and franchising agreements, other contractual entry modes have become prominent in international business, particularly with the developing countries. We offer here some comments on the more important ones.

Contract Manufacturing

Contract manufacturing is a cross between licensing and investment entry. In contract manufacturing, an international firm sources a product from an independent manufacturer in a foreign target country and subsequently markets that product in the target country or elsewhere. To obtain a product manufactured to its specifications, the international firm ordinarily transfers technology and technical-assistance to the local manufacturer. These transfers may be formalized in a separate licensing/technical-assistance agreement between the two parties.

Contract manufacturing can bring the international company several advantages. It requires a comparatively small commitment of financial and management resources, allows for quick entry into the target country, avoids local ownership problems, and—unlike standard licensing—permits the international company to exercise control over marketing and after-sales service. Contract manufacturing is especially attractive when the target market is too small to justify investment entry (assuming it is possible) and export entry is blocked by restrictions or is simply too costly.

The disadvantages of contract manufacturing resemble those of licensing. It may be difficult or impossible to find a suitable local manufacturer. Once a manufacturer is found, substantial technical assistance may be required to bring it up to the desired quality and volume levels, and to keep it at those levels. Finally, the international company runs the risk of creating a future competitor.

Turnkey Construction Contracts

A turnkey contract carries the standard construction contract a step further by obligating the contractor to bring a foreign project up to the point of operation before it is turned over to the owner. A further step is the contractor's obligation to provide services, such as management and worker training, after construction is completed in order to prepare the owner to operate the project, an arrangement sometimes called "turnkey plus."

It is impossible to use a standard turnkey contract, because each project is unique in one of more respects. Negotiations between the two parties are complex, involve large sums of money, take considerable time, and require sophisticated legal assistance. But whatever the details of a specific turnkey contract may be, experience demonstrates that the contractor should make certain that the contract clearly stipulates the project's plant and equipment, the obligations and responsibilities of each party, the meaning of *force majeure* and contract violations and their legal consequences, and procedures for the resolution of disputes.

Many turnkey contracts are with host governments. As such, they are particularly exposed to political risks of contract revocation, compulsory renegotiation, and the arbitrary calling of bank guarantees. A brief discussion of the latter will indicate the political risks assumed by a company in construction contracts with host governments.

Middle Eastern governments commonly refuse to accept surety bonds from surety or insurance companies. Instead they demand bid, advance payment, maintenance, and performance bonds guaranteed by banks (standby letters of credit) that are callable at the discretion of the host government. This situation poses a formidable risk to the contractor, who would experience an immediate loss of funds in the event of a calling: the guaranteeing bank would quickly exercise recourse on him or her. With on-demand guarantees, the host government can call a guarantee even if the contractor is not in default of the contract, and there is very little a company can do about it. It follows that this particular risk should be carefully assessed by the international company, along with other political risks (such as general political instability).[12]

It is not sufficient to make certain that cash flow exposure is minimized with payments over the contract life. Expected cash flows should also be set against liabilities in the event of sudden contract termination by action of the host government or political upheaval. Even with favorable cash payment terms, exposure to political risk can be a large fraction of the full contract value since it is the sum of bank guarantees, cancellation fees owing to subcontractors, and other termination expenses. International companies can get some protection against political risks through arbitration and *force majeure* clauses in the contract, through spreading the risk by the formation of consortia, and through insurance with a government or private agency.[13] In most instances, however, contractors will need to assume some political risk, and their only protection will be their own assessment of political risk in deciding whether to enter the contract.

Management Contracts

An international management contract gives a company the right to manage the day-to-day operations of an enterprise in a foreign target country. Ordinarily, such contracts do *not* give a company the authority to make new capital investments, assume long-term debt, decide on dividend policy, initiate basic management or policy changes, or alter ownership arrangements. Management control therefore is limited to ongoing operations.

Manufacturers seldom enter management contracts in isolation from other arrangements with a foreign enterprise. That is to say, they do not view themselves primarily as suppliers of management services. Rather, management contracts are used mainly to supplement an actual or intended joint-venture agreement or a turnkey project.[14] In this way, an international company can obtain management control over a foreign venture. Fees from management services may contribute only modestly to income derived from a joint venture, but they may be an important fraction of the income derived from a turkey-plus contract.

Viewed in isolation, a management contract can provide low-risk entry into a foreign target market, but income is limited to fees for a fixed duration of time. From an entry strategy perspective, management contracts are unsatisfactory because they do not allow a company to build a permanent market position for its products. Other disadvantages include time-consuming negotiations and the commitment of scarce management talent. But when combined with other arrangements, management contracts can sometimes help fashion a better package for both parties.

Countertrade

In doing business with developing countries, international firms are commonly pressed to accept all or part of their compensation in the form of goods, a practice called *countertrade*. Broadly defined, countertrade may be described as a contractual entry mode that involves some combination of trade, licensing, investment, and finance. The principal forms of countertrade are (1) barter (the exchange of goods or services without the use of money), (2) counterpurchase (an agreement under which an exporter undertakes to buy goods from an importer or third party designated by the importer equal to the value of an agreed percentage of the original export), (3) compensation or buyback (an agreement under which an exporter of industrial equipment agrees to buy products manufactured with that equipment), and (4) offset (an agreement whereby an exporter of, say, aircraft agrees to buy from the importer, or a third party designated by the importer, components of the aircraft up to a certain percentage of the aircraft's value). International firms that want to take full advantage of opportunities in developing countries need to consider countertrade agreements because they may be the only way to gain access to a country market.[15]

Summary

1. International licensing includes a variety of contractual arrangements whereby domestic companies (licensors) make their intangible assets (patents, trade secrets, know-how, trademarks, and company name), available to foreign companies (licensees) in return for royalties and/or other forms of payment. Commonly, the transfer of these intangible assets or property rights is accompanied by technical services to ensure the proper use of the assets.

2. The most obvious advantage of licensing as an entry mode is the circumvention of import barriers that increase the cost (tariffs) or limit the quantity (quotas) of exports to the target market. The foremost disadvantage of licensing from an entry strategy perspective is the licensor's lack of control over the marketing plan and program in the target country.

3. A company can use licensing to enter a foreign market only if it can secure legal protection of its industrial property rights in the target country. In the country-by-country quest for industrial property rights, a company faces many legal pitfalls.

4. The legal complexities in obtaining, maintaining, and enforcing patents make it all the more urgent for companies to have an international patent strategy. The same is true for trademarks. It is important that a licensor take contractual safeguard measures to prevent the disclosure or unwarranted use of trade secrets by a licensee before, during, and after a licensing agreement.

5. Managers can rationally choose licensing as a primary entry mode only when they compare the expected profitability of a proposed licensing venture with the expected profitability of alternative entry modes, notably export and

equity investment. There are many kinds of licensing income and costs.

6. If the manufacturer decides to go ahead with a licensing venture, its profitability analysis will also provide guidelines for negotiating the licensing agreement. The first task is to select the prospective licensee in the target country. Although international licensing negotiations have been conducted entirely by correspondence, it is always advisable to have face-to-face negotiations. So many points must be settled that the ensuing agreement will most probably be unique. Terms must be negotiated before the value of the technology package to the recipient can be ascertained in fact.

7. Three elements of the licensing contract are of key importance: territorial rights, performance requirements, and the settlement of disputes. The licensing contract marks the conclusion of formal negotiations, but it is only the start of the licensing venture.

8. Licensing may be combined with other entry modes to create a mixed entry mode that is superior to any of its constituents.

9. Franchising is a form of licensing in which a company (franchisor) licenses a business system as well as industrial property rights to an independent company or person (franchisee). International franchising is particularly attractive to a company when it has a product that cannot be exported to a foreign target country, it does not want to invest in that country as a producer, and its production process (business system) can be easily transferred to an independent party in the target country.

10. Other contractual entry modes include contract manufacturing, turnkey construction projects, management contracts, and countertrade agreements.

CHAPTER 6

Entering International Markets Through Investment

Companies invest in foreign production for three basic reasons: to obtain raw materials, to source products at a lower cost, and to penetrate local markets.

Extractive investors establish foreign subsidiaries to exploit natural resources in order to acquire raw materials for their own industrial operations (backward vertical integration) or for sale on world markets. Ordinarily, these investors sell only a small fraction of their raw-materials output in the foreign country of extraction. The steel, aluminum, and petroleum industries offer classic examples of this kind of direct foreign investment.

Sourcing investors establish foreign operations to manufacture products that are entirely or mainly exported to the home country or to third countries. The purpose of sourcing investments is to obtain lower-cost supplies of components, parts, or finished goods by taking advantage of abundant endowments of labor, energy, or other inputs in a foreign country. U.S. companies in the consumer electronics industry have been particularly active as sourcing investors, obtaining assembled products from plants in Mexico, Taiwan, and elsewhere for sale in the United States.

Market investors account for most investment abroad. Their objective is to penetrate a target market from a production base inside the target country. This group of investors, which regards investment as a foreign market entry mode, is the subject of this chapter.

General Appraisal of the Investment Entry Mode

As is true of other entry modes, investment offers both advantages and disadvantages to a company. The probability of a successful investment entry can be enhanced by building on experience gained through prior export to the target country/market. The investment entry decision is a complex process that requires an evaluation of both the investment climate in the target country and the intended investment project.

Advantages of Investment Entry

Fundamentally, investment entry involves the transfer to a target country of an entire enterprise. In contrast, exporting is essentially the transfer of products, while licensing is the transfer of technology and other industrial property. By allowing a company to transfer managerial, technical, marketing, financial, and other skills (its "knowledge assets") to a target country in the form of an enterprise under its own control, investment entry enables that company to exploit more fully its competitive advantages in the target market.[1] As we have observed previously, licensing entry does not allow a manufacturer to control the production and marketing of the licensed products. And although branch/subsidiary exporting offers the manufacturer full control over marketing, it does not offer the possible logistical advantages of investment entry.

Local production may lower the *costs* of supplying a foreign target market as compared to export entry, because of savings in transportation and customs duties and/or lower production costs resulting from less expensive local inputs of labor, raw materials, energy, and so on. Local production may also increase the *availability* of supply if quotas limit imports or if a company's supply of export products is constrained by plant capacity in the home country. Moreover, investment entry may enable a manufacturer to obtain a higher or more uniform *quality* of supply in the target country than would be possible through licensing an independent local company.

Investment entry can also create *marketing* advantages. Ordinarily, local production provides far more opportunity than domestic production to adapt a company's product to local preferences and purchasing power. For example, long before they started to downsize automobiles manufactured at home, U.S. automobile companies were manufacturing smaller vehicles in Europe in response to higher fuel costs, shorter distances, and other market factors. In addition, investment entry can offer quicker and more reliable delivery of products to middlemen and customers, better provision of after-sales service, direct distribution through a subsidiary's own sales force, and a local-company image. Last but not least, investment entry usually increases the resources devoted to marketing in the target country, because the investor has more to lose from marketing failure than with export or licensing entry.

When its product is a service whose production and marketing require face-to-face relations between producers and customers (such as health care, restaurants, retailing, advertising, banking, or business consulting), then the firm *must* find a way to create and deliver its product locally. If the service requires high-level skills or strong controls, franchising or licensing may be unattractive. In that event, some form of investment entry becomes the only viable entry mode.[2]

Disadvantages of Investment Entry

The advantages of investment entry must be set against its disadvantages. Compared to other modes, investment entry requires substantially more capital, management, and other company resources.[3] This higher resource commitment also means higher exposure to risks. Moreover, investment entry is subject to a wider range of political risks than other modes. Because of its high capital requirements and risks, strategic planning for investment entry becomes exceptionally important.

Since the ultimate success of a production subsidiary is dependent on many political, economic, sociocultural, and market factors, the information necessary for good entry investment decisions is far greater than for exporting or licensing. To put the matter in another way, the probability of poor investment decisions is magnified by the lack or misinterpretation of information, more so than with alternative entry modes. Other possible disadvantages of investment entry include high start-up costs, long payback periods, and the difficulty of disinvestment in the event of failure or a change in strategy.

The Time Path of Investment Entry

Because of the demanding information requirements of investment entry, it is usually unwise for a company to make its first entry investment abroad without a prior penetration of the target country through exports. One study of the initial foreign manufacturing subsidiaries of forty-three small British companies found that success was correlated with prior export entry. Companies that established a subsidiary in a target country without earlier export experience demonstrated the lowest success rating. Moreover, companies that had built up a prior export entry with the greatest number of incremental steps (using foreign agents or distributors and later their own sales subsidiaries or branches) showed the highest success rating.[4] In sum, a company's first investment abroad is likely to be more successful as a *subsequent* entry mode than as an *initial* entry mode. Prior export experience lessens a key uncertainty in the investment entry decision: the sales potential in the target market for the company's product.

After a company has gained experience from its first investment entry in a target country, the establishment of production subsidiaries in other target countries without prior export or other entry experience becomes less risky. The first investment experience instructs a company in the information it needs to make a good investment decision, develops in-house managers who can better assess the significance of that information, and instills confidence in the company's ability to manage foreign operations. Subsequent investment entry decisions therefore are apt to be made with more intelligence and skill than the first one. It does not follow, however, that investment experience in one country is fully transferable to another country. Investment climates, in

In just over a decade, Arvin Industries (U.S.) moved from being a local auto-parts manufacturer to a worldwide enterprise with one-third of its sales abroad. In 1981, auto parts (mainly mufflers and catalytic converters) accounted for about 60 percent of Arvin's sales, mostly to U.S. auto companies. But when executives in the auto industry began talking about a "world car," Arvin concluded it had to become an international company to survive. Today the company has factories in 16 countries and markets its products in 130 countries. Its sales have more than tripled since 1981. Arvin began its international expansion by acquiring auto-parts firms in Latin America. Then, in anticipation of a consolidation of the European auto-parts industry, it acquired companies in the United Kingdom, France and Spain. Because catalytic converters are relatively new in Europe, Arvin built plants to manufacture them in the United Kingdom and the Netherlands. Although the company does not sell much in Japan, it has two joint ventures with Japanese companies: Kayaba has a 25 percent stake in Arvin's shock absorber subsidiary in Spain, and Sango is an equal partner in supplying mufflers to Toyota in the United States. Arvin managers believe they are learning from these joint ventures and gaining acceptance in the international auto-parts industry, in which Japanese firms are prominent. International expansion has hurt Arvin's profits (acquisitions were financed with debt), but the company appears well positioned to grow substantially in the 1990s.

Adapted from "A Quick Course in Going Global," *Fortune,* January 13, 1992, p. 64.

particular, vary strikingly across countries. Whenever possible, a company would be wise to gain experience in a target country through exports before it undertakes an investment entry.

The Decision to Invest in a Target Country

The investment entry decision process involves several subdecisions taken over a lengthy period of time, with multiple feedbacks that stimulate the reconsideration of earlier decisions. Figure 14 suggests a way to structure this complex decision process by means of a sequence of checkpoints that must be passed if an investment proposal is to gain acceptance.

The decision to investigate a foreign investment proposal is the first and most important checkpoint. Not only will a decision to investigate require substantial management time and money, it will also tend to generate a commitment to invest in those managers carrying on the investigation. The decision to investigate, therefore, should be taken only after an appraisal of alternative entry modes and alternative forms of investment entry. If managers agree that the most appropriate way to enter the target country/market is through investment, they should then go on to

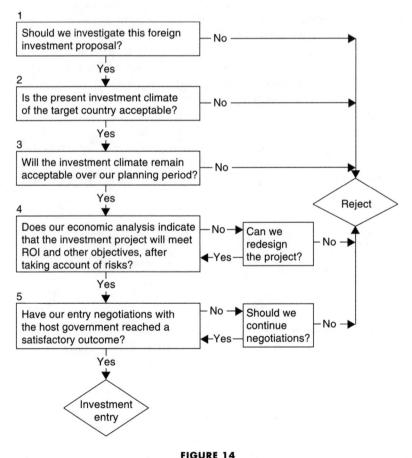

FIGURE 14

Checkpoints in the Foreign Investment Entry Decision Process

appraise alternative forms of investment entry: acquisition versus greenfield, and sole venture versus joint venture. This entry strategy review ensures against too early a commitment to investment entry or to a particular form of investment entry. Too commonly, companies respond to an outside investment proposal by setting up an investigation team that thinks only in terms of the proposal and is open to the danger of tunnel vision.

Once the decision to investigate an investment proposal is made, the next step is a thorough assessment of both the present and expected investment climates of the target country. Investment climate embraces all the environmental factors and forces—political, economic, and sociocultural—that can have a significant influence on the profitability and safety of the proposed investment project. Although the present investment climate of a target country is fully knowable to managers because it already exists, the future investment climate can be assessed only in probability terms. Since the most critical features of the future investment climate are political in nature, the dominant concern of managers is the question of political risk.

When investment-climate checkpoints are passed, managers turn to a full-scale economic analysis of the proposed project. If the project fails to meet profitability or other objectives, it may be possible to redesign the project to make it acceptable. Redesign may be intended to raise profitability (say, by reducing plant scale or adapting technology to local labor and other factor costs), to lower risk (for example, by switching from a sole venture to a joint venture), or both. The political analysis of step 3 should be integrated with the economic analysis of step 4 to ascertain the risk-adjusted profitability of the project.

If the project passes the profitability/risk checkpoint, the next step is entry negotiations with the host government.[5] In negotiations, the host government may press for certain changes in the project that managers may need to evaluate with a new economic/risk analysis. If negotiations reach a satisfactory outcome, the company proceeds to make the investment entry.

Figure 14 is intended to identify the key steps in the investment decision process, but we do not want to suggest that the actual process is a unidirectional sequence of checkpoints. In practice, the decision process is likely to take many twists and turns. In the early phases of the decision process, managers are inclined to make crude judgments of the investment climate and the economic viability of the project in order to decide if any further investigation is desirable. More refined analyses of the investment climate and the project in later phases may confirm or deny these earlier judgments. Thus managers may run through steps 2, 3, and 4 several times before deciding to proceed to negotiations with the host government. These negotiations, in turn, may cause managers to reassess the investment climate and/or the project.[6]

We now turn to a closer look at several aspects of investment entry: analyzing the investment climate, analyzing the investment project, entry through acquisition and entry through joint venture.

Analyzing the Foreign Investment Climate: Assessing Political Risk

A foreign investment project must be analyzed in the context of its political, legal, economic, social, and cultural environments—the investment climate of the target country. Although sensitivity to particular environmental factors varies from one project to another, all projects are subject to the influence of some set of environmental factors. Managers therefore should raise three questions about a country's investment climate: (1) Which variables in the investment climate are critical to the success of the project? (2) What is the present behavior (value) of these critical variables? (3) How are these critical variables likely to change over the investment planning period?

In making domestic investment decisions, U.S. managers seldom pay much attention to the investment climate, implicitly assuming that it will remain constant or change only slowly over the investment's life. But it is dangerous to extend this approach to foreign investment decisions, because in many foreign countries the investment climate is far more dynamic than in the United States. Furthermore, American managers are far less knowledgeable about foreign investment climates than about the U.S. climate, in which they have functioned as persons all of their lives.

The checklist below presents the many features of a target country's investment climate that need to be assessed by managers. The checklist is only suggestive, for each investor should develop his or her own checklist to make certain it covers all the critical variables of the project's contextual environment. Of special note is the fact that all the items in the checklist depend directly or indirectly on the behavior of the political system in the host country. For that reason, changes in the investment climate will proceed mainly from changes in the behavior of the host government or from general political instability. Because the future is uncertain, management's assessment of prospective political behavior in the host country can be expressed at most in probability terms. Hence the assessment of a country's future investment climate is an assessment of the project's *political risk*.

Checklist for Evaluating the Investment Climate of a Foreign Target Country

A. General political stability
   1. Past political behavior
   2. Form of government
   3. Strength/ideology of government
   4. Strengths/ideologies of rival political groups
   5. Political, social, ethnic, and other conflicts
B. Government policies toward foreign investment
   1. Past experience of foreign investors
   2. Attitude toward foreign investment
   3. Foreign investment treaties and agreements
   4. Restrictions on foreign ownership
   5. Local content requirements
   6. Restrictions on foreign staff
   7. Other restrictions on foreign investment
   8. Incentives for foreign investment
   9. Investment entry regulations
C. Other government policies and legal factors
   1. Enforceability of contracts
   2. Fairness of courts
   3. Corporate/business law
   4. Labor laws
   5. Taxation
   6. Import duties and restrictions
   7. Patent/trademark protection
   8. Antitrust/restrictive practices laws
   9. Honesty/efficiency of public officials

D. Macroeconomic environment
    1. Role of government in the economy
    2. Government development plans/programs
    3. Size/growth rate of gross domestic product
    4. Size/growth rate of population
    5. Size/growth rate of per capita income
    6. Distribution of personal income
    7. Sectorial distribution of industry, agriculture, and services
    8. Transportation/communications system
    9. Rate of inflation
   10. Government fiscal/monetary policies
   11. Price controls
   12. Availability/cost of local capital
   13. Management-labor relations
   14. Membership in customs unions or free trade areas
E. International payments
    1. Balance of payments
    2. Foreign exchange position/external indebtedness
    3. Repatriation restrictions
    4. Exchange rate behavior

What Is Political Risk?

For the international manager, political risk arises from *uncertainty* over the continuation of present political conditions and government policies in the foreign host country that are critical to the profitability of an actual or proposed equity/contractual business arrangement. In most instances, political risk proceeds from uncertainty that the host government or a successor government will arbitrarily change the "rules of the game" so as to cause a loss or freezing of earnings and assets, including the entire foreign venture in the event of expropriation.[7]

Political risks are conventionally distinguished from *market* risks, which derive from uncertainty about future changes in cost, demand, and competition in the marketplace. All other uncertainties (apart from insurable casualty risks) are regarded as political. But this distinction breaks down in practice; so pervasive is the role of government today that conventional market risks are often more the consequence of political than economic forces. Given this interdependence between and market phenomena, managers are called upon to evaluate *all* project risks without arbitrary distinctions between political and market risks.

Having made this point, we nonetheless need to define political risk if we are to talk about it. A pragmatic definition is as follows: political risk is created by a foreign investor's uncertainty about (1) general instability in the host country's political system in the future and/or (2) future acts by the host government that would cause loss to the investor. In terms of their potential impact on an investment entry project, political risks may be grouped into four classes: general instability risk, ownership/control risk, operations risk, and transfer risk.

General instability risk proceeds from management's uncertainty about the future viability of the host country's political system. The civil wars in what was Yugoslavia illustrate this class of risk. When it occurs, general political instability may not always force the abandonment of an investment project, but it will almost certainly interrupt operations and lower profitability. *Ownership/control risk* proceeds from management's uncertainty about host government actions that would destroy or limit the investor's ownership or effective control of its affiliate in the host country. This class of risk includes several kinds of expropriatory acts by (or sanctioned by)the host government that deprive the investor of its property.

Operations risk proceeds from management's uncertainty about host government policies or acts sanctioned by the host government that would constrain the investor's operations in the host country, whether in production, marketing, finance, or other business functions. *Transfer risk* derives mainly from management's uncertainty about future government acts that would restrict the investor's ability to transfer payments or capital out of the host country—that is, the risk of inconvertibility of the host country's currency. A second type of transfer risk is depreciation of the host currency relative to the home currency of the investor. Exchange depreciation (or, more generally, exchange rate behavior) is almost always the result of government action or the consequence of government policies.

Evaluating Political Risks

Evaluation of the political risks of a proposed foreign investment requires managers to get answers to questions such as the following:

- How likely is general political instability in the host country over our investment planning period (say, five years)?

- Barring a general political collapse, how long is the present government likely to remain in power?
- How strong is the present government's commitment to the current rules of the game (for example, ownership rights) in light of its attitude toward foreign investors (ideology) and its power position?
- If the present government is succeeded, what changes in the current rules of the game would the new government be likely to make?
- How would likely changes in the rules of the game affect the safety and profitability of our investment project?

Getting answers to these questions is seldom easy, particularly for a developing country. But it is possible to collect relevant information from both secondary and primary sources and to evaluate that information in a systematic way.[8] To help managers structure the collection and analysis of information on political risks, Figure 15 offers a four-hurdle model. This model is an elaboration of step 3 in Figure 14.

The first hurdle is an assessment of general instability risk in the target country. If managers anticipate a chaotic political situation over the planning period, they will stop any further investigation of the investment entry proposal. Otherwise, they will go on to an assessment of ownership/control risks—the probability of expropriatory actions taken by the host government toward the investor's project. Expropriation is the compulsory or coercive deprivation of foreign-owned property by action taken, or sanctioned by, a host government. *Nationalization* is the taking of foreign-owned property with transfer of title to the host government.[9] *Intervention* is the seizure of foreign-owned property either by the government or by a private group (such as workers) supported by the government. *Requisition* is similar to intervention, but it is undertaken by a government (often, the military) in response to an emergency situation, with the expectation that the property will be returned to its foreign owners at a later time. *Coerced sale* is action by the host government to compel foreign investors to sell all or part of their property to a government entity or to local nationals, usually at less than market value. *Coerced contract renegotiation* is action by a host government to compel a foreign investor to agree to changes in its contract with that government. Finally, *contract revocation* is the unilateral termination by the host government of its contract with a foreign investor.

In the majority of expropriation cases, foreign investors sooner or later receive some compensation, but it seldom meets the international standard of "prompt, effective, and adequate." Since expropriation is about the worst action a host government can take

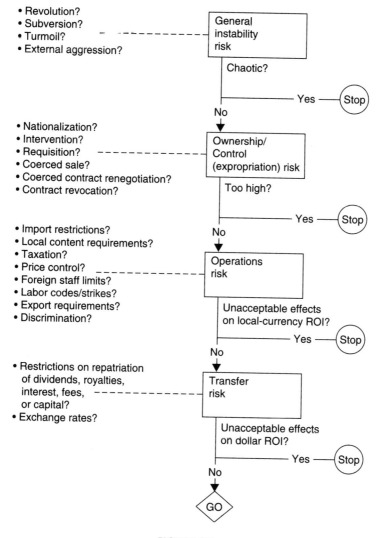

FIGURE 15

Evaluation of Political Risks of a Foreign Investment Entry Decision Process

against an investor, the expropriation risk of a project should be carefully assessed by managers. Unwarranted fear of expropriation is as much to be avoided by managers as is an unexamined belief that expropriation is something that happens only to other investors.

If the expropriation risk is judged acceptable, managers move to the third hurdle—*operations risk*. To assess operations risk, managers must first determine the character of the project's operations (inputs, outputs, size, and so on), as well as its expected cash flows over the planning period, so that they can then evaluate the probable effects of risk factors on local-currency ROI. What is required, therefore, is an integration of the risk and profitability assessments of the project, a subject taken up in the next section.

The final hurdle is *transfer risk*. Managers in companies that insist on periodic dividends and other payments from a foreign affiliate are particularly concerned with transfer risk. In contrast, managers in companies that plan to reinvest earnings in the target country for some time into the future will pay far less attention to the transfer risk, recognizing that transfer restrictions come and go with changes in the balance of payments. Ultimately, of course,

---

The revolution in Iran, which erupted in 1978, became a nightmare for the three hundred U.S. companies operating there. The most obvious victims were the big defense contractors, such as Bell Operations Corporation (a subsidiary of Textron), which suspended a $575 million contract to build a helicopter plant in Isfahan because of the Iranian government's failure to meet payments. In addition to military suppliers, the other major losers were heavy-equipment suppliers and construction companies. Westinghouse, for example, lost the sale of nuclear power plant generators worth several billion dollars. All in all, American companies had about $700 million of direct investment in Iran. By the end of 1978, most U.S. operations in Iran were brought to a halt by violence, strikes, the exodus of foreign managers and technical staff, the unavailability of supplies, and the collapse of the banking system.

Adapted from "Iran Unrest a Nightmare for Many U.S. Concerns," *New York Times*, December 22, 1978, p. 1.

all investors want to repatriate earnings and capital. In contrast to repatriation restrictions, the exchange rate risk is seldom critical to the success of a project. But to assess that risk, managers need to forecast the likely direction of changes in the dollar value of the host country's currency over the planning period and then to estimate the *net* effects of those changes on the cash flow of the project. Ordinarily the net effects will be inconsequential, because the exchange rate will reflect the internal rate of inflation, and thus higher prices in the local market will act to offset the lower dollar value of the host country currency.

If the project passes the four political risk hurdles and satisfies the investor's required rate of return, then it is ready for approval by top management.

Political Risk Insurance

In some instances, the final approval of a foreign investment project may hinge on the availability and cost of insurance against political risks. U.S. companies may be able to obtain insurance against the risks of inconvertibility, expropriation, and war, revolution, and insurrection in some eighty-five developing countries from the Overseas Private Investment Corporation (OPIC), a U.S. government agency in Washington. Political risk insurance may also be purchased from private insurers, notably the American International Group (AIG) and Lloyd's of London.

The general availability of political risk insurance, however, does not relieve managers from the responsibility of making their own assessment of a project's political risks. For one thing, OPIC insurance is available only for developing countries and then only for a new investment that is judged beneficial to the host country and not detrimental to U.S. employment or the balance of payments. Second, political risk insurance can be costly, ranging from annual OPIC rates of 1.5 percent for combined coverage up to 10 percent for private insurance. Third, insurance covers only book-value loss, which is often considerably less than market-value loss. For these reasons, investors will have to shoulder at least some exposure to political risk. In any event, they will need their own risk assessment of a project to make an informed decision on whether and how much to insure.

Analyzing the Foreign Investment Project:
Assessing Profitability

The investment project has passed the first three checkpoints in Figure 14: management has decided that investment is the most appropriate entry strategy to build or strengthen a long-term market position and that the actual and prospective investment climates of the target country are acceptable. Now management can move on to checkpoint 4 in Figure 14: does our economic analysis indicate that the investment project will meet ROI and other objectives, after taking account of risks?

Checklist for Assessing Profitability

To assess the project's profitability, managers need to identify and measure all the many factors that will collectively determine the project's size and its operating revenues and costs. The checklist below summarizes these factors.

The sales potential of the project's product line is the logical place to start the profitability analysis for an investment intended to exploit a target market in the host country. Since the evaluation of foreign market opportunity was the subject of Chapter 3, there is no need to discuss it here. Investigation of the marketing/distribution infrastructure—the availability, quality, and cost of channel intermediaries, advertising agencies, promotional media, and the like—is also necessary to determine the scope and cost of the marketing effort.

**Checklist for Evaluating the Profitability of an Investment
Entry Project in a Foreign Target Country**

A. Market factors
1. Size and prospective growth (sales potential) of target market for project's product line
2. Competitive situation
3. Marketing/distribution infrastructure
4. Required scope/cost of marketing effort
5. Export sales potential of project's product line
6. Displacement of investor's (parent company's) exports to target market

7. Projected new export sales to target market of investor's finished products
B. Production/supply factors
   1. Required capital investment in production facilities
   2. Availability/cost of plant site
   3. Availability/cost of local raw materials, energy, and other nonlabor inputs
   4. Availability/cost of imported inputs from parent company
   5. Availability/cost of imported inputs from other sources
   6. Transportation, port, and warehousing facilities
C. Labor factors
   1. Availability/cost of local managerial, technical, and office staff
   2. Availability/cost of expatriate staff
   3. Availability/cost of skilled, semiskilled, and unskilled workers
   4. Fringe benefits
   5. Worker productivity
   6. Training facilities and programs
   7. Labor relations
D. Capital-sourcing factors
   1. Availability/cost of local long-term investment capital
   2. Availability/cost of local working capital
   3. Availability/value of host government financial incentives
   4. Required investment by parent company
E. Tax factors
   1. Kinds of taxes and tax rates
   2. Allowable depreciation
   3. Tax incentives/exemptions
   4. Tax administration
   5. Tax treaty with investor's country

Although the project is intended to serve the market in the target country, its revenues may not be limited to local sales. Additional revenues may come from export sales to third countries by the project (affiliate) and from new export sales of finished products to the target country by the investing (parent) company through the project's more effective marketing organization. Conversely, the parent company may lose revenues if the project displaces existing exports of products that will now be manufactured in the target country. All these factors should be considered to arrive at a projection of the project's revenues and its marketing costs over the planning period. These same factors also influence the project's size.

The size of the project, together with the capital intensity of the production process, determines the required investment in land, plant, and equipment. The project's running production costs will depend on the availability and cost of all inputs needed to achieve the planned level or levels of production. Calculating the cost of imported inputs requires a determination of transportation costs and import duties. If the project uses certain inputs (for example, components) from the parent company, then the latter will earn a net profit contribution, which should be taken into account when estimating the net cash flow from the project to the parent company. In some instances, import restrictions may compel the use of locally sourced inputs, whose availability or quality may be less satisfactory than that of inputs from abroad.

In many foreign projects, the principal operating costs are labor inputs. In general, the use of expatriate personnel should be kept low because of its high cost and host government policies that favor local nationals. But in most instances, the parent company will need to send its own people to the target country to get the project off the ground. Estimates of unit labor costs require information on wage rates, productivity, and fringe benefits. Training facilities and programs may be necessary to upgrade labor skills, particularly in developing countries. Managers should also assess prospective relations with the project's local workers—the ideology and strength of unions, the right to hire and fire, the role of labor in management, and so on. The availability of labor may constrain the project's size, and labor costs may also influence capital requirements through their effect on the optimum mix of capital and labor inputs. In developing countries it may be profitable to substitute local labor for capital.

Capital-sourcing factors in the target country will bear strongly on the financial structure of the project, namely, the parent company's capital contribution relative to the contribution of local sources.[10] The availability of long-term loan or equity capital from local sources can reduce the size of the parent company's own investment outlay. Host government financial incentives (such as construction grants, low-interest loans, and plant leasing) can have the same effect. Local equity contributions usually occur in the form of a joint venture. In the case of sole ventures, parent companies generally finance plant and equipment expenditures with their own funds but rely on local sources to cover working capital requirements.

Since managers need to assess the project's profitability on an after-tax basis, they must calculate the effect of all local taxes (including depreciation rules) on the project's cash flow and, where applicable, of local taxes on the transfer of income from the project to the parent company. They must also calculate the effect of home country (U.S.) taxes on income repatriated from the project to estimate the project's after-tax *dollar* return. Because of the complexities of host and home country tax systems and the relations between them (which may or may not be formalized in a treaty), the determination of an after-tax project return can benefit from the expertise of an international tax analyst. In some countries, taxes are negotiated with authorities who are not always competent or honest.

As is true of the investment climate checklist presented earlier in this chapter, the project profitability checklist is only suggestive. Company management should develop its own checklist to make certain it covers all the factors critical to the project's profitability.

Discounted Cash Flow Analysis

The results of the investigation outlined in the previous section need to be brought together in a financial analysis of the project. The recommended form of capital budgeting is a discounted cash flow analysis that takes into account the time value of money. It is not our purpose to trace the financial analysis of a foreign investment project, but rather to identify the special features that distinguish capital budgeting for a foreign project from that for a domestic project.[11]

Table 5 presents the summary cash flow analysis of a foreign investment project in local-currency terms, that is to say, from the perspective of the project rather than from the perspective of the parent company. The investor's time horizon is ten years, but estimated cash flows are shown for only five years, with a terminal value indicating the project's market value at the end of the fifth year.

The estimated net post-tax cash inflows are the financial expression of the project's ten-year operations plan, involving esti-

TABLE 5

*Summary Cash Flow Analysis of a Foreign Investment Project in
Local-Currency Terms*

(millions of pesos)

| | End of Year | | | | | | Terminal |
	0	1	2	3	4	5	Value[a]
Net post-tax cash inflows	(200)	25.0	50.0	100.0	100.0	100.0	335.2
Present-value factor at 15%	1.0	0.870	0.756	0.658	0.572	0.497	0.497
Net present value of post-tax cash inflows	(200)	21.8	37.8	65.8	57.2	49.7	166.6
Cumulative net present value of cash inflows	(200)	(178.2)	(140.4)	(74.6)	(17.4)	32.3	198.9

[a]Present value of 100 million pesos earned for five more years (end of year 10) discounted at 15%.

mates of both operating revenues and costs. The negative cash inflow in year 0 represents the initial investment outlay in the host country currency (pesos). The investor's required rate of return (hurdle rate) on domestic investments is 15 percent, and this same rate is used to discount the foreign project's net cash inflows over the planning period. The cumulative net present value of net cash inflows becomes positive in year 5, indicating that the project's return exceeds the 15 percent hurdle rate.[12] Including terminal value, the internal rate of return is close to 38 percent.[13]

Managers are advised to make a local-currency cash flow analysis from the standpoint of the foreign project so that they can judge the sensitivity of local-currency cash flows to expropriation and operations risks.[14] But the critical measure of profitability is the project's rate of return to the investor or parent company, as determined by repatriable cash flows expressed in the investor's home currency (dollars).

The cash flow analysis from the standpoint of the investing company focuses only on the company's original cash outlay (equity and loan capital contributions to the project) and the cash flows that it receives, or that are freely available, from the project in dollars. It therefore includes the parent company's initial investment in the project and all net cash inflows from the project (dividends, interest, royalties, management/technical fees, profits on export sales net of any profits lost through export displacement, and so on) that are available to the parent company in dollars, whether or not they are actually transferred to the home country. It is evident that this dollar cash flow analysis can be completed only by assessing all limitations on the repatriation of funds from the target country and by assuming exchange rates to convert from the local currency to dollars. By its very nature, therefore, dollar cash flow analysis must adjust for transfer risks (Figure 15). It must also adjust for any withholding taxes imposed by the host government on the repatriation of funds and for U.S. taxes on repatriated funds.[15] After these adjustments are made, the net present value of the dollar cash flows should be calculated by using the parent company's domestic hurdle rate as the discount factor. If the net present value is zero or positive over the planning period, then the foreign investment project passes this last financial test.

Adjusting Cash Flows for Political Risk

Managers can use two different approaches to adjust project cash flows for political risk. One approach is to lump together all the project's political risks by adding a *risk premium* to the investor's domestic hurdle rate and then calculating the net present value of the foreign project at the higher rate.[16] Thus the investor would discount cash flows at, say, 25 percent rather than 15 percent. The second approach is to adjust the project's estimated cash flows period by period for specific political risks.

The only advantage of the risk-premium approach is its ease of application, a feature that explains its popularity. But it suffers from several drawbacks. First, the risk premium can be determined by managers arbitrarily without any systematic appraisal of political risks. Its use, therefore, encourages a casual treatment of risk. Second, this approach assumes that political risk will be uniform over the entire planning period, an assumption that is patently in error. Expropriation risk, for example, is lower in the early years of an investment than in the later years, and inconvertibility risk usually responds to shifts in the balance of payments. By ignoring the time pattern of uncertainties, the risk-premium approach tends to reduce early cash flows too much and later cash flows too little. After all, the investor ordinarily has less uncertainty about political changes in the host country over the next few years than at a more distant time. Third, this approach assumes that it is possible to capture the effects of different political risks in a single discount rate. As the earlier discussion of political risks indicates, however, different classes of political events do not pose the same risks for a project's viability and profitability.

Year-by-year adjustment of cash flows for political risk has none of the drawbacks of the risk-premium approach. The application of this approach requires managers to assess the sensitivity of the project's cash flows to possible political events or situations in the host country. One way to do this is to estimate the probability of a specific political event (say, expropriation) for each year of the investment planning period, and then to weight the annual cash flows by these probabilities to get their expected values or "certainty equivalents." Many techniques are available to improve probability judgments—for example, decision trees, Bayesian statistics, and computer simulation. Another way is to assess the sensitivity of the project's cash flows to different political scenarios of the host country by asking "what if" questions. When used systematically, the scenario technique will provide a range for the project's cash flows. It may be used by managers who are uneasy working with probabilities, or it may be combined with probability analysis. Whatever techniques they use, managers should assess the sensitivity of the project's cash flows to specific political risk with the same care they use to assess market risks.

The argument for directly adjusting cash flows is strongest for operations and transfer risks and weakest for general political risk, with expropriation risk somewhere in the middle. It makes little sense to adjust cash flows for general instability risk, because that risk is a threat to the entire investment project. Rather, general instability risk should be considered in a go/no-go decision framework. Many companies would also treat expropriation risk in the same way, but there is good reason to assess the sensitivity of cash flows to this class of risk. Managers may conclude, for example, that expropriation is not a threat until *after* the discounted payback period of the investment project. A simple go/no-go decision on the expropriation risk may therefore prevent a company from making a desirable investment.

Investment Entry Through Acquisition

Many investment proposals are proposals to acquire a foreign company rather than start a new foreign venture. Although the steps outlined in Figure 14 apply to acquisition entry as well as new-venture entry, acquisitions have special features that deserve some additional comment.

An investor may acquire a foreign company for any of several reasons or mix of reasons: product diversification, geographical diversification, the acquisition of specific assets (management, technology, distribution channels, workers, and others), the sourcing of raw materials or other products for sale outside the host country, or financial (portfolio) diversification. The resulting acquisition may be classified as *horizontal* (the product lines and markets of the acquired and acquiring firms are similar), *vertical* (the acquired firm becomes a supplier or customer of the acquiring firm), *concentric* (the acquired firm has the same market but different technology, or the same technology but different market), and *conglomerate* (the acquired firm is in a different industry from that of the acquiring firm).

We are concerned here only with horizontal acquisitions by investors whose primary purpose is to enter a foreign target market. In this context, acquisition is a form of investment entry—an alternative to investment entry through a new venture.

Possible Advantages and Disadvantages of Acquisition Entry

Compared to new-venture entry, acquisition entry offers several possible advantages. They are possible rather than certain because the success of an acquisition depends critically on the selection of the acquired company. A poor selection—for whatever reason—can turn any advantage into a disadvantage for the unwary firm.

The most probable advantage of acquisition entry is a faster start in exploiting the foreign target market, because the investor gets a going enterprise with existing products and markets. In contrast, it could take three to five years for an investor to achieve the same degree of exploitation if he or she were to start from scratch. For the same reason, acquisition entry promises a shorter payback period by creating immediate income for the investor. But even this advantage can prove illusory in specific instances. The acquisition process can easily take a year or more, and the post-acquisition process of fitting the acquired company to the operations and policies of the investor can constrain performance and earnings. Acquisition entry substitutes the problem of transferring ownership and control for the problem of starting a new venture. Which problem is more severe depends on the circumstances.

Another possible advantage of acquisition entry is that it may provide a resource that is scarce in the target country and is not available on the open market. Usually this resource is a human skill, notably of a managerial or technical nature. Difficulties in staffing a new venture, therefore, favor acquisition entry. It has been said that an acquisition is fundamentally an acquisition of the people in the acquired company. But this advantage can be dissipated if the staff subsequently leaves the acquired company.

A third possible advantage is the acquisition of new product lines. But once again, this advantage can turn into a disadvantage if the investor has no experience in the new product lines. If acquisition is used as an entry mode, it is vital that the acquired company have a product line that is similar to or compatible with the investor's. Otherwise the acquired company will fail to provide a vehicle for a transfer of the investor's knowledge and skills needed to exploit the target market. Indeed, a new problem is created: managing at a distance a foreign enterprise whose product line and market are strange to the investor. Insofar as foreign acquisition is conceived as an entry mode, its basic purpose is geographical diversification, not product diversification.

Apart from advantages that can become disadvantages, acquisition entry may have distinctive drawbacks. Locating and evaluating acquisition candidates can be extraordinarily difficult. In some countries where good candidates do not exist, the investor may end up with a poor prospect in the expectation of improving its performance or else turn to new-venture entry. Even when an apparently good candidate is identified, secrecy, different accounting standards, false or deceptive financial records, and the concealment of problems can all pose obstacles to an objective evaluation

In 1980, Bridgestone, Japan's biggest tire producer, had only a small foreign presence, largely confined to exporting tires from Japan to support Japanese automobile exports. But when Japanese auto companies started building factories in the United States, Bridgestone felt that it needed to do the same to keep its customers. Bridgestone had the option of investing in its own U.S. plant or buying a U.S. tire company. Earlier, Michelin (France) had built eight new factories in the United States; also, Japanese companies tended to favor investment in new plants to avoid possible problems with acquired plants: a clash of cultures, a history of labor disputes, outdated work practices, and/or antagonistic local managers. Nonetheless, Bridgestone decided on an acquisition strategy in the belief that a new plant would take too long to get the 10 percent of the U.S. tire market needed to justify that plant.

Still it hesitated, turning down an opportunity to buy Firestone in 1984 and 1986. Then in 1987 Sumitomo, Bridgestone's only major rival in Japan, acquired the Dunlop (U.K.) business in North America. Later that same year, Continental (Germany) entered a joint manufacturing/marketing venture with two Japanese firms, Toyo and Yokohama, to push sales to Japanese auto plants in the United States. Fearful of being left behind, Bridgestone in March 1988 offered $1.25 billion for a 75 percent share of Firestone's tire business. Much to Bridgestone's surprise, Pirelli (Italy) bid a higher price. This started a bidding war that Bridgestone ultimately won with an offer of $2.6 billion for all of Firestone.

Bridgestone planned to raise productivity and quality in Firestone's factories, expand output, and build U.S. market share. Instead Firestone incurred enormous losses ($350 million in 1990 and $400 million in 1991) and required massive injections of new capital. Two years after acquisition, Firestone's productivity was still only 60 percent of Bridgestone's productivity in Japan. What went wrong? First, Bridgestone paid too much for Firestone. Second, Firestone was very big, with twenty tire plants, twenty other plants manufacturing synthetic rubber and fibers, and fifty-three thousand employees. Bridgestone simply did not have enough managers to quickly turn around Firestone's high-cost, inefficient operations. More fundamentally, it did not know how to bring Firestone into its own management structure. For instance, Bridgestone rejected the idea of integrating the marketing of Bridgestone and Firestone brands to U.S. customers. A third problem was Bridgestone's slowness in replacing Firestone's top

American managers with its own managers because it feared bad publicity. A fourth problem was cultural differences, particularly in language and work styles. Japanese managers who commonly worked to 9:00 P.M. or later could not understand why their American colleagues would not do the same. Americans complained about open offices and desks facing each other. In sum, the sorry story of Bridgestone's purchase of Firestone emphasizes how contingent are the advantages of acquisition entry into foreign markets.

Adapted from "Spinning Wheels," *Wall Street Journal*, April 1, 1991, p. 1; and "When the Bridge Caught Fire," *Economist*, September 7, 1991, p. 72.

of the candidate. Other possible drawbacks include antiquated plant and other facilities that will require substantial new investment to bring them up to standard, and poor geographical location in the target country.

Finally, acquisition entry may be disadvantageous because of host and home government policies. In general, host governments view the acquisition of local companies by foreign investors in a less favorable (or more unfavorable) light than new ventures started by foreign investors. This is true even for industrial countries such as Australia, Japan, and France. The belief is widespread in host countries that acquisitions do not make much economic contribution and certainly not enough to offset the undesirable displacement of local ownership with foreign ownership. Thus negotiations are apt to be more arduous than for new ventures, and the risk of official rejection is higher. Acquisition entry may also be disapproved in some industrial host countries on antitrust grounds. Moreover, the U.S. investor needs to consider the application of U.S. antitrust policy to a foreign acquisition.

There is some evidence that managers are more inclined to make quick, arbitrary decisions on foreign acquisitions than on investments in new foreign plants. Certainly many U.S. manufacturers have become unhappy with foreign acquisitions. Some years back, while interviewing the top managers of a billion-dollar corporation, the author discovered that all eight of the corporation's European acquisitions were in deep trouble, even though they were located in different countries and had dissimilar product lines. The explanation for this unfortunate situation was that the former chairman of the board had picked up the European companies on trips to Europe entirely on his own, without any prior investigations or consultations with his staff. Surely the chairman was unlucky, but no manager can reasonably expect to do much better with purely subjective decisions.

The Need for an Acquisition Strategy

Managers should recognize that foreign acquisition is a high-risk entry mode that needs an acquisition strategy to guide decisions. These decisions ought to be made in the context of a company's entry planning system (the elements of which are identified in Figure 2). Acquisition investments should be evaluated by checkpoints used for an investment entry decision, as shown in Figure 14. An acquisition strategy specifies objectives (ranked by importance); the desired features of an acquisition candidate (size, product line, sales and profit potentials, quality of management, technological sophistication, manufacturing and other facilities, distribution channels, and so on), which constitute the acquisition profile; and guidelines for pricing, financing, and assimilating the acquisition.

The acquisition profile guides the search for candidates and their subsequent screening to identify the most attractive candidates. The profile should include the same factors used by the investor to assess the profitability of any investment entry project in the target country (see the project profitability checklist). Armed with the profile, managers can start the search for candidates. Search information may come from several sources: the press, trade journals, business contacts, company directories (such as Moody's in the United States), special industry surveys, annual reports, bankers, consultants, brokers, agents, distributors, and others. After successive screenings have narrowed the choice to a single candidate, it is necessary to investigate all aspects of that candidate's business to answer the following questions: (1) How well does the candidate fulfill our entry strategy requirements for the target country/market? (2) How well does the candidate fit the product line, technology, markets, management style, and other features of our company? (3) What can we expect to achieve with ownership of the candidate that we could not achieve with a new-venture investment? (4) What is the dollar value of the candidate to our company?

Full answers to these questions will require personal visits to the candidate. It is desirable to establish friendly personal contact with the candidate prior to any negotiations, but full access to the candidate's records and facilities may not be possible until both sides sit down to negotiate. Often a third party (such as a banker or broker) can facilitate the collection of information as well as negotiations.

Financial analysis of an acquisition investment is much like that of any investment entry project. To estimate the value of an acquisition candidate, it is recommended that managers undertake a discounted cash flow analysis along the lines discussed earlier in the chapter. The projected cash flows express what the investing company expects to achieve over, say, the next five years if the candidate were to come under its management control. Perceived opportunities to cut costs or increase sales of the candidate are therefore brought into the cash flow projections. Similarly, the latter would include any additional investment needed to attain planned performance. In brief, cash flow analysis should answer the following question: what net cash flows will be contributed to the investing company by the acquisition candidate under the investor's control over the planning period?

Capitalization of expected cash flows (adjusted for risk) at the investing company's hurdle rate gives managers a value estimate of the candidate. Valuation methods that rely exclusively on the candidate's past performance (book value of assets, past earnings, and so on) should be avoided, because the candidate's future prospects under the investor's management may be very different from its past performance. The capitalization of expected cash flows should be regarded as the investor's ceiling price in negotiations with the candidate.[17] Of course, managers will try to acquire the candidate at a lower price, and they may succeed if the owner discounts future earnings more heavily than the investing company, a not uncommon situation with individual and family owners.

Careful negotiations are time-consuming, but managers should guard against overeagerness to reach final agreement. Acquiring a company in a week's visit to the target country is an almost certain road to later disappointment. But handled right with the right candidate, negotiations can bring the investor a going enterprise that will stand a good chance of achieving his or her objectives at an acceptable profit.

Investment Entry Through Equity Joint Venture

Joint-venture entry takes place when an international company shares in the ownership of an enterprise in a target country with local private or public interests.[18] Most commonly, an international company agrees to share capital and other resources with a local company in a common endeavor. Depending on the equity share of the international company, joint ventures may be classified as majority, minority, or fifty-fifty ventures. They may be started from scratch or by the foreign partner's acquisition of a partial ownership interest in an existing local company.

An international company has less control over a joint venture than over a sole venture, particularly when it has only a minority equity position. With a sole venture, full control enables a company to carry out its own strategy in the target country and gain all the profits. It also facilitates parent company management by bringing the venture into common financial and other reporting systems, allows better protection of industrial property, encourages transactions between the parent and the venture, and eases the integration of the venture with the parent's operations in other countries. In contrast, a joint venture can frustrate a foreign partner's strategy when the local partner's interests conflict with his or her own. At the very least, the foreign partner needs to accommodate the fundamental interests of the local partner if the joint venture is to survive. Why, then, should a company choose a joint-venture entry?

Reasons for Joint Venture Entry

A common reason for joint-venture entry is the prohibition or discouragement of sole-venture entry by the governments of some developing countries. Such joint ventures represent a second-best investment entry strategy, a strategy dictated by government rather than business policy. For most companies that want to invest abroad, the first-best entry strategy remains the sole venture.

Although joint ventures may be a response to host government policies, they can also bring positive benefits to the foreign partner through the local partner's contributions: local capital (which reduces both the investment and the risk exposure of the foreign partner); knowledge of the host country environment and business practices; personal contacts with local suppliers, customers, banks, and government officials; management, production, and marketing skills; local prestige; and other resources. In most instances, the key contribution is the local partner's knowledge of the local environment and skills in dealing with it. It is why some companies have chosen joint-venture entry in Japan even when a sole-venture option was open to them. It is also why joint-venture entry may appeal to companies with little experience in operating on their own abroad. The local partner's contributions, when combined with the foreign partner's (especially technology and related skills), can sometimes exploit a target market more effectively than a sole venture. It would therefore be a mistake for international managers to pick a local partner simply to satisfy the host government and thereby ignore the contributions that a partner can bring to the joint venture.[19]

Picking the Right Partner

The most critical decision in joint-venture entry is the choice of the local partner. For that reason, joint ventures are often compared to marriages. And like marriages, joint ventures frequently end in divorce when one or both partners conclude they can benefit by breaking their association. Once a company has decided on a joint-venture entry for a target country, its managers must initiate a search/evaluation process very much like that for acquiring a foreign company: (1) drawing up a joint-venture profile that specifies the desired features of a candidate, (2) identifying/screening candidates, and (3) negotiating the joint-venture agreement. The accompanying checklist is offered to assist managers in screening and negotiating joint ventures.

Borden, a U.S. dairy products company, started a joint venture in the early 1970s with Meiji Milk Products, Japan's biggest dairy firm. The joint venture proved successful: it manufactured an ice cream product carrying the Lady Borden brand name that captured half of Japan's premium ice cream market. Also, Borden was able to market its own products throughout Japan by using Meiji's distribution network. But Borden decided in the early 1990s to break away from Meiji. Since the 1980s Lady Borden's market share has been falling as Japanese and foreign firms have entered the premium ice cream market. A notable new competitor is Pillsbury (U.S.) with its Haagen-Dazs brand. Borden became unhappy with this deterioration in market share, accusing Meiji of being slow in responding to the new competition. When Meiji refused to give Borden more control over operations, Borden dissolved the joint venture. Fearing a loss of sales, Meiji then entered the ice cream market with its own brands, one of which (called Breuges) is in direct competition with Lady Borden. Borden now faces the task of marketing Lady Borden and other Borden products in Japan on its own. Lacking production facilities in Japan, Borden also needs to import its products from other countries. Evidently, the company concluded that gaining greater managerial control over marketing in Japan will pay off in the longer run.

The breakup of joint ventures in Japan happens quite often. For instance, Ralston Purina (U.S.) replaced its twenty-year venture with Taiyo Fishery (Japan) with its own pet-food subsidiary in Japan. Microwave Systems (U.S.) ended a seven-year partnership with Microboards, a Japanese software company. Bayer, a German pharmaceutical firm, and Monsanto, a U.S. chemical company, recently dissolved joint ventures in Japan in favor of wholly owned subsidiaries. Although joint ventures offer a relatively easy entry into the Japanese market, the Japanese partner usually keeps tight control over production and marketing. Also, the Japanese partner may become less dependent on its foreign partner through a learning experience. In this case, Meiji learned from Borden how to process cheese, margarine, and ice cream, a technology once unknown to Japanese firms. In sum, if foreign partners have nothing to contribute beyond the original product, then the Japanese partner is likely to take control of the venture.

Adapted from "Borden's Breakup with Meiji Milk Shows How a Japanese Partnership Can Curdle," *Wall Street Journal*, February 21, 1991, p. B1.

After growing at home from 238 stores in 1987 to 2,989 stores in 1992, Blockbuster Entertainments (U.S.) is now entering foreign markets. It plans to get 25 percent of its revenues from international operations by 1995. To do so, Blockbuster needs to add at least 1,200 stores to the 952 stores it now has in nine foreign countries. Its first entry in England in 1990 proved to be too small to establish its identity, so in 1992 Blockbuster acquired Citivision, Britain's biggest home-video company. Under the Ritz name, Citivision operates 775 stores in Britain and 23 in Austria. Blockbuster plan to convert Ritz outlets into Blockbusters and use the chain as a springboard for entry into continental Europe. Blockbuster is also negotiating joint ventures in France, Germany, and Italy. In Latin America, it is expanding its franchise systems in Mexico, Chile, and Venezuela. In Japan, Blockbuster has entered a joint venture (with Den Fujita, who runs McDonald's Japan and has a stake in Toys 'R' Us) that has opened 15 stores and plans to have 1,000 stores in ten years.

Adapted from "They Don't Call It Blockbuster for Nothing," *Business Week*, October 19, 1992, pp. 113–114.

Checklist for Joint-Venture Entry

A. Purpose of joint venture
   1. Objectives/strategy of foreign partner
   2. Objectives/strategy of local partner
   3. Reconciliation of objectives
B. Contributions of each partner
   1. Knowledge of local environment
   2. Personal contacts with local suppliers, customers, and so on
   3. Influence with host government
   4. Local prestige
   5. Existing facilities
   6. Capital
   7. Management/production/marketing skills
   8. Technical skills and industrial property
   9. Other
C. Role of host government
   1. Laws/regulations/policies
   2. Administrative flexibility

      3. Interest in this joint venture
      4. Requirements for approval
  D. Ownership shares
      1. Majority (foreign partner)
      2. Minority (foreign partner)
      3. Fifty-fifty
      4. Other arrangements
  E. Capital structure
      1. Legal character of venture
      2. Equity capital
      3. Loan capital (local and foreign)
      4. Future increase in equity capital
      5. Limits on transfer of shares
  F. Management
      1. Appointment/composition of board of directors
      2. Appointment/authority of executive officers
      3. Expatriate staff
      4. Organization
  G. Production
      1. Planning/construction of facilities
      2. Supply/installation of machinery and equipment
      3. Operations
      4. Quality control
      5. R & D
      6. Training
  H. Finance
      1. Accounting/control system
      2. Working capital
      3. Capital expenditures
      4. Dividends
      5. Pricing of products provided by partners
      6. Borrowing and loan guarantees by partners
      7. Taxation
  I. Marketing
      1. Product lines, trademarks, and trade names
      2. Target market(s) and sales potentials
      3. Distribution channels
      4. Promotion
      5. Pricing
      6. Organization
  J. Agreement
      1. Company law in host country
      2. Articles and bylaws of incorporation
      3. Contractual arrangements (licensing, technical assistance, management, and so on)
      4. Settlement of disputes

Managers should start by defining what they want the joint venture to accomplish in the target country/market over the strategic planning period and how the joint venture will fit into their company's overall international business strategy. Managers also need to know the objectives and strategy of the prospective local partner. It would be rash to assume that the two partners would have the same or compatible interests in the joint venture. What is called for is an open, thorough discussion between the two parties about the purpose of the joint venture and how it will be attained. Agreement on these fundamental issues can be formalized in a memorandum of agreement signed by both parties, but mutual trust and understanding are the true foundation of a successful joint venture.

Each partner enters a joint venture to gain the skills and resources possessed by the other partner. Hence the contributions of the international company to a joint venture depend on both its own capabilities and those of the local partner, as well as on the joint venture's purpose and scope. Usually the key combination of the international partner is technology or products, while that of the local partner is the knowledge and skills to manage the venture in the host country. When a joint venture must be approved by the host government (as is true in developing countries), the partners' respective contributions—particularly the ownership share of the foreign partner—may also be influenced by public policy.

Apart from settling the question of ownership shares, managers need to resolve many other issues in negotiations: the allocation of responsibilities in management, production, finance, and marketing; day-to-day operations; and planning for the future. Frequent problem areas of joint ventures include profit reporting, dividend policy, capital expansion, the pricing of inputs sourced from either partner, and executive compensation. If these issues are not resolved by the partners during negotiations, they will almost certainly return to haunt them at a later time.

Negotiations end in written agreements that determine the legal and substantive nature of the joint venture (articles of incorporation, bylaws, memorandum of agreement, and so on) and in written agreements (such as licenses, technical-assistance contracts, and management contracts) concerning the provision of industrial property or services by one or both partners to the joint venture.

The Question of Control

The most common criticism of joint ventures by international companies is the loss or dilution of management control. As noted earlier, the importance of control to a company ultimately depends on its strategy. Control for the sake of control is hardly a satisfactory policy. Instead, managers should decide how much control is needed to accomplish their objectives in the target country. A follow-on question is how they should obtain the desired control.

The most direct way to gain control over a joint venture is through majority ownership. But when majority ownership is ruled out by government policy, control may still be exercised in other ways by the minority partner. This is most evident when the joint venture is critically dependent on a continuing flow of technical assistance from the foreign partner. By holding the power of

---

Over the past few years, Toys 'R' Us, the biggest toy chain in the United States (with more than a fifth of the domestic market), has spread rapidly abroad. By 1997 it plans to have more than four hundred international units generating annual sales of over $4 billion. Toys 'R' Us's basic strategy (proven in the United States) is creating huge stores that support a high-volume, low-price approach to marketing Nintendo games, Ninja Turtles, Monopoly sets, Barbie dolls, and thousands of other products fascinating to children. The company chairman, Charles Lazarus, believes that "kids are the same all over the world." Toys 'R' Us went international in 1984, first in Canada, then in Europe, Hong Kong, and Singapore, and most recently in Japan.

To enter foreign markets, Toys 'R' Us has overcome many obstacles. Its first store in Germany provoked open hostility from local toy manufacturers who feared it would drive down prices, while German toy retailers warned about the "dangerous" self-service concept. Toys 'R' Us needed to overcome much higher barriers in Japan, where it spent three years negotiating with Japanese bureaucrats over the Large Company Law, which protected shopkeepers from big retailers. To gain approval to open its stores in Japan, Toys 'R' Us entered a joint venture with Mc-Donald's Japan, with the latter taking a 20 percent interest in the Japanese toy operation. (McDonald's Japan itself is a fifty-fifty joint venture between McDonald's U.S. and a Japanese entrepreneur, Den Fujita). While Toys 'R' Us lobbied the U.S. government to pressure the Japanese government to approve its entry, McDonald's Japan lobbied the Japanese government. To gain approval, Toys 'R' Us agreed to close its stores at 8:00 P.M. and close them thirty days a year like other Japanese stores. At the end of 1991 the firm opened its first Japanese store, and it plans to open ten stores a year through the 1990s.

Apart from overcoming barriers to international expansion, Toys 'R' Us has needed to adapt to local cultures and buyer preferences. Because the company logo can perplex non-English speakers, it has complemented the American logo with local versions, such as "Big Toy City" in Hong Kong, "Spielwaren Das Sind Wir" in Germany, and "Les Jouets C'est Nous" in France. The company has also adapted its merchandise to local tastes by, for instance, offering porcelain dolls in Japan and wooden toys in Germany. Vice chairman Robert Nakasone, who is in charge of the company's international expansion, says, "We try to think globally and act locally."

Adapted from "Guess Who's Selling Barbies in Japan Now?" *Business Week*, December 9, 1991, pp. 72–76; "The World 'S' Ours," *Newsweek*, March 23, 1992, pp. 46–47; and "Den Fujita, Japan's Mr. Joint Venture," *New York Times*, March 22, 1992, p. F1.

life or death over the joint venture, the minority partner can easily exert a dominant influence on its policies and operations.

The minority partner can also exercise control through bylaws that grant it certain rights (for example, the selection of key executives) or through a management contract. Another control device is the issuance of voting and nonvoting stock shares, with a majority of the latter held by the foreign partner. The minority partner's interest may also be protected by holding veto rights over key decisions in the joint venture, such as dividend declarations or new capital investments.

Enough has been said to indicate that an international company can exercise a substantial degree of control over a joint venture even when the company is a minority partner. Managers should recognize that a minority position need not mean a lack of control, and that they can negotiate good joint-venture agreements as a minority partner. For that reason, it would be shortsighted for managers to insist on full or majority ownership at the cost of losing the only opportunity to enter an attractive target country as an investor.[20]

Summary

1. Companies invest in foreign production operations for three basic reasons: to obtain raw materials, to acquire products at a lower cost, and to penetrate local markets. Investment as a foreign market entry mode is the subject of this chapter.

2. Investment entry offers both advantages and disadvantages to a company. The investment entry decision is a complex process that requires an evaluation of both the investment climate in the target country and the intended investment project.

3. Because of the demanding information requirements of investment entry, it is usually unwise for a company to make its first entry investment abroad without a prior penetration of the target country through exports.

4. The decision to investigate a foreign investment proposal is the first and most important checkpoint.

5. A foreign investment project must be analyzed in the context of its political, legal, economic, social, and cultural environments—the investment climate of the target country. The assessment of a country's future investment climate is an assessment of the project's political risk.

6. For the international manager, political risk arises from uncertainty over the continuation of present political conditions and government policies in the foreign host country that are critical to the profitability of an actual or proposed equity/contractual business arrangement. Political risks may be grouped into four classes: general instability risk, ownership/control risk, operations risk, and transfer risk. If a project passes the four political risk hurdles and satisfies

the investor's required rate of return, it is ready for approval by top management.

7. To assess the project's profitability, managers need to identify and measure all the many factors that will collectively determine the project's size and its operating revenues and costs. The recommended form of capital budgeting is a discounted cash flow analysis that takes into account the time value of money. Managers should adjust the project's estimated cash flows period by period for specific political risks.

8. Many investment proposals are proposals to acquire a foreign company rather than start a new foreign venture. The most probable advantage of acquisition entry is a faster start in exploiting the foreign target market. Managers should recognize that foreign acquisition is a high-risk entry mode that needs an acquisition strategy to guide decisions.

9. Joint-venture entry takes place when an international company shares in the ownership of an enterprise in a target country with local private or public interests. The most common reason for joint-venture entry is the prohibition or discouragement of sole-venture entry by governments in developing countries. The most critical decision in joint-venture entry is the choice of the local partner. The most common criticism of joint ventures by international companies is the loss or dilution of management control.

CHAPTER 7

Deciding on the Right Entry Mode

We have now explored the several entry modes that are actually or potentially available to companies seeking to exploit international market opportunities. In this chapter, we return to the question raised in Chapter 2: how should managers decide on the right entry mode for a given product and given target country/market?

Three different decision rules for entry mode selection can be distinguished by their degrees of sophistication: the *naive rule* (use the same entry mode for all foreign markets), the *pragmatic rule* (use a workable entry mode for each target market), and the *strategy rule* (use the right entry mode for each target market).

The Naive Rule

Managers follow the naive rule when they consider only one way to enter foreign markets.[1] Statements such as "We only export" or "We only license" are examples of the naive rule. Commonly, this rule is implicit in the behavior of managers rather than explicit in a policy statement. Whatever its expression, the naive rule ignores the heterogeneity of country markets and entry conditions. Managers using this rule are guilty of tunnel vision. Sooner or later, they will make mistakes of two kinds: either they will give up a promising foreign market that cannot be penetrated with their only entry mode, or they will enter a market with an inappropriate mode. If managers learn in time that the "only" entry mode is simply unprofitable for a target country, they cease any further effort to enter that market. In effect, they are selecting foreign markets not for their sales potential but rather for their accommodation to the company's entry mode. Entering a foreign market with the wrong mode is also a likely consequence of the naive rule, because managers acting on the presumption that their preferred mode is also the right one do not bother to assess the long-run profitability of the preferred mode for a particular target country. In sum, the inflexibility of the naive rule prevents a company from fully exploiting its foreign market opportunities.

The Pragmatic Rule

Most firms appear to start their international business careers by using the pragmatic rule. In discussing the dynamics of entry mode decisions in Chapter 2, we pointed out that a company ordinarily initiates international business with a low-risk entry mode, which is almost always some form of export. The outstanding advantages of export as a learning experience were described in Chapter 4. In practice, therefore, new international managers begin their search for an entry mode by assessing export prospects in a target country. Only if export entry is not feasible or profitable do they continue to look for a workable entry mode.[2]

The pragmatic rule holds certain advantages for a company and its managers. The risk of entering a target market with the wrong mode is minimized, because managers reject any mode that is not workable. This rule also saves on the cost of gathering information on alternative entry modes and the management time to assess them. After all, why take the time and trouble to investigate other entry modes if one finds a workable mode, especially when the consequences of *any* entry mode are uncertain in some degree? And if managers are rewarded for positive results but are not punished for failing to do something that would bring better results, why search for the right or best entry mode?

These advantages are hardly trivial, but neither is the cost of lost opportunity. The fundamental weakness of the pragmatic rule lies in its failure to guide managers toward a determination of the entry mode that would best match the company's capabilities with opportunity in a foreign target market. In short, an entry mode that works may not be the *right* entry mode.

The Strategy Rule

The strategy decision rule—use the right entry mode—is more difficult for managers to follow than the pragmatic rule, because it demands systematic comparisons of alternative modes. But it also guides managers to better entry decisions.

The discussion of entry modes in the previous chapters should convince anyone that the entry decision process cannot be reduced to a formula, a set of rules, or even a complex computer model. Chapter 2 described the many external and internal factors that can influence the entry mode decision: environmental, market, and production factors in the target foreign country; home country factors; and company product and resource/commitment factors. As stated then, a company's choice of its entry mode for a given product/target country is the net result of several often conflicting forces.

As the reader can now recognize, another difficulty is the *multiplicity* of entry modes: the several variations of export, contractual, and investment modes and the several combinations of these modes to form mixed modes. It is by no means certain, therefore, that managers are always aware of the many entry modes available to them.

A comparison of alternative entry modes is also complicated by the need of managers to assess the advantages and disadvantages of each mode in terms of a company's multiple objectives in the target market, objectives that are seldom fully consistent. An entry mode that scores highly on one objective (say, rate of growth in sales) may score low on another objective (say, profitability). Somehow, managers must decide on trade-offs among their several objectives. Managers may also find it hard to identify some of the advantages or disadvantages of a particular entry mode, to say nothing of measuring them. For example, the discussion of licensing indicated the possible cost of creating a competitor in third markets or the foreclosure of opportunity to enter a target market with a new entry mode at a later time.

This last remark points to another difficulty, one that is common to all strategic decisions. Entry mode comparisons need to be made between projected benefits and costs over a future period. Managers therefore are comparing *expected* benefits and costs of alternative entry modes, benefits and costs that are uncertain in some degree. Moreover, different entry modes (and the company assets associated with them) are subject to different market and political risks. Managers therefore need to adjust expected benefits and costs for risk.

Figure 16 brings these considerations together in an entry mode comparison matrix. To fill out each row, managers should assess the specific entry mode in terms of the criteria listed at the top of the matrix. Next, they should use the columns to compare the alternative entry modes in terms of each criterion. To decide on the right entry mode, managers should then determine the relative importance or trade-offs among the criteria (which were identified earlier as important to the company), because an entry mode could rank highly on one criterion and low on another. Of course, the entry decision would be greatly facilitated by a quantitative measure that captured all the criteria values for each entry mode—that is to say, a "summary" entry in a final column. Unfortunately, no such summary measure is likely to carry much credibility. But, as the reader shall see, it is possible to go partway in that direction.

Managers may view the strategy decision rule as too arduous or time-consuming to apply in the "real world." But it is hard to deny the proposition that managers should try to find the most appropriate entry mode for a target foreign market. Even a crude use of an entry strategy matrix holds the promise of better entry decisions. Given the complexity of the entry mode decision, what is demanded is not the abandonment of the strategy decision rule but rather an approach that facilitates systematic comparisons of alternative modes.

Comparing Entry Modes: An Approach

The approach offered here interprets the strategy decision rule as follows: choose that entry mode that maximizes the profit contribution over the strategic planning period within the constraints

Criteria / Modes	Investment	Sales	Costs	Profit Contribution	Market Share	Reversibility	Control	Risk	Other
Indirect Export									
Agent/Distributor Export									
Branch/Subsidiary Export									
Licensing									
Franchising									
Other Contractual Agreements									
Investment: New Establishment									
Investment Acquisition									
Joint Venture									
Mixed									

FIGURE 16

Comparison Matrix for Entry Modes

imposed by (1) the availability of company resources, (2) risk, and (3) nonprofit objective's. Figure 17 depicts this approach.

Managers start by reviewing all entry modes for *feasibility* with respect to the foreign target country/market and with respect to the company's resources and commitment. Is it possible for our company to enter the target market in this way? Feasibility screening is negative screening. Some entry modes may be ruled out for external reasons—for example, export entry may be blocked by import restrictions in the target country. Or they may be ruled out for internal reasons, notably the resource/commitment factor. Ordinarily, feasibility screening can be done quickly, but it should be done on the basis of reliable information.

The feasible entry modes justify a systematic comparative evaluation, because they are all within the company's resource/commitment capability and they are all possible ways to penetrate the target country. Three kinds of comparative analyses are called for: profit contribution, risk, and nonprofit objectives. Managers should then bring the results of these analyses together in an overall comparative assessment that ranks the feasible entry modes. The highest-ranking mode is the right, or most appropriate, mode for the company.

Comparative Profit Contribution Analysis

The profit contribution of a foreign market entry mode is the *net* revenue it will earn for a company over the strategic plan. Estimation of the profit contribution requires that managers project all costs and revenues that will result directly or indirectly from using an entry mode for a target country.[3] Different entry modes will have different time profiles for revenues and costs. Export entry, for example, will ordinarily bring quicker returns than investment entry. To standardize time profiles for comparative analysis, it is necessary to calculate the present values of estimated profit contributions over the same number of years.

Profit contribution analysis is identical to the cash flow analysis described in Chapter 6. Its use is justified here by regarding all entry mode decisions as investment decisions. Broadly defined, *investment* includes all once-for-all allocations of a company resource that are intended to generate income over a lengthy future

period. Hence start-up costs that are incurred to enter a new foreign market (learning about and organizing for a new business environment, hiring personnel with new skills, negotiating with foreign businessmen and host government officials, undertaking
market research, adapting the product, developing distribution
channels, securing permanent working capital, and so on) are as
much part of a company's "entry investment base" as an investment in a new foreign plant. Although start-up expenditures may
be charged off against current income as expenses, they are
nonetheless investments in an economic sense if their benefits can
be realized only over several years.

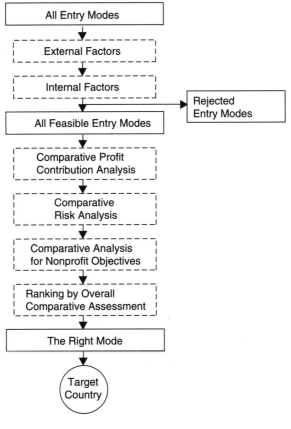

FIGURE 17
Deciding on the Right Entry Mode

To estimate the net profit contribution, managers need to identify and measure all revenues and costs that would arise from the use of an entry mode—that is to say, all *incremental* revenues and costs, whether directly or indirectly resulting from the entry mode. If, for example, an investment entry mode is expected to create net export revenues, then these revenues should be added to the direct revenues of that mode. Conversely, if an investment entry mode is expected to lower current export earnings by displacing exports to the target country, then the forsaken export earnings should be added to the costs of that entry mode. In short, profit contribution analysis boils down to two questions: if we choose this entry mode, what will happen to our revenues? What will happen to our costs?

Summing up, comparative profit contribution analysis requires five steps: (1) identify/measure/project over the planning horizon (say, five years) all revenues (net of foreign and U.S. taxes) that would be received by the company from the use of each feasible entry mode; (2) do the same for start-up and operating costs; (3) using projections from the first two steps, calculate the net profit contributions for each year of all the feasible entry modes; (4) adjust the expected profit contributions for the time value of money by calculating their net present values at the company's hurdle rate; and (5) rank order the feasible entry modes by the size of their net present values.

Tables 6 and 7 illustrate a comparative profit contribution analysis in a situation where only two entry modes have passed the feasibility test. This example is simplified, because, as the reader

TABLE 6

Estimated Net Profit Contributions of Feasible Entry Modes by Each Year of the Strategic Plan: Target Country Y

(thousands of dollars)

| | End of Year | | | | | | |
	0	1	2	3	4	5	Cumulative
Export entry	(25)	15	30	50	50	50	170
Investment entry	(200)	10	50	150	250	300	560

TABLE 7

Net Present Values of Estimated Net Profit Contributions,
Discounted at 15 Percent: Target Country Y

(thousands of dollars)

			End of Year				
	0	1	2	3	4	5	Cumulative
Export entry	(25)	13.0	22.7	32.9	28.6	24.9	97.1
Investment entry	(200)	8.7	37.8	98.6	142.9	149.2	237.2

knows, there are several forms of export and investment entry. The planning horizons of the different entry modes can always be made the same by using terminal values, but here we simply assume identical horizons.

It is evident from Table 7 that investment entry offers the highest profit contribution after discounting at the company's hurdle rate. At this stage of the analysis it therefore becomes the preferred entry mode. This choice rests on an interpretation of the strategy decision rule: choose the feasible entry mode that maximizes profit contribution. This interpretation implicitly assumes that a company can obtain at its hurdle rate all the capital it needs for any entry mode. If this is not the case and managers need to ration capital, they may prefer to rank entry modes by their rates of return on investment. One way to do this is to calculate the cumulated net present value per dollar of investment entry base; another way is to calculate the internal rate of return. In Table 7 the per-dollar profit contribution of export entry is $97.1/25, or $3.9, and that for investment entry is $237.2/200, or $1.2. The internal rate of return is also higher for export entry. Managers trying to maximize the rate of return, therefore, would prefer export entry over investment entry.

Comparative Risk Analysis

In Chapter 5 we discussed the adjustment of cash flows for political risk. We propose here that the same approach be used, namely, adjusting the yearly profit contributions of each feasible entry mode for both market and political risks.

Generally, political risks are greater for investment entry than for export entry. In most instances, therefore, a comparative risk analysis would lower the cumulative profit contribution (net present value) of investment entry relative to that of export entry. It could even reverse the ranking of the two modes.

Comparative Analysis for Nonprofit Objectives

Managers need also to analyze feasible entry modes in terms of nonprofit objectives. The entry mode that ranks highest on risk-adjusted profit contribution may not rank highest on certain nonprofit objectives. Nonprofit objectives vary from company to company: targets for sales volume, growth, and market share; control; reversibility (the degree to which an entry mode can be undone if a mistake is made); establishment of a reputation; and so on. Managers should be clear about their nonprofit objectives and the importance of those objectives to the company.

Ranking by Overall Comparative Assessment

In the final stage, managers should bring together the results of their analyses of profit contribution, risk, and nonprofit objectives to make an overall comparative assessment of the feasible entry modes. As stated earlier, there is no objective procedure to capture the three analyses in a single number. Inevitably, therefore, managers must use their own judgment in making the overall assessment.

A Last Observation

For one reason or another, managers may fail to carry out profit contribution analysis to the degree shown in Tables 6 and 7. But even so, the approach presented here should help them make better entry decisions. Its key advantage is the forcing of a comparison of feasible entry modes so that managers do not accept a workable mode when a better mode is available. A crude use of this approach will still encourage managers to raise the necessary questions about entry modes, and thereby will guide them in the direction of the right entry mode for a target country. Managers using this approach will design flexible entry strategies for heterogeneous and changing international markets. To use a colloquial expression, flexibility is the name of the game.

Summary

1. Three different decision rules for entry mode selection can be distinguished by their degrees of sophistication: the naive rule (use of the same entry mode for all foreign markets), the pragmatic rule (use a workable entry mode for each target market), and the strategy rule (use the right entry mode for each target market).

2. The inflexibility of the naive rule prevents a company from fully exploiting its foreign market opportunities.

3. Most firms appear to start their international business careers by using the pragmatic rule. Using this rule minimizes the risk of entering a target market with the wrong mode, because managers reject any mode that is not workable. But an entry mode that works may not be the right entry mode.

4. The strategy decision rule demands systematic comparisons of alternative modes, but it also guides managers to better entry decisions. What is involved in the strategy decision rule is depicted in an entry mode comparison matrix.

5. The approach offered here interprets the strategy decision rule as follows: choose the entry mode that maximizes the profit contribution over the strategic planning period within the constraints imposed by (1) the availability of company resources, (2) risk, and (3) nonprofit objectives.

6. Managers start by reviewing all entry modes for feasibility. Feasible modes justify three kinds of comparative analysis: profit contribution, risk, and nonprofit objectives. The results of these analyses are then brought together in an overall comparative assessment that ranks the feasible entry modes.

7. Profit contribution analysis regards all entry mode decisions as investment decisions.

8. Even a crude use of the approach presented here should guide managers in the direction of the right entry mode for a target country.

CHAPTER 8

Designing the International Marketing Plan

I n Chapter 3 we pointed out that company sales potential (CSP) in a target market depends on both the entry mode and the marketing effort. We have now reviewed the several entry modes and their systematic comparison to decide on the right entry mode. In this chapter we turn to the design of the foreign marketing plan, which is represented by box 4 in the entry strategy model depicted in Figure 2.

The International Marketing Plan

The scope of an international marketing plan was indicated in Chapter 2, and there is no need to repeat what was said there. To design a marketing plan managers must make decisions, both individually and collectively, on policies relating to the product, pricing, channels, promotion, and logistics. These policy areas (commonly referred to as the marketing mix) are defined in Table 4 in Chapter 2. The international marketing effort, then, is the sum total of a company's resources committed to marketing mix policies in the target market.

International Marketing Concept

In designing international marketing plans, managers should be guided by the international marketing concept. This concept is a philosophy asserting that the long-run profitability and ultimate survival of a company in world markets depends on its capacity to provide a continuing stream of benefits to customers at a competitive price. To apply this concept, managers need to (1) find out what foreign customers want, (2) try to give them what they want by adapting old products or developing new products, (3) try to formulate other marketing policies (such as distribution channels) that satisfy customer wants, and (4) ascertain the costs of adapting products and marketing policies to a particular target market, so as to ensure that those policies are cost-effective.

In sum, application of the international marketing concept requires managers to make trade-offs between the consumer/user benefits of adaptation (enhancing marketing effectiveness) and the costs of adaptation. But the fundamental contribution of this concept to a company lies in its stimulation of an outward orientation to world markets. Animated by this philosophy, managers are more likely than otherwise to design cost-effective international marketing plans.

Determining the International Marketing Mix

Managers should determine the marketing mix for a target country over a strategic planning period of three to five years. They need to decide, therefore, not only the initial mix but also changes in its aggegate level and composition over time. Apart from the difficulties inherent in all strategic planning, determining the marketing mix for a target country poses particular difficulties for managers.

The several mix elements are highly interdependent: no single element can be fully effective in generating sales or accomplishing other marketing objectives without the support of other elements. Hence managers need to make *joint* decisions on mix policies in order to design an integrated marketing plan. This means, for example, that they should not decide on pricing policy without taking into account other mix policies. Unfortunately, this joint decision making can seldom be based on precise knowledge of the relationship between any single mix element and sales in the target market, or of the relationships among the mix elements. One must rely mainly on informed judgments for answers to such questions as, What will happen to sales if we raise advertising expenditures by 10 percent? Will it be more cost-effective to join a high price with heavy promotion or to join a low price with modest promotion?

Figure 18 is intended to help managers improve their decisions on the international marketing mix. Each mix element is appraised by reference to factors in the target country/market that can influence its effectiveness or cost. A *vertical* appraisal of each marketing mix element represents management's judgment of the most appropriate policy for that element without regard to other mix elements. The resulting *individual summary profile* may be a compromise policy, because some of the country/market factors may point toward different policies. The next step is a *horizontal* appraisal across all the mix elements. This appraisal spots inconsistencies (such as a high-quality-product policy and a low-price policy) that need to be removed and indicates other changes that will improve the cost-effectiveness of the marketing plan. The result of this second appraisal is an *aggregate summary profile*. Profile appraisal should consider not only the initial marketing mix but also mixes over the entire strategic planning period.

The optimum international marketing plan is the one that maximizes profit contribution over the planning period. Optimality requires that the level of total marketing effort be increased up to the point where its incremental cost equals its incremental revenue, but not beyond the point where its incremental cost exceeds its incremental revenue. As a corollary, optimality also requires that incremental costs and revenues be equal for each element of the marketing mix; otherwise, the profit contribution can be increased by reallocating effort among the several elements.[1] It follows that the optimum mix may not be achieved because total marketing effort falls short of the optimum level and/or the allocation of marketing effort among the mix elements is suboptimum.

Clearly, to say that managers should design the optimum foreign marketing plan is a counsel of perfection.[2] But by trying to

Target Country/Market	Product			Promotion			Channel	Price	Logistics
	Physical	Package	Service	Personal Selling	Advertising	Other			
A. Market 1. IMP 2. Competition 3. Structure 4. Consumer/User 5. Other									
B. Marketing Infrastructure 1. Transportation 2. Communication 3. Warehousing 4. Other									
C. Legal Factors									
D. Macroenvironment 1. Economy 2. Culture 3. Society 4. Polity 5. Other									
E. Other Factors									
Individual summary profile									
Aggregate summary profile									

FIGURE 18

Designing the International Marketing Plan: Marketing Mix Profile of Target Country/Market for a Candidate Product move toward optimality, managers can reasonably anticipate a more cost-effective plan than otherwise. And this can give them a decisive advantage over competitors whose plans are grounded on tradition, wishful thinking, or short-run prospects rather than on market knowledge coupled with a strategic approach to foreign market entry. Managers can move toward optimality by raising two questions about the marketing mix for a target market: (1) If we increase the overall level of our marketing effort, will it add more to revenues than to costs? (2) Given our overall level, can we increase the profit contribution by shifting resources from one element to another?

No one should pretend that factual answers to these questions are easy to come by. Even comprehensive information on the target country/market is not likely to give managers precise, reliable estimates of the market's responses to the various mix elements. The design of an international marketing plan therefore always carries a heavy load of judgment and risk. But even approximate answers to these questions are better than none at all, and they are possible only if the questions are raised in the first place.

Segmenting the Target Country Market

Only after carefully defining the foreign target market—the prospective household consumers or industrial/government users of the candidate product—can managers design the most appropriate marketing plan. The target market may be conceived as the total market covering all possible consumers/users throughout the target country or, alternatively, as part of the total market that includes only a particular group of consumers/users. I refer to the first concept as *market aggregation,* and to the second as *market segmentation.*

Concept of Market Segmentation

The concept of market segmentation derives from the proposition that consumers/users in a country market have different needs and preferences, which in turn create differences in demand for a candidate product. Meaningful segmentation, therefore, is feasible for a given country market only when consumer/user needs and preferences are truly heterogeneous with respect to a candidate product. Furthermore, it must be possible to classify heterogeneous consumers/users into homogeneous segments, and these segments must vary significantly in their responses to the candidate product and/or other marketing mix policies. Finally, at least one segment must have a big enough sales potential to justify a special marketing mix.

In segmenting a target country market, managers may be raising several questions. First, is there an identifiable group of consumers/users that offers a special opportunity for my product? If the answer is yes, it may be possible to obtain a competitive niche in the country market, especially if the segment in question is ignored or poorly served by competitors. This search for an *opportunity segment* is a continuation of the target market selection model presented in Figure 8 in Chapter 3. After identifying an opportunity segment, managers can raise a follow-on question: what particular mix of marketing policies (including the possible development of a new product) addressed to that segment will be most cost-effective? The answer to that question relates to a third question, namely, will a segmentation strategy be more cost-effective than an aggregate marketing strategy?

Generally speaking, the scope for segmentation is greater in large-country markets than in small-country markets; in high-income, technologically sophisticated markets than in low-income, low-technology markets; and for highly differentiated products than for standard or commodity-like products. But segmentation may be profitable in any heterogeneous market, as for instance in developing countries, where consumers fall into distinctive income groups with different patterns of consumption, store patronage, responsiveness to advertising, and other buying behavior.

The Choice of Segmentation Criteria

The key criterion of market segmentation is the response of consumers/users to the candidate product and its pricing, promotion, distribution, and logistics. But it is seldom possible for managers to obtain reliable direct measurements of response functions, although they should try to do so. Instead, other variables are used as segmentation criteria, on the assumption that they are highly

Thirty-eight companies in the world make electric drills, and twenty-eight of them are based in West Germany. But when Black & Decker (U.S.) entered that country in the late 1950s, it found that drill manufacturers were selling only to professionals. So B & D decided to focus its marketing effort on the do-it-yourself market segment. Using heavy advertising, the company was able to build a strong market position before local firms reacted to its presence. In the 1990s Black & Decker continues to dominate the consumer tool market in Europe and the United States, but its share of the professional tool market is weak because carpenters view B & D products as "amateurish." In focusing on the consumer tool segment, the company has hurt its image in the professional tool segment. Hence in 1992 B & D decided to differentiate its tool models for the two segments. Consumer models keep the B & D name, but professional models carry the De-Walt brand name, taken from a company acquired by B & D that manufactures high-quality stationary saws. Black & Decker rebuilt all 33 DeWalt tools—painted an industrial yellow—to match or beat Makita's (Japan), which dominate the professional tool market.

Adapted from "Tool Maker Thrives in Europe," *New York Times,* July 7, 1980, p. D1; and "Black & Decker, New Selling Tool: The Acura Concept," *Fortune,* February 24, 1992, pp. 88–90.

correlated with market response variables. These substitute criteria fall into two broad categories: general criteria and situation-specific criteria.

For consumer goods, *general criteria* include attributes relating to geographical location, socioeconomic status (such as age, sex, income, education, family size, and occupation), culture (such as language, race, religion, customs, and attitudes toward foreigners and foreign-made products), and psychology (such as personality and life-style). General criteria used for industrial goods include industry classification, customer size, nature of operations, buying organization, geographical location, and private versus public sector identity. One general criterion peculiar to international marketing is buyer attitudes toward foreign-made products.

Situation-specific criteria pertain to buyer behavior with respect to the candidate product. For consumer goods, they include attitudes toward and impressions of the products, benefits sought, purchase motivations, purchase occasions, usage rates, and brand loyalty. Situation-specific criteria commonly used for segmenting industrial-goods markets are product requirements, usage rates, benefits sought, purchase motivations, and buying practices.

The foregoing criteria are useful in segmenting country markets only to the extent that they correlate with market responses to the candidate product and other mix elements. Even situation-specific criteria may fail to distinguish different needs and preferences. For example, heavy users of a product may not always seek benefits different from light users. Of fundamental importance, therefore, is the choice of the segmentation criteria. Sophisticated techniques, such as multidimensional scaling and factor analysis, have been used to derive segmentation variables from consumer/user survey data. But for the most part such data are not available to international managers, who must instead rely mainly on judgment for criteria selection. To partly overcome the weakness of a priori segmentation criteria, managers should use several criteria for grouping consumers/users.

Market Segmentation Strategy

Even though a foreign country market can be segmented, it by no means follows that managers should adopt a segmentation strategy rather than an aggregate-market strategy. The advantages of a segmentation strategy need to be weighed against its possible disadvantages. A major obstacle to segmentation strategies is the need for large amounts of information to identify and measure market segments. High research costs can be a severe constraint for a smaller company. Also, in deciding to serve a single segment instead of the total market, a company may give up volume sales and thereby lose economies of scale in production and marketing.

The main advantage of a market segmentation strategy is greater marketing effectiveness. Managers are able to design a marketing program that is responsive to the needs and preferences of a certain group of customers. This strategy may offer a company an opportunity to become the market leader in a target segment rather than a market follower in the aggregate country market. In sum, a market segmentation strategy is most attractive when it promises to achieve greater satisfaction of customer needs and, at the same time, better utilization of a company's scarce resources than an aggregate-market strategy, for then it will be a company's most cost-effective foreign marketing plan. A final point: identification and measurement of market segments must be a continuing activity, because segments, like other market phenomena, are almost certain to change over time.

We now turn to some considerations in planning price and promotion policies for a foreign target market. We have already spoken about product policies in Chapter 3 and channel policies in Chapter 4.

Pricing for International Market Entry

How should managers price a candidate product for international market entry? Few questions in international marketing are more troublesome. Managers must decide on a pricing policy that will enable their company to attain its several goals in the target market (such as market share, sales volume, and growth) over the strategic planning period, and to do so at an acceptable level of profits or return on investment. Moreover, they must make pricing decisions with some uncertainty about their own costs and about demand and competition in the target market. Also, they need to consider antitrust, tariff, and other legal and policy constraints of both home and target country governments. They need to reconcile the often divergent interests and perspectives on international pricing held by different functional groups in the company, notably marketing and finance. Finally, managers need to integrate pricing with the rest of the foreign marketing plan.

In view of this complexity, a systematic approach to entry pricing is hardly a waste of time.[3] This section identifies the questions that should be raised in planning entry pricing strategies, examines different basic approaches to pricing, describes several entry pricing strategies, calls attention to some special factors in international pricing, and concludes with a multiple-stage entry pricing model.

Entry Pricing Strategy: Some Questions

In pricing for foreign market entry, international managers face several interdependent questions:

- How sensitive will the sales volume of the candidate product be to its price in the target market? What other factors influence buying decisions, and in what degree? What are the pricing policies of competitors? How much pricing discretion do we have in the target market?
- In light of our answers to these questions and other considerations, what should be the role of price in our foreign marketing plan? Aggressive? Passive? What pricing strategy best fits our strategies for product, promotion, channel, and logistics? What should be our pricing objectives?
- What is the probable life cycle of the candidate product type in the target market? How should we price over the entire strategic planning period?
- What should be our price to middlemen in the target market? Should we try to control or influence the final-buyer price? How?
- How should we allow for tactical pricing flexibility?
- Will our pricing policy be legal in the target country? Will it attract government investigation and possibly regulation?

Fundamental Approaches to Entry Pricing

Fundamentally, entry pricing decisions involve costs, sales volume, and revenues. But decision makers may treat these variables in radically different ways depending on their approach to entry pricing.

Full-Cost Pricing. Full-cost pricing is the most common approach of U.S. companies in pricing products for foreign markets. A full-cost price is simply the sum of total unit costs attributed to a product and a profit margin: direct production costs *plus* direct marketing costs *plus* allocated production and other overheads *plus* a profit margin. The full-cost approach is attractive to companies because it is easy to understand and the availability of conventional accounting data makes it comparatively easy to calculate. Moreover, it seems to ensure that each sales transaction will be profitable. But full-cost pricing has serious weaknesses. As a purely cost-oriented approach, it ignores demand and competition in the foreign target market, assuming implicitly that price will have no effect on sales volume. It also requires an arbitrary allocation of indirect costs (overheads) to the candidate product, even though such costs will remain unaffected by sales of that product. Again, by failing to consider the influence of price on sales volume, it fails to consider the effect of price on production volume and therefore on total unit costs.

Because of these weaknesses, the full-cost approach cannot lead managers to the profit-maximizing price or, more generally, to the most appropriate price to attain strategic goals in a foreign target market. Full-cost pricing, moreover, does not provide assurance of profits, which depend not only on a profit margin but also on sales volume. Since a certain level of production is assumed in the allocation of overheads (so-called standard costs), failure to reach the corresponding sales volume can cause losses over an accounting period.

Quite frequently, U.S. companies set export prices by simply adding an "export margin" to a domestic full-cost price. The result is not a true full-cost price, because direct costs incurred in domestic sales may not be incurred in export sales, and vice versa. Full-cost pricing, especially the "domestic-plus" variant, is quite likely to overprice a product in export markets because of price escalation, namely, the addition to the FOB export price of several subsequent charges (such as shipping, insurance, forwarding fees, duties and border taxes, and channel markups). Escalation can make the final-buyer price in the international target market several times the FOB price.

When full-cost pricing proves to be uncompetitive in a target market, profit margins may be cut with a resulting less-than-full-cost price. Such ad hoc adjustments reflect a back-door consideration of market demand and competition that is forced on managers by poor market performance. In sum, the use of a full-cost approach to pricing for international market entry is particularly undesirable in view of escalation effects and the often slow feedback of information on market performance, which delay ad hoc price adjustments. Instead, what managers need is an approach that pays explicit attention to demand and competition in the foreign target market.

Incremental-Cost Pricing. The incremental-cost approach distinguishes between *variable costs* (such as labor, materials, and some marketing costs), which vary directly with production and sales, and *fixed costs,* which remain unaffected over a specified planning period. (In the very long run, of course, all costs are variable.) The incremental costs of foreign market entry therefore are the *new* costs of that entry that would not exist in its absence.[4] An incremental-cost price, then, is the sum of variable production and marketing costs plus a profit contribution.

Incremental costs alone should not be used by managers to determine entry prices, because, like full costs, they do not take account of demand and competition in the target market. But incremental costs do indicate a *floor price* that a company could accept for its candidate product without incurring out-of-pocket cash losses. Indeed, any price above the incremental floor price generates a positive cash flow even if it is below the full-cost price. The difference between full costs and incremental costs, therefore, defines a range of prices over which a company would make some contribution to overhead costs, although it would not make an accounting profit.

The principal use of costs should be to determine the profit consequences of alternative prices. For this use, incremental costs are superior to full costs. But to determine the most profitable price, managers also need to know the demand facing the candidate product in the foreign target market.

Profit-Contribution Pricing. A product's demand schedule shows the amounts that can be sold at different prices. Its two key features are (1) the amounts demanded at different prices and (2) the sensitivity of the amounts demanded to price changes. Sensitivity, known as *demand elasticity,* is defined as the ratio of the percentage change in amount demanded to the percentage change in price. If the absolute value (ignoring sign) of this fraction is greater than one, then demand is elastic: a decrease in price will increase total sales revenues, and vice versa. If it is smaller than one, then demand is inelastic: a decrease in price will decrease total sales revenues, and vice versa. Elasticity, then, is also a measure of the sensitivity of total sales revenues to price changes.

The demand schedule facing a candidate product in a foreign target market may be very unlike its demand schedule in the home market. This will be the case when the target market differs substantially from the home market in size, preferences, income, the differentiation of the candidate product as perceived by consumers/users, and competition. To estimate the demand schedule in a target market, managers can use three general methods: (1) buyer surveys, (2) market testing, and (3) statistical analysis of past relationships between sales and price in other markets similar to the target market. Clearly, demand estimation is most difficult when the product is generically new to the target market and that market does not resemble other markets in which the company has sales experience. Nonetheless, it is important that managers make explicit judgments about the shape and elasticity of a candidate product's demand schedule in a target market rather than assume implicitly that demand is wholly price insensitive, as is done with full-cost pricing.

The *profit contribution* of a candidate product in a target market is its incremental revenues minus its incremental costs over the planning period. Incremental revenues are all the revenues created by product sales; they would not exist in the absence of those sales. Incremental costs were defined earlier. The most profitable price is the price that generates the highest profit contribution. Table 8 offers a hypothetical example of how managers can identify the most profitable price among alternative prices by using the profit-contribution approach.

Here the manager has established a range of alternative prices for the candidate product that extends downward from a $6 price, which he or she estimates the target market would fully reject, to a floor price, which equals unit incremental costs of $1. Among these alternative prices, which price would maximize profit (or minimize loss)? The answer is the price that offers the highest profit contribution, namely $4 with a profit contribution of $15 (indicated by an asterisk in the table).

Profit-contribution pricing is often confused with incremental cost pricing and therefore rejected on the ground that it fails to cover fixed costs, which must be covered if a company is to survive in the long run. Actually, the profit-contribution price may or may not cover full costs, depending on the market. The profit-contribution approach is based on the economic truth that fixed costs have nothing to do with the determination of the most profitable price. *The price that maximizes profit contribution is the best a company can choose in the target market in the context of a given marketing plan.*

If the highest profit contribution is positive but smaller than the overhead charges allocated to a product, then managers may respond to the prospective accounting loss in several ways: (1) abandon market entry, although by so doing the company will have lower cash flow unless it can obtain a higher profit contribution by selling the same product in another market; (2) go ahead with the entry strategy because it will provide a positive cash flow; (3) alter the entry strategy by changing other elements of the marketing plan (such as advertising effort) that, by raising revenues more than costs, create the opportunity for a price that will both maximize profit contribution and cover full costs; (4) reduce incremental production costs at home in one or more ways or reduce them by sourcing the product within the target country or from a third country (that is to say, by changing the entry mode); or (5) reduce the product's overhead burden by changing the allocation rule.

TABLE 8

Profit-Contribution Analysis of Alternative Entry Prices for an International Target Market

Price	Estimated Unit Sales Volume	Incremental Revenue	Incremental Cost	Profit Contribution
$6	0	$0	$0	$0
$5	2	$10	$2	$8
$4	5	$20	$5	$15*
$3	7	$21	$7	$14
$2	9	$18	$9	$9
$1	10	$10	$10	$0

Note. * denotes the most profitable price.

Courses of action (3), (4), and (5) may, of course, be taken to-gether.

Entry Pricing Strategies

Entry pricing strategy is intended to obtain the maximum profit contribution for the entire marketing plan over the planning period, taking into account risks and other internal or external constraints. It follows that pricing strategy can be decided only along with distribution, promotion, and other marketing mix strategies. Managers may be seeking any one or more of several specific pricing objectives in the target market, including quick profits (payback), minimum risk, target sales growth, target market share, gaining support of middlemen, enhancing a high-quality image, meeting competitors, "buying" market entry, and avoiding government investigation. Whatever the objectives may be, they should be consistent with the objectives of the overall international marketing plan.

Pioneer Pricing Strategies. Pioneer pricing strategies are strategies for introducing a product that is generically new to the target market, that is to say, one that is in the introductory phase of its life cycle. Two very different pioneer strategies can be distinguished: skimming and development.

A *skimming* price strategy sets a high entry price for the new products, with the intent to earn quick profits before rivals respond with substitute products at a lower price. This strategy is especially attractive when a company is unwilling (or unable) to finance the cost of long-run market development and/or views market potential as highly uncertain. It is also appealing when a company has only a modest production capacity to serve the target market.

The profitability of a skimming strategy depends, of course, on the willingness of enough "early adopters" to pay a high price for the candidate product. But a high price also encourages competitors to enter the market with comparable products at lower prices. A skimming strategy therefore cannot build a long-run market position and may, for that reason, be less than optimum over the entire planning period. Anything that will slow down competitors' responses (such as patent protection) is favorable to this strategy. In sum, a skimming price strategy can be judged a low-risk strategy because it aims at a quick return with minimum marketing effort, but over the longer run it may turn out to be a high-risk strategy because it loses the market to competitors.

A *development* price strategy deliberately uses a low entry price to build up a dominant market position that can be defended against competitors. With this strategy, a company is willing to accept losses in early years because it views them as an investment in market development. As a long-run strategy, development pricing is most attractive when market potential is large, development costs are reasonable, substantial economies of scale are experienced in production, and the company has the production and marketing capacity to support volume sales. This strategy discourages potential competitors because the price is so low that profits can be made only at high sales volumes.

A pricing strategy that tries to combine the advantages of both the skimming and development strategies is *life-cycle* pricing. Although a company introduces its pioneer product at a high skimming price, it plans to lower the price in the successive stages of the product's life cycle in order to maintain market dominance. The success of this strategy depends on the correct timing of successive price reductions. Failure to anticipate changing market and competitive conditions can transform this strategy into a sequence of reactions to competitive moves, reactions that come too late to avoid an erosion of market position.

Other Entry Pricing Strategies. Companies with highly differentiated products are inclined toward a pricing strategy that enhances a *high-quality product image.* However irrational their attitudes might be, consumers/users tend to discredit high-quality claims for a product that is priced near (or especially below) the prices of average-quality competitive products. Hence the creation of a high-quality image ordinarily requires a comparatively high price, which may be suboptimal in profitability until that image is established in the market. Forgone short-run profits therefore are considered an investment in image development. For this strategy to work, a company must serve a market segment that is willing to pay for high quality, and it must be able to persuade consumers/

users that its product has that quality. With respect to the latter, it is a mistake for a company to believe that its high-quality image in the home market can be easily transferred to a foreign target market. In general, a high-quality image in a market can be achieved only through marketing effort in that market.

An entry pricing strategy to reach a *target market share* will not be successful if competitors in the target market quickly match the strategy. This is the common situation when a large company enters a market with a small number of major competitors (that is to say, an oligopolistic market); instead, the company must try to get its target market share through nonprice marketing efforts, such as product improvements, promotion, and distribution. But this strategy may work for a smaller company that is not viewed by major competitors as a threat to their own market shares.

Pricing to achieve a target market share should not be confused with a strategy to undercut competitors with an entry price below a company's costs. This is a high-risk strategy, because it invites price retaliation by competitors (with resulting losses for everyone) and/or antidumping actions and other forms of protection by the host government. This strategy, which may be labeled *buying international market entry,* is therefore unlikely to eliminate local competitors. In sum, buying international market entry is an unprofitable entry strategy not only in the short run but most likely in the long run as well.

Pricing to achieve *target sales* may deliberately sacrifice short-run profits for sales growth. This strategy works best in a price-elastic, high-growth market, which allows a company to obtain volume sales without taking them away from competitors. Pricing for growth can be justified as a long-run strategy only if volume sales will lead to profits through economies of scale in production and/or marketing.

Competitive pricing strategy matches the prices of competitors in the foreign target market. It is the only possible strategy for commodity-like products that are mildly differentiated in the eyes of buyers. Price then becomes the critical variable in purchase decisions, and a company has little pricing discretion, acting more as a price taker than a price maker. A competitive pricing strategy is also needed for sales to government agencies and industrial users under conditions of competitive bidding.

Planning the Discount Structure

Up to this point we have been talking about the *final-buyer* price of the candidate product, for it is this price that influences the buying decisions of consumers/users in the target market. In many instances, however, companies will be using indirect channels with independent intermediaries (agents, distributors, wholesalers, or retailers) to reach final buyers. Hence managers need to determine the price discounts that they should offer these middle-men.

Channel discount policy derives from both pricing and channel strategies. Discounts must be sufficient to attract good middlemen and to stimulate their marketing efforts, but at the same time they should be compatible with the final-buyer price desired by the international company. Since few countries allow manufacturers to establish legal controls on resale prices, getting middlemen to resell at the proper price can be accomplished only by convincing them that they will gain more by following the manufacturer's pricing strategy than by setting prices on their own.[5] This is seldom an easy task, but if international managers cannot control resale prices, then they also cannot control final-buyer prices.

Functional discounts are the most important discounts in entry pricing. They have two purposes: (1) payment to middlemen for their ordinary marketing efforts (personal selling, stocking, delivery, and so on) and (2) payment to encourage them to undertake extraordinary marketing efforts on behalf of the client company. In deciding on a functional-discount policy, therefore, managers need to decide first on the channel performance they want in the target market (see Chapter 4).

Quantity discounts may also be offered to middlemen as well as others. They should be justified by savings in order taking, transportation, handling, and other costs. *Cash* discounts intended to accelerate payment are more useful as a tactical instrument than as a strategic one.

Some Special Factors in International Pricing

Throughout this text we have called attention to special factors in international business. Many of these factors influence entry pricing strategies; here we merely identify the more prominent ones.

Chapter 4 discussed export price quotations, foreign exchange risks, and terms of payment, which include credit arrangements. Other price-related factors are tariffs and nontariff trade barriers, antitrust laws, and price controls. These factors can add to costs, limit pricing discretion, restrain sales, or introduce risks. They should be considered along with ordinary costs and market factors in planning entry pricing strategies.

The Need for Tactical Pricing Flexibility

An entry pricing strategy is intended to give a company the most appropriate pricing system in the target foreign market after full account is taken of market objectives, costs, demand, competition, and special factors over the planning period. When translated into policy, written manuals, and directives, entry pricing strategy becomes a set of guidelines for operating managers. As strategic guidelines, they should allow those managers some tactical flexibility in negotiating with middlemen and final buyers, meeting short-run market developments, or countering sporadic competitive activity. At the same time, tactical flexibility should be consistent with pricing strategy; otherwise, flexibility may achieve a tactical victory at the cost of a strategic defeat.

To conclude this section on pricing, we offer in Figure 19 a multistage model that brings together in a systematic way the several factors that managers should consider in planning entry pricing strategies.

Deciding on an International Promotion Strategy

In Chapter 2 we defined promotion as all communications initiated by a seller that are addressed to final buyers, channel members, or the general public with the intent to create immediate sales or a positive image for the seller's product or company. Promotion includes personal selling, advertising, sales promotion, and publicity.

Promotion in international marketing is one form of *cross-cultural* communication, because it involves a message sender belonging to one national culture and a message receiver belonging to a second national culture. Actually, all international business activities depend on cross-cultural communication in one way or another. This subject is so important that Chapter 9 is entirely devoted to planning entry strategies across cultural differences. Suffice it to say at this point that effective cross-cultural communication for promotional or other purposes is more difficult to achieve than effective communication within the same culture.

"Made-In" Product Images

When entering a foreign market for the first time, managers should understand that consumers/users in that market are likely to know little or nothing about the product and company, however well known they may be in the home market. But this does not mean that managers can write their promotional messages on a clean slate, particularly when they are entering the market

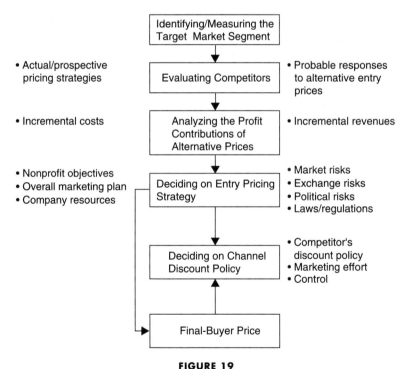

FIGURE 19

Multistage Determination of Pricing Strategy for International Market Entry

through exports. They will find that foreign consumers/users have already formed judgments about the managers' country and the products it manufactures. In short, they will confront "made-in" images that may be beneficial or detrimental to their own promotion effort. These images may be factual, fanciful, or most likely, a mixture of facts and conventional stereotypes. But whatever they may be, they will condition responses to the promotional messages of an international company.

Several studies have established the significance of made-in images for international marketing. A pioneer study published in 1963 showed that Europeans have favorable national self-images but less complimentary images of citizens of other countries.[6] For example, the French described themselves as pleasure loving, hardworking, and conscientious, but they were described by the Italians as pleasure loving, frivolous, and amorous. This inclination to ascribe favorable characteristics to one's own countrymen and less favorable characteristics to others also extended to products. Nonetheless, the Europeans often held similar images of the products manufactured by a particular country. For example, respondents in all seven survey countries viewed U.S. products as up-to-date but of lower quality and less reliable than German products.

Made-in images can change over time. Perhaps the most striking change has occurred for Japanese products, which before World War II were regarded by Western consumers as shoddy imitations of Western products. In sharp contrast, two surveys undertaken eight years apart indicate a deterioration in the image Japanese businessmen hold of U.S. products.[7] In 1967 Japanese businessmen considered American products superior in reliability to those of Japan and France, although inferior to those of West Germany and England. But in 1975 Japanese businessmen rated the reliability of American products at the bottom along with those of France. Although "made in the USA" remained highly rated for technical advancement and worldwide distribution, it lost first place to Germany in the former attribute and to Japan in the second. Overall, the U.S. made-in image had declined substantially for Japanese businessmen between 1967 and 1975. A more recent study found that Finnish perceptions of *both* U.S. and Japanese consumer products have improved over the period 1975 to 1985 but that the improvement was substantially greater for

Japanese products. Furthermore, these perceptual changes correspond to changes in the relative market shares of U.S. and Japanese consumer products in Finland.[8]

Knowledge of made-in images can be very helpful to international managers in planning promotion strategy for a foreign target market.[9] Ordinarily, these images are a mixture of both positive and negative attitudes toward products identified with the managers' country. By appealing to positive attitudes, managers stand a better chance than otherwise to create an attractive *brand* or *company* image with their own promotion. An awareness of made-in images can also be a powerful corrective to managers' ethnocentric biases. As mentioned above, people in industrial

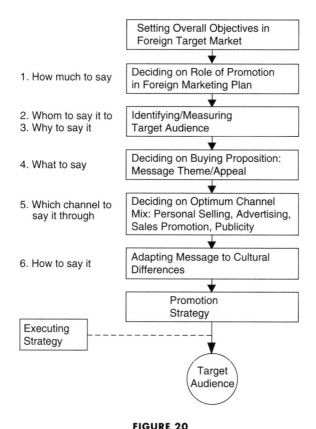

FIGURE 20

Deciding on Promotion Strategy in the Marketing Plan

countries usually have a more favorable image of their own country's products than foreigners do.[10]

Deciding on a Promotion Strategy: A Planning Model

Figure 20 identifies the key decisions that must be made in designing a company's promotion strategy for a foreign target market.

How Much to Say. The first and most fundamental decision concerns the role promotion should have in the international marketing plan. The starting point is the target market objectives established by managers over the entry planning period, a subject treated earlier. What level of promotion effort is required to attain those objectives? Several considerations bear on the answer to this question. Consumer goods usually need more promotion effort than industrial goods because there are many consumers dispersed over a sizable geographical area. Furthermore, sellers of consumer goods may have to create psychological benefits in the minds of consumers through promotion, while sellers of industrial products can appeal to rational buying motives by communicating information mostly on product features, performance, and cost. Apart from these general considerations is the company's own product. As remarked earlier in this chapter, if a product is highly adapted to a particular market segment, it requires less promotion than a product not so adapted.

Other factors include the size of the target market, the phase of the product's life cycle, competition, and the entry mode. A market with a high company sales potential clearly justifies more promotion effort than one with a smaller potential. Heavier promotion is called for by new-product introduction than by later phases of the life cycle. Again, if competitors promote heavily in the target market, the international company is compelled to match them in some degree. Promotion effort also depends on the entry mode. For instance, a company using foreign distributors may leave promotion entirely or partly to them, but with its own sales subsidiary it must assume the full promotion effort.

To overcome ignorance of their company and product, managers should plan *more* intensive promotion in markets abroad than at home. But a survey of U.S. industrial companies found that only one-tenth of the surveyed companies were spending more than 1 percent of their international sales on print advertising, while three-tenths were spending more than 1 percent of their domestic sales on print advertising.[11] This finding suggests that many U.S. manufacturers would substantially increase their international promotion if they were simply to match their domestic promotion.

Whom to Say It To and Why to Say It. Managers need to specify the target audience or audiences. Should we address our channel members? Or should we address the final consumers or users of our product? Or should we address both? Should we address the general public? The identity of the target audience largely deter-

Instead of using a single global advertising campaign (something that has become fashionable in the advertising industry), Heineken tailors its advertising to each country market. Beer, Heineken managers believe, has cultural idiosyncrasies. In some traditional wine-drinking countries like Italy and France, Heineken's advertising tries to make beer converts. In Italy, its TV commercials promote Heineken beer as a drink for all occasions, including a romantic stay at a ski chalet. One of its French commercials shows a distinguished middle-aged actor holding a glass of Heineken to the light, as if it were a fine wine. In Japan, Heineken appeals to young professionals as a taste of refined European culture with TV commercials showing tuxedoed gentlemen and elegant ladies sipping Heineken aboard the fabled Orient Express. Heineken's strategy in the United States is to position its brew as a foreign status symbol, the Rolls Royce of beers. Although different, these approaches are all based on Heineken's "holy principles": Heineken beer is brewed to look the same and taste the same nearly everywhere, and it is sold as a prestige beer worth its high price. Heineken is Europe's largest brewer and the third biggest in the world. It brews beer in fifty countries and is America's favorite imported beer.

Adapted from "Competition Gets Scrappy in Heineken's Beer Markets, *Wall Street Journal,* August 24, 1984, p. 24; and "Cheers to Heineken," *Fortune,* November 19, 1990, p. 172.

mines the *general* purpose of promotional messages: managers want channel members to sell more, they want final consumers/ users to buy more, and they want the general public to regard their company and product more favorably.

Specific promotion objectives derive from the objectives of the foreign marketing plan. Common objectives include introducing a new product or new product features, developing a favorable brand image, supporting present or obtaining new channel members, gaining immediate sales, matching the promotion of competitors, and building goodwill toward the company and its product. Whatever the objectives may be managers should know *why* they want to communicate with a target audience. Clearly, the more managers know about that audience—buying motivations and behavior, purchasing power, demographic characteristics, cultural values, and other features—the better they can design their promotion strategy: deciding on the buying proposition, determining the optimum channel mix, and adapting the promotional message to cultural differences. Acquiring information on target audiences is the job of market research, as discussed in Chapter 3.

What to Say. The next step in the model is to decide on the buying proposition, namely, the dominant theme or appeal that managers want to communicate to the target audience. The buying proposition is the *idea* content of the promotional message—persuasive selling points of the product or company. How the buying proposition is to be presented is contingent on the choice of promotion channels. The creation of an effective buying proposal requires that managers view their product and company from the perspective of the intended receivers in the target market, who belong to a different culture and society. Although a buying proposition used in domestic promotion may be fully transferable to a foreign market, it would be rash for managers to assume that this is always the case.

Which Channel to Say It Through. Basically, communication channels are either personal or impersonal. Personal selling, as the name implies, relies on the personal, face-to-face channel; advertising and publicity rely on impersonal channels that reach a mass audience; and sales promotion relies on both personal and impersonal channels depending on its specific nature.

When international companies use foreign agents or distributors, *personal selling* in the target market is largely left to those representative.[12] They assume the responsibility for the recruitment, training, and supervision of a sales force. Although an international company may provide technical and sales training and sales aids to its agent/distributor, ordinarily it has little control over the personal selling effort in the target market. Its most active participation occurs when its own missionary salesmen assist foreign representatives.

International companies take on the personal selling function when they establish sales branches/subsidiaries in a target market or when corporate persons undertake missions to foreign markets for face-to-face contacts with prospective final buyers.[13] This latter channel is used principally by companies that negotiate high-unit-value transactions (whether of tangible products or of services) with foreign industrial users or governments.

Advertising, the dominant channel for mass promotion, may be defined as any paid form of nonpersonal communication by an identified sponsor to promote a product or company. Advertising employs several specific channels or media, including direct mail, newspapers, magazines, trade journals, radio, television, cinema, and outdoor posters. In deciding on advertising media, managers are concerned with *effectiveness* (as indicated by coverage, audience selectivity, frequency, and other features) and *cost*. In general, cost-effectiveness inclines consumer-products companies toward radio, television, and widely distributed print media, while it inclines industrial-products companies toward direct mail, trade journals, and other specialized print media that are aimed at a relatively small number of business prospects. Commonly, the function of industrial advertising is to back up personal selling efforts.

It is seldom possible for a company to duplicate in foreign markets the advertising media mix used in the home market. Countries differ widely in the availability, quality, coverage, audience, and cost of advertising media. Also, national laws regulate advertising in many ways: choice of media, comparative claims, required information, trademarks and labels, and promotion methods, such as contests and premiums. For example, media availability is quite different in Western Europe from what it is in the United States, even though the economies are similar. Television advertising is not allowed in Belgium, Denmark, Sweden, and Norway, and regulations restrict the time allowed for television advertising in other European countries. Media availability is most limited in the developing countries, where the choice of a media mix is also complicated by the common lack of reliable information on media coverages and audiences.

When used in a specific sense, *sales promotion* covers all promotion intended to supplement or strengthen personal selling, advertising, and publicity. It includes exhibitions and shows, demonstrations, seminars, contests, sales aids (letters, catalogs, technical bulletins, films, sales kits, and so on), point-of-purchase displays, samples, gifts, premiums, special allowances, and, in general, any promotion effort that is not designated as personal selling, advertising, or publicity. Much sales promotion is used to improve the performance of a company's own salesmen or of its foreign distributors and agents.

One kind of sales promotion is far more important in international than in domestic marketing: trade fairs. International trade fairs are a special kind of market that brings buyers and sellers from different countries together at one place and time. The *general* trade fair is a big event (usually annual) exhibiting the products of several different industries. The other and more common type of fair is the *specialized* fair, which displays the products of a single industry of closely affiliated ones, such as Photokina in Cologne. All in all, nearly one hundred cities throughout the world host international trade fairs, covering virtually every industry.

Companies entering foreign markets for the first time may find trade fairs a valuable experience. Exhibitors can quickly generate awareness of their product brands and company names, and because visitors come to buy on the spot, they can also test the acceptability of their products before launching a full-scale marketing effort. Exhibitors can also learn much about competitors' products at first hand. Channel arrangements may also be negotiated with agents and distributors who visit fairs. Finally, exhibitors can use the promotional advantages of personal selling, and, unlike in the usual personal selling situations, they can talk with many potential buyers within a short time and at one place. Furthermore, they can make more striking presentations of their products than possible in ordinary personal selling. In sum, international trade fairs offer the advantages of both personal selling and advertising. As noted in Chapter 4, the U.S. Department of Commerce actively encourages the participation of U.S. companies in international trade fairs by sponsoring exhibits.

Like advertising, *publicity* is a channel for mass promotion. But unlike advertising, it is commercially significant news about a company or product, disseminated to the general public and not paid for by a sponsor. Because publicity messages are perceived as news, they may have more credibility than advertising messages. We are speaking here of publicity initiated by the international company, not inadvertent publicity that the company does not control and that may be beneficial or detrimental to its interests in the target country/market. Publicity promotion is seldom used with export and licensing entry modes; it is used mostly with investment entry and contractual arrangements with host governments. For instance, the start of new-plant construction in a target country may be turned into a ceremonial occasion with the attendance of leading government officials and full media coverage.

Each promotion channel has its own comparative advantages and disadvantages. Personal selling is generally the most effective channel, as measured by the ratio of sales made to the number of sales contacts. But the cost per sales contact can be very high, because international sales representatives must often travel great distances and remain away from the home country for extended periods. In contrast, advertising offers comparatively low cost per contact, but it also usually generates lower average sales per contact than personal selling. It is impossible to generalize about the advantages and disadvantages of the many forms of sales promotion, some of which closely resemble personal selling or advertising. Earlier we noted the several advantages of trade fairs. Because the many promotion channels are complementary as well as substitutive, a mix of channels is almost certain to provide a more cost-effective promotion program than a single channel.

How to Say It. Effective presentation of the buying proposition in promotional messages can be achieved only through a full understanding of the foreign target audience. Assuming that the buying proposition addresses the needs and motivations of that audience, the question of presentation at the strategic level becomes mainly one of adaptation to the national culture. We therefore defer further discussion on presentation until Chapter 9, which treats cross-cultural communication.

Promotion Strategy. Deciding international promotion strategy is a planning process that is recursive with multiple feedback loops. Although all the questions raised in Figure 20 may not be fully answerable, nonetheless they must be answered if managers are to design a cost-effective promotion strategy. This becomes evident when one considers the several possible sources of failure in promotion: (1) The message does not get through to target receivers because the channel does not reach them. (2) The message is received but is misunderstood, either because of ambiguous content (buying proposition) or, more commonly, because of a presentation that is not responsive to cultural differences. (3) Although understood, the message fails to persuade receivers to change their behavior in the way intended by the sender because of a weak appeal, a weak presentation, or external factors (such as lack of purchasing power). Only a comprehensive approach to international promotion strategy can deal with these several obstacles to effective promotion across economic, political, and cultural differences.

A Note to the Reader

We have now completed an elaboration of the first four boxes in the entry strategy model depicted in Figure 2 in Chapter 2. The focus of this model is on planning entry strategies for a single candidate product in a single target country/market. As stated in Chapter 2, this is the constituent international market entry strategy. But it is not the whole story. As a company evolves in international business, its managers must make entry decisions in the context of an ongoing multiproduct/multicountry enterprise system. Entry decisions can no longer be made for a single product and target country in isolation from other products and countries. Some key issues that arise in planning and controlling entry strategies in a multiproduct/multicountry context (including monitoring and revising entry strategies—box 5 in Figure 2) are taken up in Chapter 10. Also, in elaborating the entry model, we have not systematically examined the role of cultural differences in planning and controlling entry strategies. That is done in Chapter 9.

Summary

1. To design an international marketing plan, managers must make decisions, both individually and collectively, on policies relating to the product, pricing, channels, promotion, and logistics. In so doing, they should be guided by the international marketing concept.
2. Managers need to make *joint* decisions on mix policies in order to design an integrated marketing plan. Analyzing the marketing mix profile can help in this endeavor. The best plan is one that maximizes profit contribution over the planning period.
3. The concept of market segmentation derives from the proposition that consumers/users in a country market have different needs and preferences that, in turn, create differences in demand for a candidate product. Segmentation criteria may be general or situation specific. The advantages of a segmentation strategy must be weighed against its possible disadvantages.
4. Few questions in international marketing are more troublesome than pricing. Fundamental approaches to entry pricing are full-cost pricing, incremental-cost pricing, and profit-contribution pricing. The profit-contribution approach is recommended because the price that maximizes profit contribution is the best choice a company can make in the target market in the context of a given marketing plan.
5. Entry pricing strategy is intended to obtain the maximum profit contribution for the entire marketing plan over the

planning period, taking into account risks and other internal or external constraints. Thus pricing strategy can be decided only along with other mix strategies.

6. Entry pricing strategies include skimming pricing, development pricing, high-quality-image pricing, target-market-share pricing, pricing to buy market entry, target-sales pricing, and competitive pricing. Managers also need to formulate channel discount policies. Special factors in international pricing, such as tariffs and nontariff trade barriers, add to costs, limit pricing discretion, restrain sales, or introduce risks. A model brings together in a systematic way the several factors that managers should consider in planning entry pricing strategies.

7. Promotion comprises all communications initiated by a seller that are addressed to final buyers, channel members, or the general public with the intent to create immediate sales or a positive image for the seller's product or company. It is one form of cross-cultural communication in international business.

8. In entering foreign markets, companies confront "made-in" images that may be beneficial or detrimental to their own promotion efforts. These images are preformed judgments held by foreign consumers/users about a company's country and the products of that country. Ordinarily these images are a mix of both positive and negative attitudes.

9. Managers need to answer several questions in planning promotion strategy for a foreign target market: how much to say, whom to say it to, why to say it, what to say, which channel to say it through, and how to say it.

10. The most fundamental decision concerns the role that promotion should have in the foreign marketing plan. To overcome ignorance of their company and product, managers should plan more intensive promotion abroad than at home. Specific promotion objectives derive from the objectives of the foreign marketing plan.

11. The creation of an effective buying proposal requires that managers view their product and company from the perspective of the intended receivers in the target market, who belong to a different culture and society.

12. Promotion channels are personal selling, advertising, sales promotion, and publicity. It is seldom possible for a company to duplicate in foreign markets the advertising media mix in the home market. A particularly important form of sales promotion in international marketing is the international trade fair. Because many promotion channels are complementary as well as substitutive, a mix of channels is almost certain to provide a more cost-effective promotion program than a single channel.

CHAPTER 9

Designing and Managing
Entry Strategies Across
Cultural Differences

B lunders in international business are commonly traceable to
ethnocentric assumptions unconsciously held by managers,
especially the belief that foreigners think and behave much like
people at home even though they may speak another language. Because they are usually wrong in one respect or another, ethnocentric assumptions lead to poor strategies in both design and execution. They act to distort communications with foreign nationals,
whether they be government officials, licensees, joint-venture
partners, agents, distributors, suppliers, employees, customers, or
the general public. Cultural differences can affect any and all entry
strategy decisions: the choice of target country markets (or segments within those markets), the choice of a candidate product
and its adaptation to foreign markets, the choice of an entry
mode, the formulation of a foreign marketing program, and the
control of entry operations. All these decisions depend on cross-
cultural communication of one sort or another. In sum, cross-
cultural communication is the lifeblood of international management. But any time a message crosses cultural boundaries, there is
a potential for misunderstanding arising from largely unconscious
cultural differences.

International managers are communicators across cultures,
transmitters of their own culture, and agents of change in foreign
cultures. They need to deal with foreign nationals in face-to-face

encounters and through letters, faxes, telephone calls, and other means. They also need to design and execute marketing communications, such as advertising, addressed to foreign nationals. The expatriate manager is most directly involved in managing cultural differences, followed by headquarters managers who make frequent business trips abroad. But in an international company, even home country managers should learn to appreciate cultural differences, because at the very least they are members of a communications system that includes foreign nationals. A frequent complaint of country managers is their inability to communicate with ethnocentric managers at the corporate level.

In Chapter 2 we spoke about cultural distance as an influence on the choice of an entry mode, and throughout the text we have mentioned cultural factors. But the pervasive influence of cultural differences on communication in international business merits a more thorough treatment. We first describe the nature of culture and then examine its bearing on cross-cultural communication, including negotiations. We close with some pointers on how managers can develop the cultural understanding so necessary to success in international business.

What Is Culture?

Culture may be defined as the unique life-style of a given human society: a distinctive way of thinking, perceiving, feeling, believing, and behaving that is passed on from one generation to another. Anthropologists agree on three features of every human culture.[1] First, culture is not something that is inherited; rather, it is learned by individuals as they grow up in their society, a process called *enculturation*. Second, the knowledge, values, beliefs, customs, and mores that make up the culture are interrelated to form a more or less *integrated whole*. Third, culture consists of learned behavior traits that are shared by members of a *social group* and distinguish that group from other groups with different cultures. In sum, a given culture offers a complete set of rules for living that enables its members to cope with physical and social environments. As a total way of life with existential values that shape perceptions of the world and with norms that guide social behavior, culture patterns not only our behavior but also how we expect others to behave.

Cultural Personality

Different cultures foster different personality types. They do so by postulating an ideal personality type ("the good person") and then rewarding behavior consistent with the ideal type while punishing behavior inconsistent with it. For the most part a culture's desired behavior is learned early in life, and the totality of the resulting behavior traits constitutes the core of the individual's personality, which persists throughout his or her life. Consequently, personality norms vary from one culture to another. That is why one can speak of a French personality, a Japanese personality, an American personality, and so on. This does not mean, of course, that all French nationals have the same personality; genetic inheritance and individual life experience also influence the formation of personality. It is for that reason that the members of a given culture exhibit a range of personality types that matches the range in other cultures. But the *representative* personality type differs from one culture to another, because different cultures encourage different personality types.

Cultural Universals

Despite their profound differences, all cultures have many general features in common—the so-called *cultural universals,* which reflect the common biological nature of humans and their common needs to cope with physical and social environments. Some of these universals are age grading, community organization, cooking, dancing, education, ethics, family, funeral rites, games, government, greetings, housing, marriage, medicine, mythology, personal names, property rights, religious ritual, residence rules, sexual restrictions, tool making, and trade. Probably the most important single universal is language, for much of culture is transmitted by word of mouth. Indeed, some anthropologists, notably Hall, define culture as a total communications system: words, gestures, facial expressions, posture, and other behaviors that convey meaning, including the use of time, space, and materials.[2]

Cultural universals are similarities across cultures in types of behavior rather than in specific behavior traits. These traits may be classified into different systems, such as political, economic, religious, kinship, educational, health, and recreational.

Another approach to cultural universals is to consider the limited number of questions that all peoples need to answer in one way or another. Five fundamental questions are listed here, followed by some alternative responses enclosed in parentheses. (1) What is the essence of human nature? (Good? Evil? A mixture of the two?) (2) What is the relationship of man to nature? (Subject? Master? Part of?) (3) What is the temporal focus of life? (The past? The present? The future?) (4) What is the modality of man's behavior? (Spontaneous expression? Self-actualization? Measurable accomplishment?) (5) What is the relationship of man to man? (As an individual? As a member of a permanent group? As a member of a transitory group?) The preferred responses of a society to these questions make up its ideal cultural values that shape the thinking, feeling, and behavior of its members.

Cultural Self-Awareness

The cultural patterns that govern our perception of the world and our social behavior function mostly below the level of conscious awareness. Only when we come into contact with persons of other cultures who have different perceptions and behavior traits do we become aware of cultural differences and, in that way, of our own cultural uniqueness. To achieve cultural self-awareness, therefore, we must learn about other cultures and how they differ from our own. Those who know no other culture cannot know their own.

In the absence of cultural self-awareness, we unconsciously assume that people in other cultures experience the world as we do, an assumption termed *projective cognitive similarity* or, more popularly, the *self-reference criterion*. Unconscious references to our own cultural values cause no problem when we are interacting with persons of our own culture; indeed, they facilitate social interactions by creating congruent expectations. But the self-reference criterion can play havoc when we interact with persons of another culture. We shall say more about this when we discuss cross-cultural communication; suffice it to say at this point that cultural self-awareness is a necessary condition for successful intercultural relations.

Cultural self-awareness goes beyond the mere recognition of cultural differences. It also requires the abandonment of the belief, often accompanied with strong emotions, that one's own culture is superior to others. All cultures tend to breed ethnocentric people.

When such people encounter a foreign culture, they observe behavior that not only makes little sense to them but also appears "wrong": "Why can't these people behave like we do, like reasonable humans should behave?"

Ethnocentric attitudes of superiority, disdain, and rejection are a potent and all too common source of barriers in cross-cultural relations. Moreover, they are simply wrong. It makes no sense to judge a foreign culture inferior to one's own, because each culture is unique. Hence the assignment of inferiority to a foreign culture

---

More and more foreign managers and technicians are coming to the United States either to staff the U.S. subsidiaries of foreign-based parent companies or to receive training from U.S.-based parent companies for positions in foreign subsidiaries. To most of these European, Asian, and Latin American business people, the United States is a foreign country possessing a strange culture that can sometimes cause painful problems of maladjustment. A manager raised in the Dominican Republic, where business people start meetings with relaxed chitchat, found that Americans view such behavior as a waste of time. He still feels uncomfortable starting abruptly with business matters because it strikes him as "cold-blooded." Europeans are often fooled by the informality of their American managers, not understanding that a request may be urgent even when expressed in an informal style. One U.S. firm runs role-playing sessions for its Japanese managers, many of whom are upset by American bluntness. The Japanese must learn how to interrupt conversations at, say, a manufacturing plant when there is trouble. Families of foreign managers can also suffer from culture shock, and many U.S. companies now try to help them. Without the benefit of a strong U.S. presence, many foreign-based companies overlook cultural differences. Says Sir Gordon White, chairman of Hanson Industries (U.K.): "I don't believe you can run a major U.S. company from abroad. George III tried to run the United States from Britain, and look what happened to him."

Adapted from "American Culture Is Often a Puzzle for Foreign Managers in the U.S.," *Wall Street Journal,* February 12, 1986, p. 33; and "For More and More Foreign Companies America Isn't Paved with Gold," *Business Week,* February 3, 1986, pp. 84–85.

is nothing more than a projection of one's own cultural values, which are also unique. This is not to gainsay that the values of a given culture may be more or less congruent with the values, say, of Western-style science or Western-style economic organization. But that is a question of cultural distance, not one of cultural inferiority.

Cultural self-awareness makes us conscious of the norms and rules that govern our thinking, feeling, and behavior. It is a process of learning about our own culture through learning about other cultures. In this way we gradually gain an outsider's perspective on our culture and some release from an emotional attachment to our cultural values. Cultural self-awareness is an affirmation, not a rejection, of our own culture. By knowing our culture, we know more about ourselves and in that sense become liberated persons. We put aside our "cultural blinders."

How do we achieve cultural self-awareness? Ultimately, only through personal interactions with individuals who belong to other cultures, which is to say that cultural self-awareness is *experiential* learning. But this learning can be facilitated by gaining intellectual knowledge of foreign cultures, most notably through language study. Table 9 offers a modest contribution to such knowledge by comparing some Sinic culture traits shared by the Chinese, Japanese, Koreans, and Vietnamese to American culture traits.[3] Although the comparison is superficial, it should make evident that Americans need to understand their own cultural uniqueness if they are to relate successfully with persons of other cultures.

Communicating Across Cultures

Communication can be successful in conveying an intended meaning only when the sender's perceptual field—his or her experience of the world—is congruent with the receiver's perceptual field. That is to say, communication is a process of sharing perceptions. A message falling outside the receiver's perceptual field, therefore, cannot transmit the sender's meaning, although it may well transmit a meaning not intended by the sender. But this congruity of perception, although necessary, is not a sufficient condition for successful communication. In addition, the sender needs to "encode" his or her message in words, other linguistic symbols, ges-

TABLE 9

A Comparison of Some American and Sinic Cultural Traits

	American	Sinic
Man and Nature	Mechanistic worldview: world is material, not spiritual. Man stands outside nature and should dominate it.	The world is essentially spiritual. Man is part of nature and should be in harmony with it.
Philosophy of Life	The individual is all-important. Individualism is preferable to conformity. Life is competitive; it rewards effort with material success. All activity should have a purpose. Man is perfectible.	The group is all-important. Conformity and compromise to maintain group harmony are preferable to individualism. Life is cooperative; it rewards effort with the esteem of one's fellows. Man is a mixture of bad and good and always will be.
Relations with Others	One should be open and direct with others. Communication should be explicit; one should get to the point quickly. Informality is good.	It is dangerous for one to be open and direct with others. To keep relations harmonious and avoid embarrassment, indirect, ambiguous language is often necessary. Formality is good.
Time	Time is unilinear. Activities should be scheduled; it is good to plan ahead. Time is valuable; punctuality is important.	Time is elastic: it can be stretched or contracted depending on the circumstances. Punctuality is not important of itself; long delays are sometimes necessary before taking action.
Social Structure	All persons should have equal opportunity. Class distinction is undesirable; status should be earned. Persons should accord each other equal treatment.	Social inequalities are to be expected; society is hierarchical, with clearly defined reciprocities and appropriate behavior between inferiors and superiors. Men are superior to women.
Agreements	Agreements should be verbal and explicit. Business contracts should specify the mutual obligations of each party in detail, and they should be legally enforceable.	Agreements should be based on mutual understanding. The written expression of the agreement is not very important and should be flexible. Disputes should be settled by negotiation, not by law.

tures, facial expressions, or other forms of behavior that can be "decoded" by the receiver to obtain the sender's meaning.[4] The encoding/decoding processes are not confined to linguistic symbols; all forms of behavior may carry a meaning. Indeed, almost every verbal message is accompanied by a nonverbal message.

Perceptual and Encoding/Decoding Gaps

Communication between persons belonging to the same culture benefits from a high degree of congruence in their perceptual fields and of commonality in their message codes. Contrariwise, communication between persons belonging to different cultures is distorted by perceptual and encoding/decoding gaps that derive from the cultural distance between sender and receiver. The greater the cultural distance, the greater the gaps. Furthermore, because of the unconscious nature of much of culture, communication distortion is intensified by a common failure of both the sender and receiver to recognize the existence of perceptual and nonverbal encoding gaps. Consequently, a sender may believe he or she has communicated successfully when he or she has not, and correspondingly, a receiver may believe he or she has understood a message when he or she has not. The feedback process, therefore, is also subject to cultural distortion.

The distinction we have drawn between perceptual gaps and encoding/decoding gaps is more analytical than behavioral. Not only is our native language in which we encode or decode a message a means of communication; it also profoundly structures our perception of the world.[5] For that reason, perceptual and encoding/decoding gaps usually occur together in cross-cultural communication, especially when cultural distances are large. It follows that the most direct way for a sender to overcome both perceptual and encoding/decoding gaps is to learn the language of the receiver. By so doing, he or she is able to use the receiver's linguistic code and, more important, to share in some degree the receiver's perceptual field as shaped by his or her language.

A sender may try to overcome cultural gaps *indirectly* by using another person to encode or interpret a message to a foreign receiver. This indirect approach must be used by international managers at least some of the time, because no single manager can know the languages of all the foreign nationals he or she must deal with. It must be recognized, however, that the use of an interpreter (or translator) places another mind between those of the sender and receiver, a mind that may distort rather than transfer a message. The more senders know about the culture of the receiver, the better they can guard against interpreter distortions and the better they know what to say at what time and how to behave in general, something they cannot (and should not) expect to get from an interpreter. In sum, interpreters at best can only partly compensate for the sender's (or receiver's) ignorance of a foreign culture.

Figure 21 depicts the congruence between the perceptual fields and encoding/decoding behavior of a message sender and a message receiver at different cultural distances. The greater the congruence, as shown by the cross-hatched overlaps, the lower

---

Facing saturated domestic markets, Campbell Soup (U.S.)—a maker of soups, cookies, frozen foods and other prepared food products—is determined to become a global enterprise. Its chief executive wants one-half of company sales, which totaled about $6 billion in 1992, to come from outside the United States compared to about one-quarter at present. This will not be an easy task: prepared food products are not as easily marketed abroad as soap, cigarettes, or soft drinks, for they are more sensitive to local tastes. Campbell is a latecomer to international markets compared to its major U.S. competitors, CPC International and H. J. Heinz. In 1992 60 percent of CPC's sales were outside North America, and Heinz entered the British market in 1895. Furthermore, Nestlé (Switzerland) dominates world markets in prepared foods. In many countries, consumers have never heard of Campbell or its products. To become a global enterprise, Campbell is pursuing a multidomestic strategy: it is busy creating new products that appeal to distinctive local tastes (for example, a cream of chile poblano soup in Mexico, a watercress/duck gizzard soup in Hong Kong, and a peppery tripe soup in Poland). In 1991 the company opened a taste kitchen in Hong Kong to develop soups that will appeal to 2 billion Asian consumers.

Adapted from "Campbell: Now It's M-M-Global," *Business Week,* March 15, 1993, pp. 52–53.

the probability of cultural distortions in communication. When sender and receiver belong to the same culture, the congruence is complete, which is to say there is no cultural distance.[6] Although incomplete, congruence is substantial when the sender and receiver are separated by a small cultural distance but use the same language. This situation pertains to, for example, the Americans and the British, the Germans and the Austrians, the French and the Walloon Belgians, the Egyptians and the Saudis, and the Argentinians and the Colombians. Congruence shrinks noticeably when the sender and receiver speak different languages even though they are separated by only a medium cultural distance. This situation characterizes Americans and Europeans, who share the same Western macroculture, and the Japanese and Chinese, who share the same Sinic macroculture. With large cultural distances, congruence becomes marginal. At the extreme, communication may be confined to primitive gestures, such as pointing at

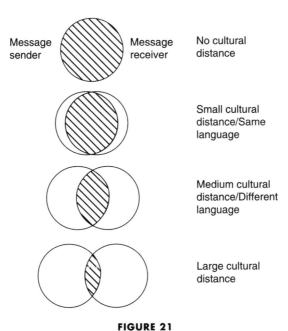

FIGURE 21

Congruence of the Perceptual Fields and Encoding or Decoding Behavior of Message Sender and Message Receiver at Different Cultural Distances

the mouth to indicate a desire for food. The large cultural distance between the Western and Sinic macrocultures is of particular importance to international business managers.

The foregoing discussion of perceptual and encoding/decoding gaps in cross-cultural communication may strike some readers as merely academic. To remove that impression, eleven examples of international advertising blunders follow, four demonstrating perceptual gaps and seven illustrating encoding/decoding gaps. We leave it to the reader to decide which is which!

1. An American airline in Brazil advertised "rendezvous lounges" on its jets. In Portuguese, *rendezvous* means a room hired for lovemaking.
2. A leading producer of farm equipment built an advertising campaign in the United States around testimonials of small farmers. But this campaign fell flat in Europe, where dealers found it to be insulting because "small farmers" were viewed as peasants. Who wants advice from peasants?
3. In many regions of Southeast Asia where betelnut chewing was an elite habit and black teeth were a symbol of prestige, Pepsodent's promise of white teeth did not help. Nor did its slogan, "Wonder where the yellow went."
4. "Body by Fisher" became "corpse by Fisher" in Flemish.
5. Parker Pen Company once launched an ad campaign in Latin America that unintentionally claimed that its new ink would help prevent unwanted pregnancies.
6. McDonnell Douglas Corporation created an aircraft brochure for potential customers in India depicting men wearing turbans. The Indians politely pointed out that turbans were Pakistani Moslem, not Indian.
7. When Pepsi-Cola Company ran an ad in the Taiwan issue of the *Reader's Digest,* it used the slogan, "Come alive with Pepsi!" Unfortunately, the Taiwanese translation told its readers, "Pepsi brings your ancestors back from the dead!" In Germany, the same slogan was translated, "Come out of the grave with Pepsi!"
8. General Mills advertised its breakfast cereal in Britain showing a freckled, red-haired, crew-cut, grinning kid saying, "See kids, it's great!" But the cereal was almost un-

touched on retail shelves. The stereotyped American boy with the banal expression did not appeal to the British ideal of a child.

9. When Kentucky Fried Chicken used its famous slogan, "It's finger-licking good!" in Iran, it came out in Farsi as "It's so good you will eat your fingers!"

10. General Motors dealers in Puerto Rico were not happy with the new Chevrolet Nova automobile. The reason? When pronounced in Spanish, *no va* means "it does not go." GM quickly changed the name to Caribe.

11. An Oriental translator transformed Northwest Orient Airlines' slogan—"Give wings to your heart"—into "Tie feathers to your blood pump."

Low-Context and High-Context Cultures

Distance is greatest between cultures that rely heavily on *words* for communication (low-context cultures) and cultures that rely heavily on *nonverbal behavior* (high context cultures).[7] In a low-context culture, most of the information in most messages is contained in an explicit linguistic code, that is to say, spoken or written words. In a high-context culture, however, most of the information in most messages is contained in the physical context or in the receiver's internal context, and very little is explicitly coded in words. American culture is low context (and even more so the Scandinavian and German cultures); the Chinese and Japanese cultures are high context. While an American looks for meaning in what is being said, a Japanese looks for meaning in what is *not* being said—the silences, the gestures, the situation, and so on. To the American, therefore, it is most important to send accurate verbal messages, but to the Japanese it is most important to receive messages that are only partly (or not at all) in verbal form.

In low-context cultures, communication is more abstract and impersonal than in high-context cultures. That is because any event or situation is more complex than the language used to describe it, and the written language is itself an abstraction of the spoken language. In other words, language has a "linear" dimension, since one can talk or write about only a single aspect of an event or situation at any one time. It follows that language can convey only some of the meaning of an event or situation, including some things while leaving out others. Conversely, in high-context cultures communication conveys much more of the complexity of an event or situation, because the receiver obtains meaning not only from words but, to a far greater degree than in low-context cultures, also from the sender's nonverbal behavior and from the physical setting. But high-context communication also requires that the receiver share the perceptual field of the sender much more fully than in low-context communication.

High-context messages can be understood only by someone who has been "programmed" with the necessary information (internal context) and an understanding of the setting (external context). The Japanese and Chinese, therefore, must know much more what is going on at the covert level. It is the ignorance of Americans and other Westerners of the hidden, contextual perceptions that so confounds communication with the Chinese and Japanese or with persons in other high-context cultures. That is why Hall says it is "sheer folly" to get seriously involved with high-context cultures unless one is really "contexted."[8]

Because communication is the lifeblood of any organization, it is not surprising to find that typical business organizations in low- and high-context cultures are dissimilar in many ways. In a low-context culture, such as the American, a firm depends primarily on explicit (mostly written) rules to direct and control the behavior of managers and workers, and it rewards and punishes them by reference to their accomplishment of specific performance goals. Large American firms also explicitly define many functions and activities that are linked by formal relations among specialized managers and workers. Generally only top managers plan several years ahead, while operating managers plan ahead to meet short-term budgetary goals and workers are left entirely out of the planning process. An American executive believes that few if any skills are unique to his company. Consequently, managers, technicians, and workers can be brought into the company from the outside at any time and at any level, and they will fit easily into the organization with its impersonal rules of behavior and specialized tasks. Managers and workers appear to be motivated mainly by the prospect of immediate economic reward from the sale of their job skills to the highest bidder. Hence Americans move frequently from one company to another, holding only a conditional loyalty to their present companies. Their social life is only partly, if at all, centered on their fellow employees.

In a high-context culture, such as the Japanese, the behavior of managers and workers is guided by implicit rules that are internalized through a process of enculturation in the firm's values and ways of doing things. The mutual understanding of their own and others' roles in the firm by employees who are fully contexted in the firm's own culture replaces the explicit relations and performance goals of the American firm. That is to say, in a Japanese firm, rules, roles, and expectations are communicated more through context than through words. A Japanese executive believes that managers and workers must acquire skills that are unique to the firm and can be learned only on the job. Furthermore, they must be inculcated with the firm's business ideology. Hence it is extremely important to hire the right young people, people who are chosen as persons who will fit into the organization rather than as persons who possess specialized skills. A high-context firm seldom brings in outsiders except at the starting level. The basic organizational principle is that all employees have a collective responsibility to promote the company's long-run welfare. Decision making is widely shared, and even workers are encouraged to take an interest in the long-range goals of the firm. To obtain this long-term orientation, the firm offers job security to its managers and workers. Employees center their social lives on the firm, to which they owe a lifetime loyalty.

This brief review of business organizations in low- and high-context cultures is not intended to suggest that one organization pattern is superior to the other. Nor do we want to say that every American firm is low context while every Japanese firm is high context. Instead we have tried to make the point that the *typical* American (or Western) firm, reflecting its environing low-context culture, is organized along very different lines than the typical Japanese (or Sinic) firm, reflecting a high-context culture. One of the more interesting questions in management is the extent to which high-context organizations can perform effectively in the West.[9]

Nonverbal Communication

People in all cultures use nonverbal behavior as well as words to communicate meaning, although as observed above, people in high-context cultures rely on nonverbal behavior to a far higher degree than people in low-context cultures: words are usually accompanied by some overt or covert behavior that can amplify, weaken, or even reverse their meaning.[10] Overt behavior includes posture, dress, facial expression, and gesture. The meaning of such behavior varies from one culture to another. Overt behavior is also accompanied by covert nonverbal behavior, which Hall has called the "silent language," such as the language of time, space, and agreements. Because it is hidden, the silent language is often a mysterious source of misunderstanding in cross-cultural communication. We offer below some comments on the languages of time and space, leaving the language of agreements to the next section.

Gestures carry meanings but they may not carry the same meanings across cultures. Even simple gestures of the hand can provoke misunderstandings: to a Spaniard touching the lobe of the ear is an insult, but to a Greek showing open palms is an insult. Greeks, Turks, and Bulgarians signify "yes" with a sideways movement of the head that resembles the movement signifying "no" for other Europeans. Joining the index finger and the thumb to make a circle means OK in New York or Paris, "I will kill you" in Tunisia, and "money" in Tokyo. Anthropologists say that the English move as little as possible when speaking, keeping their hands steady and holding their heads high. Also, the English seldom kiss in public. Used to open spaces, Americans walk with a swaying motion, moving their shoulders and letting their arms swing freely. In contrast the French, accustomed to less space, walk with a straight back and without much movement of the hips.

Adapted from "Hidden Messages," *World Press Review*, July 1989, p. 39.

Language of Time. Time carries different meanings in different cultures. To Americans, time might be described as a river flowing into the future, along which one moves from one activity to another. To get to where we want to arrive, we need to allocate our activities to discrete segments of time (that is, we need to *schedule* time). For that reason, Americans value promptness, and because they are very future oriented, they strike many foreigners as extremely impatient people. Americans are also uncomfortable when several things are going on at the same time.

Other cultures may perceive time quite differently. For example, the Arabs dislike planning for the future (they may even consider it blasphemous, since only Allah knows the future), and they do not take schedules as serious commitments. Making an appointment with an Arab far in advance is risky, because he is apt to consider any time beyond the next week as somewhere in a vague future. Unlike the American, the Arab is quite happy when several things are going on at the same time. Latin Americans have an elastic perception of time: "important" people, relatives, and friends get more time even during business hours than do "unimportant" people. When an American businessman has, say, a 9:00 A.M. appointment with a Latin American official, he may be kept waiting a half hour or longer. Using his own self-reference criterion, the American finds such behavior insulting, particularly since he has probably come a long way to see the minister. What he does not understand is that the official intends no insult and still wants to see him. Clearly, international managers should know the local language of time before visiting a country. American managers, in particular, need to curb their impatience when local nationals appear unwilling to "get down to business."

Language of Space. The meaning of visual and auditory space is not the same across cultures. For instance, the American belief that space should be shared with others is not accepted by the Germans. In offices, Americans keep doors open, but Germans keep them closed. The German perceives open doors to be disorderly; the American perceives closed doors as unfriendly. Not surprising, German doors are much more solid than American doors.[11]

Another aspect of space is its role in neighboring patterns. Americans expect to get to know the people who live next door, but in Denmark and many other European countries, propinquity means nothing: personal relationships are based on family and social class. In Denmark, suburban houses are protected by walls that firmly demarcate property lines. While living in a Copenhagen suburb, I watched with some astonishment the erection of a board fence around a house that was only half constructed. Incidentally, I never got to know any of my "neighbors."

The French plan much of their space in a radial pattern, as with the famous Place de l'Etoile. The manager of a French office is commonly found in the center, with his or her subordinates placed around him or her.[12] Conversational and other social distances are also influenced by culture. For instance, conversational distance is much closer in Latin America than in the United States. An American businessman talking with a Latin American may unconsciously back up to maintain his customary conversational distance.

In Asian cultures, the language of space is radically different from that in American and other Western cultures. Japanese spatial patterns, for example, emphasize centers.[13] The Japanese name intersections, not the streets leading to them. To the Westerner, a Japanese room looks bare because the sides are bare, with everything in the center. (To the Japanese, a Western room may look bare because the center is empty, with everything along the sides!) In Japan, there is a protocol of seating arrangements for business associates in a restaurant, the more formal with individual tables (the host welcoming guests in the *center* of the room), the less formal with a center table.[14] More profoundly, the Japanese, unlike Westerners, are taught to give meaning to spaces, based on the *ma* or interval. The Japanese floral arrangement and the rock garden illustrate *ma*.

Arabs also treat space differently than Westerns do. When they first encounter the Arab culture, Americans are likely to feel overwhelmed by smells, noise, and crowding.[15] Arabs appear to have no concept of a "private zone" outside the body. They breathe on a person when they talk; they want to smell the other person. The American conversational distance strikes Arabs as cold and unfriendly. When an American sees two Arab men holding hands, he or she probably draws the wrong conclusion. An executive of an American construction company told me that his foreman in Saudi Arabia, a burly Texan, asked to be sent home because he could no longer endure the friendly embraces of his Arab workers! In sum, Arabs interact with each other on several levels much more intimately than Westerners.

Blunders in Face-to-Face Communication Across Cultures

Perceptual and encoding/decoding gaps create many blunders in face-to-face interactions between persons of different cultures. Here are a few examples.

1. While walking in the park with a visiting American businessman, a Latin American official pointed to a statue, saying, "There is the statue of the great liberator of mankind!" The American asked the name of this renowned patriot and, being told, said "I never heard of him."
2. Trying to break the ice in Germany with "Wie geht's?" is twice wrong: the expression is too informal and too personal for first encounters.
3. While using first names in business situations is regarded as an American vice in many countries, nowhere is it found more offensive than in France.
4. When pressed by a U.S. sales executive for a yes or no in the construction of a factory, a procurement official in Dubai responded, "After all, Rome wasn't built in a day." The American smartly quipped back, "That's because they didn't have an American foreman on the job." The Dubai official reacted with what anthropologists call the "glass curtain"— a glazed stare that said, "The conversation is over. Please leave."
5. In the Middle East it is risky for a guest to admire something, because his or her host may feel obliged to make a gift of it. A General Motors executive told his host at an all-male cocktail party that he intended to buy an Arab robe as a souvenir. The host promptly took off his robe and, standing in pale-yellow long johns, handed it to the bewildered executive.

6. A sturdy handshake is part of the American cultural reper-
   tory. Yet in the Middle East the visitor gets a flaccid, "dead
   fish" handshake that a male may associate with femininity
   or unfriendliness. To the Arab, the hearty grasp is a sign
   that the American has more brawn than brains.
7. Crossing one's legs in front of a person or pointing the soles
   of one's feet toward him or her is regarded as insulting in
   Thailand.

The first blunder shows a gross insensitivity to the culture of
one's host—ethnocentrism at its worse. The next three blunders
are mainly linguistic in nature: using an improper form of address
or trying out American humor on a foreign national (something
always dangerous to do, because humor is so bound to a particular culture, it is apt to be misunderstood by a foreigner). But the
last three blunders have little or nothing to do with words; they
are blunders in nonverbal behavior.

Negotiating Across Cultures

Cross-cultural negotiations are a fact of life for the international
manager, whether he or she is trying to get host government approval for a project, set up a local distribution system, acquire a
local company, establish a joint venture, or start any other endeavor abroad. Indeed, it is not too much to say that international
managers need to negotiate not only their own business affairs but
their business environment as well. The ability to negotiate with
foreigners in their own countries therefore is an indispensable skill
of the international manager—a skill, moreover, that is becoming
even more important than in the past.

All business negotiations involve *common* interests (something
to negotiate for) and *conflicting* interests (something to negotiate
about). Negotiation therefore requires a clear understanding on
both sides of their common and conflicting interests, coupled with
a willingness to compromise their differences. A good negotiator
finds out as much as he or she can about the other party, not only
strengths and weaknesses but also how that party views the negotiations. Through such empathy, the negotiator is better able to
anticipate the offers and counteroffers of the other side and

thereby to formulate a superior negotiating strategy. Gaining empathy is not always easy, even when negotiating with persons of one's own culture, but it is child's play compared to gaining empathy with foreigners. For to do so, negotiators must be aware of the other side's culture as well as their own; otherwise, no matter how hard they try, they will fail to put themselves "in the other fellow's shoes."[16]

International business negotiations break down through failures in cross-cultural communication even when both sides have much to gain from an agreement. Or an agreement is reached that turns out later to be only an apparent agreement, in which each side thought it understood the other side but did not. As should be evident by now, we are not speaking simply of failures in verbal communication but also—and more fundamentally—of failures by international managers to understand the local "language of agreements," the way in which agreements are reached and the very meaning of agreement in the host culture.

Language of Agreements

Americans have a formal, legalistic approach to agreements, which is symbolized by the written contract. Indeed, Americans view the signing of the contract as marking the successful conclusion of negotiations and deserving a ceremonial recognition. According to Hall, however, the Greeks see the contract as a way station in the negotiations process, which will continue until the agreement's implementation has come to an end.[17] The point is that different cultures reveal different conceptions of what an agreement is and exhibit different negotiating styles.[18] To elaborate this point, the next section offers some observations on negotiating with the Japanese.

Negotiating with the Japanese

Because Japanese businessmen prefer face-to-face contacts, a personal call on a prospective business associate (based on an introduction) is generally more effective than trying to initiate contact through a letter. Between Japanese firms, the first contacts are ordinarily made at the top-executive levels: business cards are exchanged, along with other formalities. The purpose of the meeting is to get acquainted, establish the broad interest of the calling party, and consider whether more substantive discussions are desirable. The traditional Japanese greeting is a bow, and the Japanese appreciate a slight bow by a foreigner, although they expect to use a handshake when dealing with foreign visitors. Japanese businessmen dress conservatively, and they seldom use first names in business relationships.

When an American or other Western company decides to go to Japan to negotiate a business agreement, it should prepare its representative or representatives with (1) a full explanation of what the company is willing to offer and what it wants to get and (2) a briefing on Japanese business etiquette and behavior and, if there is time, on Japanese culture in general, as well as on the economic and political situation in Japan. It should also give its negotiating team much more time in Japan to reach an agreement than it would take back home.

The Japanese go to extraordinary lengths to create an atmosphere of utmost cordiality for business transactions. The foreign visitors may be taken through several rounds of entertainment before negotiations start, and during negotiations green tea is likely to be served every hour or so, along with dinners in the evening.

While the American negotiator is inclined to press for explicit agreement on specific issues, the Japanese prefers to feel out the other party and become rather certain of the other side's position before putting forward a proposal that he or she believes both sides can agree on. To the American, the Japanese seems to have all the time in the world and to be somewhat reluctant to get down to business. Patience not only is a virtue in Japan (as in most other Asian countries); it can also be used as a negotiating ploy, particularly with the impatient Americans. Americans often reveal their bargaining position before they start to bargain, and they may make ill-considered concessions just to keep negotiations moving along. The American negotiator, therefore, is well advised to say as little as possible and steadily pursue his or her objectives in a relaxed, friendly manner.

A common source of confusion in negotiating with Japanese is the meaning of "yes." To a Japanese, "yes" may simply mean that he or she has understood, not that he or she agreed. The Japanese "yes" can be correctly interpreted only by someone who is contexted in the Japanese culture. If the Japanese "yes" is ambiguous, the Japanese "no" is rarely expressed, because the Japanese are reluctant to embarrass themselves or the other party.

Another problem is silence. Generally, Americans do not know how to respond to silence on the part of the Japanese for what is too long a time by American standards. They are apt to interpret a long silence on the other side (after they have made a statement or raised a question) as a rejection. Often Americans then give in on a point or say something unwise just to get the conversation going again. But what is happening on the other side is quite different. For one thing, the Japanese do not have the Western compulsion to talk, because they come from a listening culture. For another thing, the Japanese are unwilling to say *anything* until all members of the negotiating team (or possibly other company executives) agree or are willing to go along.

Because the Japanese dislike high-pressure tactics and prize sincerity, the American negotiator should present his or her proposal in stages in a modest way. This approach gives the Japanese plenty of opportunity to ask questions and to feel that both sides are working together to establish the facts.[19]

Negotiating with the Japanese is a lengthy exercise not only because of cultural gaps but also because the Japanese will not take a position until they have reached an internal agreement among a great many managers. But because of this consensus, the Japanese firm can move very quickly once an agreement is made. Since the Japanese value personal relationships, they prefer a broad agreement rather than a detailed contract, on the assumption that each party is willing to negotiate in good faith on any issues arising from the agreement's implementation. Like the Greeks, the Japanese do not view the signing of a contract as the end of negotiations. Japanese firms want long-term, exclusive business relations based on *kan*, a word that can be translated as "emotional attunement."

Developing Cultural Understanding

How can international managers develop cultural self-awareness and thereby transcend ethnocentric perceptions, beliefs, feelings, and behavior in communicating with foreign nationals? As earlier observed, cultural self-awareness ultimately depends on experiential learning that is gained by interacting with persons of other cultures. It can be described as a cumulative process of learning to understand the behavior of other peoples by learning to understand one's own cultural behavior. Cultural understanding for the manager (or any other person) starts, therefore, with a *sensitivity* to cultural differences and a willingness to learn more about the cultures of host nationals. Understanding a foreign culture, of course, is not the same as understanding one's own culture, for there is no way to match the experience of growing up in a culture.

International managers cannot undertake a thorough study of every culture in which they conduct business. If they tried to do so, they would have little time for their business affairs. But they can obtain insights into a new culture through a preparation before they visit. This is sure to enhance their learning experience after arrival.

Learning a Foreign Language

Probably the single best way to gain some sensitivity to cultural differences, short of actually living in a host country, is to learn its language. Unfortunately, American managers are generally reluctant to do so, a reluctance that is rationalized by the argument that they have a better use for their time and, anyway, the international business language is English: let the foreigners learn English! But this attitude misses the point. Apart from the ability to communicate with host nationals in their own tongue (which is ordinarily pleasing to them), knowledge of the host language is a "window" for perceiving the host culture and, therefore, for perceiving one's own.

Undoubtedly, it is best to learn a foreign language when one is young, for it is hard work, with much rote repetition of words and phrases that easily bores a mature person. Most important for international managers is the ability to *speak* a host language. Learning how to speak a foreign language is facilitated by a willingness to make mistakes and laugh at them, an openness to new experience, and persistence. The more cosmopolitan a person, the better he or she will do, which is one reason why learning one foreign language makes it easier to learn a second. For the manager assigned to a host country for two years or more, learning to speak the local language is important for both professional and social reasons. A manager who spends a lengthy time in a host country without learning the language is telling host nationals, "I'm not really interested in you or your country."

Approaching a New Culture

International managers need to know how to approach cultures new to them in order to accomplish their missions with a minimum of cultural misunderstanding and conflict.

Minimizing Culture Shock. When a manager first arrives in a new culture, he is likely to experience a sense of disorientation that is called *culture shock*. Culture shock is the traumatic experience of having to cope with a bewildering array of new cultural cues and situations that differ in many overt and covert ways from those in one's own culture. It can range from mild anxiety and discomfort to severe anxiety that renders a manager unable to carry on business.Not understanding the local language or nonverbal behavior, the manager has no cues on which to base his or her own behavior. In trying to communicate with host nationals, he or she experiences frustration, irritation, anger, helplessness, and the strains of heightened attention. In short, the manager lacks a cultural map that can help predict the behavior and expectations of others and thereby guide one's own behavior and expectations.

Culture shock is most notable in the case of expatriate managers who must live and work in a new culture for a prolonged period. Indeed, the most common explanation of expatriate failure is the inability to adapt to the host culture and society. But even managers who spend only a few days in a strange culture can experience culture shock, a persistent anxiety about the unknown, although they are unlikely to develop "separation anxiety," because of the shortness of their stay. Learning how to approach a new culture, then, is also learning how to minimize culture shock.

Learning from Cultural Situations. The quicker managers learn the verbal and nonverbal behavior of host nationals, the quicker they can overcome culture shock. How should one go about learning that behavior? The best approach is to focus on *cultural situations,* especially those that frequently occur in the course of conducting business affairs.

The rules governing behavior in a host culture can be discovered only in real-life situations. Situations are the building blocks of a culture: greetings and farewells, working, eating, negotiating, governing, fighting, making love, going to school, raising children, playing, and so on. The manager should start by learning the basic verbal language to handle the situations most relevant to his or her mission and by observing the nonverbal behavior associated with them. Host nationals will appreciate the manager's efforts to speak their language even when it is confined to stock phrases. More important, the manager is on the way to cultural understanding. The checklist below offers some guidelines for approaching new cultures.

Before visiting a new culture, managers can profit by asking themselves the following questions: (1) What do I know about the behavior and, particularly, the business customs of this culture? (2) What are my beliefs about and attitudes toward host nationals? Are they based on knowledge, or are they stereotypes? (3) How do these beliefs and attitudes relate to my own cultural assumptions? (4) What understanding and skills do I need to communicate successfully with host nationals? It is the intent of the first guideline to enable the manager to get answers to these questions that will support his or her mission in the host country.

Cultural preparation for a visit to a foreign country should be more intensive for a prolonged stay than for a short trip. But in both instances preparation should lessen cultural shock and improve the chances of communicating successfully with host nationals. Preparation includes language instruction (ranging from "immersion training" to instruction in stock words and phrases), knowledge of the social and cultural history of the host country (at the very least, the names of prominent statesmen, artists, and heroes), some acquaintance with business and social customs, and, if there is time, a study of the culture as a whole. Preparation should also include knowledge of the manager's own culture and how it relates to the host culture.

The remaining guidelines are pointers on the manager's behavior in the host country. They are specific implications of the earlier discussion of culture and cross-cultural communication. Cultural blunders are inevitable, but if the manager is perceived as a sympathetic person by host nationals, they are likely to attribute such blunders to simple ignorance, which can be forgiven in a foreigner. Conversely, blunders can cause serious problems when the manager's behavior is interpreted as uncaring of the host culture and its people.

Cultural differences surely complicate the lives of international managers. But they also enrich those lives with new experiences. And by building bridges of understanding across cultures, international managers form a "third culture" that makes its own contribution to a better world. In any event, the manager has no choice: he or she must learn to design, execute, and control international market entry strategies across cultural differences if his or her company is to survive in a harshly competitive global economy. As high-growth market opportunities increasingly shift from industrial to developing countries, the management of cultural differences will become ever more critical to success in international business. No company can afford ethnocentric managers. When all is said and done, it is the task of international managers to communicate with foreign markets, and markets are people.

Some Guidelines for Managers in Approaching New Cultures

1. Make cultural preparations before your first visit.
2. In your verbal and nonverbal behavior, communicate a genuine interest in and respect for the host culture and its people. Mix with host nationals.
3. Show empathy for the attitudes, values, and ways of thinking of host nationals. Be person oriented.
4. Act with reserve until you know the rules of behavior. Listen before you talk; avoid off-the-cuff responses.
5. Avoid judgments on cultural differences, particularly invidious comparisons with your own culture.
6. Be flexible, creative, and diplomatic in relations with host nationals. Avoid dogmatic behavior; learn to tolerate ambiguity.

7. Do not expect to accomplish everything at once. Accept yourself and your hosts. Be both patient and persistent.
8. Accept the challenge of cross-cultural experience. Don't give up.

Summary

1. Blunders in international business are commonly traceable to ethnocentric assumptions unconsciously held by managers, especially the belief that foreigners think and behave much like people at home even though they may speak another language.
2. Culture may be defined as the unique life-style of a given human society: a distinctive way of thinking, perceiving, feeling, believing, and behaving that is passed on from one generation to another.
3. Different cultures foster different personality types. They do so by postulating an ideal personality type ("the good person") and then rewarding behavior consistent with the ideal type while punishing behavior inconsistent with it.
4. Despite their profound differences, all cultures have many general features—the so-called cultural universals—in common. These features reflect the common biological nature of humans and their common needs to cope with physical and social environments.
5. Only when we come into contact with people of other cultures who have different perceptions and behavior traits do we become aware of cultural differences, and in that way of our own cultural uniqueness. In the absence of cultural self-awareness, we unconsciously assume that people in other cultures experience the world as we do (the self-reference criterion).
6. Communication between people belonging to different cultures is distorted by perceptual and encoding/decoding gaps that derive from the cultural distance between sender and receiver.
7. Our native language in which we encode or decode a message is not only a means of communication; it also profoundly structures our perception of the world. Hence the

most direct way for a sender to overcome both perceptual and encoding/decoding gaps is to learn the language of the receiver.

8. Distance is greatest between cultures that rely heavily on words for communication (low-context cultures) and cultures that rely heavily on nonverbal behavior for communication (high-context cultures). High-context messages can be understood only by someone who has been "programmed" with the necessary information (internal context) and an understanding of the setting (external context).

9. In communication, words are usually accompanied by some overt or covert behavior that can amplify, weaken, or even reverse their meaning. Covert nonverbal behavior has been called the "silent language": the language of time, space, agreements, things, and other perceptions.

10. Cross-cultural negotiations are a fact of life for international managers, whether they are trying to get host government approval for a project, set up a local distribution system, acquire a local company, establish a joint venture, or start any endeavor abroad. The ability to negotiate with host nationals therefore is an indispensable skill of the international manager.

11. International managers cannot undertake a thorough study of every culture in which they conduct business. But they can obtain insights into a new culture through a preparation before the visit that will enhance their learning experience after arrival.

12. Probably the single best way to gain some sensitivity to cultural differences, short of actually living in a host country, is to learn its language.

13. Learning how to approach a new culture is also learning how to minimize culture shock.

Designing Entry Strategies for Global Competitive Advantage in Multinational Enterprise Systems

T his chapter looks at the design of entry strategies in a multinational enterprise that has reached stage 4 as described in Table 3 on page 40. Such an enterprise has penetrated scores of foreign markets with several products (or businesses) and with multiple entry modes. Managers therefore must make entry decisions in the context of an ongoing multinational enterprise system. We start by describing such a system and its organization and how one may adapt the entry planning model depicted in Chapter 2 to take advantage of the special strengths of a multinational system. We then go on to look at how managers in multinational companies can build international competitive advantages. We close with some observations on the international manager of the future.

The Multinational Enterprise System

The multinational enterprise is a company that (1) enters markets throughout the world by establishing its own sales and production subsidiaries in several countries and by using other entry modes, (2) exercises control over its subsidiaries, and (3) strives to design and execute corporate strategies in marketing, production, finance, and other functions from an international perspective that transcends national and regional boundaries. A key feature of the multinational enterprise system (distinguishing it from stage 1 and stage 2 companies as defined in Table 3) is its involvement in international production through investment entry modes.

The multinational enterprise, its country subsidiaries, and the foreign entities with which it has long-term contractual arrangements together make up the *multinational enterprise system*. This system is depicted in Figure 22. The P circle represents the multinational enterprise, the headquarters company that owns, in whole or in part, the several foreign-country subsidiaries represented by the S circles. In some countries, the global enterprise has only agent/distributor arrangements (represented by the A/D_j circle), and in other countries, only licensing or other contractual arrangements (represented by the L/C_i circle). These several elements of the global enterprise system are located in different countries, as indicated by the dashed lines in Figure 22.

As the parent company, the multinational enterprise is the control center for the entire system, setting the strategy of the system and its individual elements and controlling global and country op-

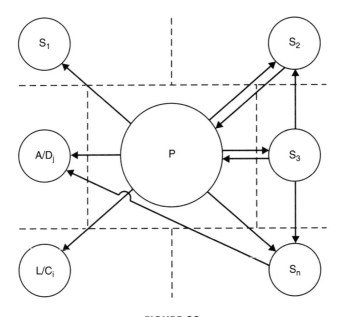

FIGURE 22
The Multinational Enterprise Systems

erations in conformance with those strategies. The legal basis for
the exercise of control over subsidiaries is the parent company's
ownership claims on them; the legal basis of control over agents,
distributors, licensees, and other independent parties is the parent
company's contractual claims on them. In general, the parent
company can exercise the most control over fully owned subsidiaries, the least control over independent contractual parties
and control somewhere between these two extremes over partly
owned subsidiaries (joint ventures). How the multinational company exercises its legal control over subordinate elements of the
system depends on its management philosophy, corporate strategy, and organization.

In designing foreign market entry strategies for a multinational
system, managers need answers to some basic questions:

- Where in the world are the actual and potential markets for
  our final products?
- Where in the world should we locate production facilities to
  supply our final products to those markets? More generally,
  where in the world should we *source* our final products for
  country markets?
- Where in the world should we acquire inputs for production
  of our final products, such as raw materials, parts, components, and capital equipment?
- What should be our marketing strategies in individual country markets? Should we design common strategies across
  country markets?
- How should we control operations at the country, regional,
  and global levels?

Decisions on these questions create a worldwide pattern of
transfers of management, technology, product, and capital, both
within the multinational enterprise system and between that system and its transactional environment (comprising customers,
suppliers, governments, labor unions, and other outside parties).
In-system transfers are indicated in Figure 22 by solid lines con-
necting the system members.

Management and technology transfers from the parent company to subordinate system members are essential features of the
multinational enterprise system. The most notable management

transfers are *entrepreneurial* decisions that initiate new ventures, *strategy* decisions, and *control* decisions. Without central planning and control, the multinational enterprise system disintegrates into something else; by its very nature, it is hierarchical. This statement does not gainsay that central planning and control are compatible with high levels of decentralized operations management at country and regional levels. Moreover, although the parent company must assume ultimate responsibility, strategy decisions may be "shared" in varying degrees with regional and country management. Indeed, a continuing issue for parent companies is how to reconcile the need for central direction and control with the need for operational flexibility.

The other indispensable transfer from the parent company to its subsidiaries and other system elements is the transfer of *technology*, broadly defined as all knowledge that pertains to the production and marketing of products. Some multinational companies are more technology intensive than others, but all must possess proprietary knowledge that allows them to compete successfully in foreign markets. To be effective, this knowledge must be transferred from the parent company to the rest of the system.

Other kinds of transfer from the parent company are contingent on circumstances: they may not occur at all, occur only occasionally, or occur only for some system members.[1] Most likely, the parent company is exporting some intermediate or finished products to some country subsidiaries, as well as to foreign agents and distributors. But product transfers from the parent company are only a probable, not indispensable, feature of the multinational enterprise system. And the same is true of capital transfers. Most likely, some capital is transferred from the parent company to its subsidiaries (particularly for start-up operations), but capital may also be sourced in a subsidiary's country or in a third country. To illustrate, the parent company in Figure 22 transfers management and technology to all system members, but it transfers products only to (say) S_1, S_3, and A/D_j, and it transfers capital only to (say) Si_1, which is a new subsidiary.

The parent company is a receiver as well as originator of transfers. Apart from financial transfers from subsidiaries and other system members, it may also receive products and technology. For instance, in Figure 22, S_2 sends finished products to P, and S_3 sends technology on intermediate products to P. But a more striking feature of the multinational enterprise system is the transfer of products and technology among the subsidiaries and other subordinate system members. When managers at the parent company design entry strategies from a global perspective, they act to build up intersubsidiary transfers at regional and global levels to take advantage of similarities among country markets, economies of scale, and international specialization. Returning to Figure 22, S_3 ships intermediate products to S_2 and S_n, and S_n ships final product to A/D_j.

Strategic Focus: Multidomestic and Global Enterprise Systems

There are two broad variants of the multinational enterprise (MNE) system, as defined by the international strategic focus of its managers. International strategic focus is the governing perception held by an MNE's managers of the geographical boundaries of the markets in which the enterprise competes in the present and anticipated future.

When managers perceive their company as competing in separate national markets, then they create a *multidomestic* system that enables their businesses to adapt to each country market. They view country subsidiaries as stand-alone operations with only modest product or other international transfers. In contrast, when managers perceive the boundaries of their company's markets and competition as coextensive with the world, then they design a *global* system. They view country subsidiaries as closely integrated by flows of products, technology, information, and other transfers.[2]

Driving Forces Favoring Global Strategies

Global strategies have no inherent superiority over multidomestic strategies. The superiority of a strategy is contingent, depending on its net advantages in specific circumstances. When environmental, market, and competitive forces are creating global markets in a particular industry, then an enterprise competing in that industry is inviting trouble if it sticks to a multidomestic strategic

Gillette no longer views itself as a multidomestic company tailoring products to different local markets throughout the world. Instead it believes that its products "travel like good Bordeaux wine" from one country to another, and hence it markets the same products to all countries and uses the same advertising message. The only concession that Gillette makes to local markets is the timing of product entry. Older,cheaper products are first sold to developing markets, such as Eastern Europe and China, before entry of newer replacement products.

This shift to a global (standardized) marketing strategy owes much to the outstanding success of the new Sensor razor launched in 1990. The Sensor was Gillette's major effort to stop the shift toward disposable razors, which threatened to turn razors into nondifferentiated commodities with low profit margins. The company faced two launching options: (1) launch in selected markets, gain experience, and gradually enter additional markets; or (2) launch throughout the United States and Europe at the same time with massive promotion. Gillette chose the second, high-risk entry strategy. Moreover, it used the same television commercials in the United States and Europe (apart from language). Indeed, Gillette went much further toward standardizing its marketing strategy by merging its U.S. and European marketing divisions into a North Atlantic group, which was given full authority over all aspects of Sensor. This group priced the Sensor at $3.75, making it less expensive than several other nondisposable razors but high enough to keep a prestige image. The blades, selling for 75 cents each, had a gross margin of nearly 90 percent. Gillette's most optimistic projections were sales of 18 million razors and 200 million blades in the first year; actual sales were 27 million and 350 million, respectively, as Sensor took an astounding 42 percent of the combined U.S. and European markets for nondisposable razors.

Sensor came out of Gillette's strong R & D program. The company's laboratories generate a continuing stream of new products: replacement products are on the way even as new products are being launched. But even more research staff is working to design new production equipment to cut manufacturing costs at least 4 percent a year. The production cost of Sensor has fallen a third since its introduction four years ago.

Adapted from "Gillette, Blade-Runner," *Economist,* April 10, 1993, p. 68; and "The Best a Plan Can Get," *Economist,* August 15, 1992. pp. 59–60.

focus. The opposite is also true: an MNE's global strategy in a particular business will come to grief if, in fact, global markets do not exist in that business. International managers cannot duck the responsibility of judging the strategic direction of their industries and their competitors. To illustrate this point, we identify several forces favoring the globalization of an industry: (1) economies of scale in production, marketing, or other functions can be achieved only at an international level; (2) costs can be reduced by locating value-added activities in different countries; (3) cross-national buyer preferences are similar; (4) transfer costs are low for products, technology, human skills, and capital; (5) communication costs are low; (6) political risks are low; and (7) major competitors are initiating global strategies.

The appearance of globalizing forces in a particular industry should alert managers to the need to adopt a global strategy if they are to remain competitive. The persistence or appearance of opposing forces (such as dissimilar buyer preferences, high transfer costs, or high political risks), should point managers toward a multidomestic strategy. But it is seldom easy for managers to discern the international direction of their industries. Often the forces at work are conflicting—some pushing for global strategies, others pushing for multidomestic strategies. Commonly, managers try to follow a mix of both strategic orientations: some of an MNE's businesses may be run more globally (or less multidomestically) than others, some functions (such as R & D, production, and marketing) may be run more globally than others and so on. But the emergence of a global economy, as described in Chapter 1, suggests that managers are more likely to err by failing to globalize rather than the opposite. (Nonetheless, the case of Parker Pen, discussed later in this chapter, shows that the opposite mistake does happen.) "Think globally, act locally" is a slogan that apparently reconciles the conflicting forces, but it is not easy to put into practice. We take up later the question of how MNEs can develop and sustain an international competitive advantage.

International Production of the World's Twenty-Five Largest Industrial Companies

To introduce actual examples of multinational enterprise systems, Table 10 shows the international production of the world's

Toyota (Japan) and Honda (Japan) are establishing the auto industry's first global manufacturing system. The fundamental conception is to try out the design and production of a car in one country and then turn out thousands of "world cars" each year that can be made in one place and marketed around the world. Such a system could cut development costs, maximize the use of assembly plants, and achieve assembly-line efficiencies. The system could be fine-tuned on a quarterly basis according to economic conditions in different markets. One Honda manager says, "Japan can supply North America and Europe, North America can supply Japan and Europe, and Europe can supply Japan and the United States." So far the first two are already happening. In 1992 Toyota's U.S. plant in Kentucky produced 240,000 Camrys, including 3,700 right-hand-drive station wagons shipped to Japan. These cars are promoted in Japan as American, with a video for customers showing the car (named the Scepter) rolling through Kentucky's horse country. The Kentucky plant also shipped 9,000 Camry sedans to Taiwan in the same year. Japan is already the biggest export market for Honda's plant in Ohio.

This global strategy stands in contrast to the traditional multidomestic strategy of U.S. auto companies, who erected foreign plants to supply local or regional markets. But this is now changing: U.S. auto manufacturers are now trying to integrate global design, manufacturing, and marketing so as to satisfy local markets better and, at the same time, exploit more effectively their resources and variations in exchange rates. Ford has developed a midsize "world car," called the Mondeo, for European and U.S. markets. (So far only the Volkswagen Beetle and perhaps the Toyota Corolla have come close to being world cars.) Three different Ford engineering centers worked on the Mondeo: Detroit designed the V-6 engine, automatic transmission system, and the heating/air-conditioning units; Dunton (England) did the interior, steering, suspension, electronics, and 4-cylinder engine; and Cologne (Germany) carried out the basic structural engineering. To coordinate the work of these centers, Ford had to develop worldwide engineering standards. Although the program cost $6 billion, Ford's world car project has achieved economies of scale in production and better prices from suppliers who could be promised a sale of 700,000 autos annually in the world market.

Adapted from "Toyota and Honda Create Global Production System," *New York Times*, March 26, 1993, p. 1; and "Ford's $6 Billion Baby," *Fortune*, June 28, 1993, pp. 76–81.

TABLE 10

International Production of the World's 25 Largest Industrial Companies, Ranked by Worldwide Sales at the End of 1990

(billions of dollars)

Rank	Company	Home	Sector	Total Worldwide Sales[a] (A)	Sales of Foreign Subsidiaries[b] (B)	B/A (Percent)
1	General Motors	USA	Motor vehicles	120.3	37.3	31
2	Royal Dutch Shell	UK/NETH	Oil	114.3	56.0[c]	49
3	Exxon	USA	Oil	105.2	90.5	86
4	Ford Motor	USA	Motor vehicles	98.5	47.3	48
5	IBM	USA	Computers	68.7	41.9	61
6	Toyota Motor	JPN	Motor vehicles	62.6	26.3	42
7	General Electric	USA	Diversified	59.3	8.3	14
8	British Petroleum	UK	Oil	59.0	46.6	79
9	Mobil	USA	Oil	57.5	44.3	77
10	Daimler-Benz	FRG	Motor vehicles	53.6	32.7[d]	21
11	Philip Morris	USA	Food, tobacco	50.7	15.2	30
12	Hitachi	JPN	Electronics	50.0	10.5[d]	21
13	Volkswagen	FRG	Motor vehicles	42.3	27.5[d]	65
14	ENI	ITA	Chemicals	41.6	7.9	19

15	Matsushita Electric	JPN	Electronics	41.5	16.6	40
16	Texaco	USA	Oil	40.9	18.0	44
17	E.I. Dupont	USA	Chemicals	40.5	17.4	43
18	Unilever	UK/NETH	Food	39.8	16.7[c]	42
19	Chevron	USA	Oil	39.2	9.8	25
20	Siemens	FRG	Electrical	37.8	15.1[b]	40
21	Nestle	SWI	Food, drink	33.7	33.0	98
22	Elf Aquitaine	FRA	Oil	32.1	12.1	38
23	Philips	NETH	Electronics	30.8	28.6[b]	93
24	Amoco	USA	Oil	28.3	8.5	30
25	Hoechst	FRG	Chemicals	28.2	14.1[b]	50

[a]Consolidated sales for the enterprise and its subsidiaries.
[b]Consolidated sales of subsidiaries outside the home country.
[c]Outside Europe.
[d]Includes exports from home country.
Key: FRA—France, FRG—Federal Republic of Germany, ITA—Italy, JPN—Japan, NETH—Netherlands, SWI—Switzerland, UK—United Kingdom, and USA—United States.
Source: Derived from data compiled by Center on Transnational Corporations, United Nations, New York.

Even when a company has little choice, the shift from a multidomestic to a global strategy can be traumatic. The story of Black & Decker is instructive. Before the 1980s, B & D followed a multidomestic strategy: its British subsidiary made tools for Britons, its Italian subsidiary made tools for Italians, and so on. This strategy worked well for B & D until Japanese competitors (especially Makita) adopted global strategies. Makita made a good professional drill for sale at a low price everywhere in the world. Makita began taking away sales from B & D, and by the early 1980s it nearly matched B & D's 20 percent market share of professional tools worldwide. B & D answered this attack with a crash program to cut costs, enabling the company to hold on to its U.S. market share. But this reactive tactic was not sufficient to meet the new global competition.

Anticipating the entry of Makita into the consumer tool market, B & D replaced its multidomestic strategy with a global strategy. When Laurence Farley became its president in 1982, B & D operated twenty-five plants in thirteen countries located on six continents. The company was organized into a U.S. headquarters group and three regional operating groups, each with its own staff. Below these operating groups, individual subsidiaries functioned autonomously in more than fifty countries. Before Farley country managers were in full charge, because headquarters assumed that those managers knew the local market better than anyone else. That is why Dustbuster, B & D's cordless vacuum cleaner, was not launched in Australia until four years after its highly successful launch in the United States. It is also why B & D's eight design centers (since reduced to two) generated more than 260 different motor sizes, even though the company needed fewer than 10. European managers refused to market B & D's housewares, arguing that the products were not suited to European tastes. Farley did not agree: he fired 25 European managers and closed the Brussels regional headquarters.

Adapted from "Black & Decker's Gamble on 'Globalization,' " *Fortune,* May 14, 1984, pp. 40–48; and "Black and Decker, New Selling Tool: The Acura Concept," *Fortune,* February 24, 1992, pp. 88–89.

twenty-five largest industrial companies. This list could easily be extended to cover several hundred MNEs.

Organizing the Multinational Enterprise

How should a multinational enterprise organize to best exploit market opportunities throughout the world? How should it group its diverse activities? How should it coordinate them? What should be the authority and responsibility of managers at corporate, regional, and country levels? What should be the reporting and control relationships between these three levels? In sum, how should a multinational enterprise manage its worldwide operations?

All multinational enterprises must resolve these questions, but they may resolve them in several different ways. To be effective, an international organization must bring to managers three fundamental competencies at the times and places they are needed for decision making: *functional* (finance, marketing, production, and others), *product* (including allied technology), and *geographical*. The most basic question in organization design therefore is whether line operations should be subdivided according to major functions, major product lines, major geographical areas, or some mix of them.

Evolution of Organization Structure

As an enterprise becomes more international, its organization structure also evolves in response to shifts in international strategies. Table 11 indicates the most common organization structures at different stages of the evolutionary scheme first introduced in Table 3 in Chapter 2.

In stage 1, a company's foreign business is marginal and probably intermittent. Since it has no international strategy, it has no need to redesign its organization. At most, a stage 1 company may set up a built-in export department, consisting of a manager and a few assistants, at a level in the corporate structure below domestic sales.

In stage 2, a company adopts a strategy of exploiting foreign markets through direct exports. This new strategy creates a need for the full-function export department at the same level as the domestic sales department or even an export division headed by a corporate vice president.

A company moves into stage 3 when it enters one or more foreign markets through investment in local production. This shift in international strategy marks a critical step in the evolution of a multinational enterprise. For the first time, the company commits substantial financial, management, and technical resources to a foreign venture. To a far greater extent than ever before, investment entry brings top corporate management into decisions about international business. As the company adds to the number of its country subsidiaries while also serving country markets with exports and contractual arrangements, the need to manage *all* its international operations under common direction is signaled by failures to coordinate export, licensing, investments, and other foreign activities. Most U.S. companies respond to this need by creating an international division headed by a director of international operations, who is also a corporate vice president, holding line authority over all international operations.

When a company enters stage 4, the international division may account for one-third or more of total corporate sales and profits. The company now fully deserves designation as a multinational

TABLE 11

Common Responses in Organization Structure in the Evolution of the Multinational Enterprise

Stage	International Strategy	Organization Response
1	None	None, or built-in export department
2	Enter foreign markets with direct exports	Full-function export department or division
3	Enter some foreign markets with investment in local production; enter other markets with noninvestment modes	International division
4	Serve markets throughout the world from multiple country sources with multidomestic or global strategic focus	Enterprise-wide structures based on area or product

enterprise with production and marketing subsidiaries in several countries. The importance of international business to the company commonly leads to the creation of an area-based or product-based structure that eliminates any corporate distinction between domestic and international business. Managers with a multi-domestic strategic focus favor area-based structures; managers with a global strategic focus favor product-based structures.

The evolutionary stages described in Table 3 are simplistic. They should be regarded as signposts of an evolutionary process taking place over an indefinite amount of time. Nonetheless, the organizational changes that occur as a company evolves into a multinational enterprise demonstrate the proposition that "structure follows strategy." Shifts in international business strategy demand changes in organization structure to manage that strategy. But organization changes do not come easily. Substantive differences among managers about the form of reorganization, as well as personalities, rivalries, politics, fears, and sheer inertia, act to delay structural responses until it becomes impossible to ignore critical failures of the existing organization. Even then, reorganization may occur piecemeal over a long period of time. To say that a company should have an organization structure that promotes and sustains its international strategy is true. But at any given time, a company's organization most probably lags behind its strategy and is in transition to a new structure. We now turn to a brief description of the principal organizational alternatives for the multinational enterprise.

International Division

Most multiproduct U.S. companies are already organized by domestic product divisions when they make their first overseas investments in foreign production. The most common organizational response to this new strategy, therefore, is the creation of an international division at the same corporate level as the domestic product divisions.[3] This form of organization is depicted in Figure 23

The formation of an international division represents a decision to place corporate business into two separate categories based on geography. This organization appeals strongly to a stage 3 company, in which few if any executives have international experience. Since the international vice president reports directly to the president, only those two top executives need to be directly involved in foreign operations. On the positive side, the international division makes possible a single, coordinated management of international business across products and countries. It develops the specialized skills and experience needed to plan, execute, and control international programs. Established as a profit center, the international division encourages a concentrated drive to expand a company's international business.

The weaknesses of the international division stem mostly from its separation from the domestic product divisions and from corporate staff. Lacking its own product/technology skills, the international division may not be able to support fully its foreign subsidiaries. Although the international division can develop its own functional staffs, they are unlikely to match the resources of corporate functional staffs, and they also represent some duplication of effort. In sum, its isolation from the rest of the corporation may render an international division unable to carry out the strategy of a stage 4 enterprise. But this is not necessarily the case, because the international division can be a very flexible organization structure. Over time, dotted-line and other arrangements can build effective

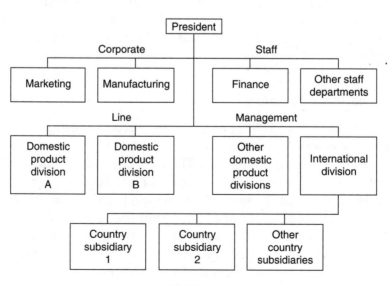

FIGURE 23

Structure of an International Division

communication channels between an international division and the domestic divisions, and corporate staff can assume international responsibilities in direct support of the international division. Again, a top-level management committee with members drawn from the domestic and international divisions can be established to coordinate operations across the entire enterprise. In short, an international division may allow a company to achieve a substantial degree of integration between its domestic and international business. Some companies in stage 4, however, may abandon the international division in favor of an organization that transfers international responsibility to all operating divisions, that is to say, companywide structure based on product or geography.

Companywide Structure Based on Product

Companies that have several product lines with distinctive technologies and end uses, such as chemical- and electrical-product companies, find a structure based on product to be more beneficial than one based on geography. This structure is shown in Figure 24.

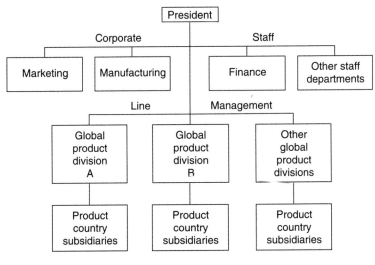

FIGURE 24

Companywide Structure Based on Product

With the product-based structure, the vice presidents of the respective product divisions become responsible for the production and marketing of their products throughout the world. These operating divisions are supported by corporate staff departments that now have a global responsibility for their functions. Hence the product-based structure enables an enterprise to undertake global strategies for diverse product lines. Country subsidiaries report directly to a corporate product division, from which they receive product and technical information and skills. In brief, this structure encourages a focus on product strategies that cover the world.

This emphasis on product means a de-emphasis of geography. Consequently, division managers may ignore country differences that limit the effectiveness of standardized global strategies. Efforts by product divisions to develop their own area specialists are apt to be uneven and duplicative for the corporation as a whole. Also, a global enterprise may end up with several subsidiaries in the same foreign country reporting to different product divisions, with no one at headquarters responsible for the overall corporate presence in that country. In sum, the product-based structure is well suited to carry out global strategies, but ill suited to carry out multidomestic strategies.

Companywide Structure Based on Area

Companies with product lines that have similar technologies and common end-use markets, such as beverage, food, automotive, and pharmaceuticals companies, are attracted to the area-based global structure depicted in Figure 25.

With this organization, the division vice presidents are responsible for operations across all product lines in their respective areas. Emphasis on geographical areas makes this structure well suited to carrying out multidomestic strategies that must be sensitive to country differences, encouraging adaptive foreign marketing programs. For that reason, consumer-products companies favor an area-based global structure. A major drawback of this structure is its de-emphasis of product/technology competencies necessary to support area manufacturing and marketing operations. Since each area division develops its own product specialists, some duplication of staff across divisions is a likely outcome. This structure also fosters area autonomy, posing obstacles to the creation of truly global strategies.

Mixed Structures

Mixed organization structures are common in multinational enterprises. Frequently, they are the adventitious consequence of piecemeal adaptions to new international strategies. In particular, an international division may be slowly dismantled as certain product divisions take on global responsibilities while others remain domestic, or certain areas are transferred to area divisions while other areas are not. But mixed structures may also represent efforts to obtain the advantages of pure forms of organization while limiting their disadvantages. For example, an international division may be retained to provide area expertise to global product divisions in a staff relationship. Or some product lines may be managed through global product divisions while other product lines are administered through area divisions.

We have observed that each of the three organization structures described suffers from weaknesses, because the choice of one com-

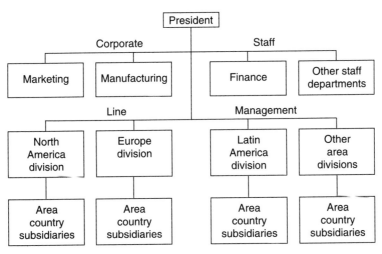

FIGURE 25

Companywide Structure Based on Area

Competition in the telecommunications industry is fast becoming global, as deregulation and privatization break down walls that have heretofore protected national markets. At the same time corporate customers are going global, demanding top-quality service from a single supplier wherever they operate. The volume of corporate voice, data, and teleconferencing traffic among countries is growing at an annual rate of 15 to 20 percent. By the end of the 1990s, annual international revenues are expected to reach $14 billion. No communications company can afford to ignore such a dynamic market. If a national company fails to provide international communication services demanded by corporations, then foreign companies will do so and also move to provide local corporate services. Although local phone services to residential customers and small firms remain a monopoly in most countries, U.S. carriers are starting to penetrate national markets with cellular systems and private data transmission services. In the United States, foreign telecommunications companies are investing in long-distance and data transmission services that do not require licenses from the Federal Communications Commission.

Leading companies—such as American Telephone and Telegraph (U.S.), Cable and Wireless (U.K.), and Nippon Telegraph and Telephone (Japan)—want to manage their customers' complete global communications systems. To do so, they must provide communication links covering the world, giving each customer a detailed accounting of services in each country's currency. The big carriers are investing heavily in new equipment (such as digital switches and fiber-optic lines), and they are planning to lay transoceanic optical cables. Smaller national phone companies do not have the resources to compete in the new global market on their own; this situation is forcing consolidation of the telecommunications industry. For instance, Telefonica de Espana has acquired telephone properties in Argentina and Chile, while Southwestern Bell (U.S.) has acquired a major ownership interest in Telefono de Mexico. Some observers believe that by the late 1990s, just four or five giant companies will dominate global telecommunications. To build global systems, telephone companies will need either to create their own networks in foreign countries or use the existing networks of national companies. The former strategy would be very expensive and time-consuming; hence acquisitions and alliances appear to be the preferred entry strategies.

Adapted from "Spanning the Globe," *Wall Street Journal*, October 4, 1991, p. R1; and "Called Together," *Economist*, October 19, 1991, p. 90.

petency as the basis of line operations means that other competencies must either be provided at lower levels in line operations (with some duplication across divisions) or be concentrated in corporate staff departments. The most ambitious structure to overcome this problem is the *matrix* organization, which gives equal importance to functional, product, and geographical competencies. But to do so, it abandons the principle of unity of command: single lines of authority and accountability in a hierarchical system. Thus, in a matrix organization, country managers are accountable to functional, product, and area managers at corporate headquarters. For the matrix structure to work, managers must be willing to participate in much committee and team management. Decision making becomes a slow process, but presumably decisions, once made, are quickly implemented, because functional, product, and area managers are involved from the start. Only a handful of global enterprises have adopted a matrix structure for the entire corporation, but many more have tried it for certain product lines or geographical areas. One thing is certain: global enterprises will continue to respond to strategy shifts in a changing world with new forms of organization. As we shall observe later, the proliferation of international strategic alliances and the fast growth of international subcontracting are raising new questions about the boundaries of multinational enterprise systems and their restructuring to accommodate other multinational enterprise systems in cooperative arrangements.

Planning Entry Strategies in a Multinational Enterprise System

The elements of a foreign market entry strategy, as depicted in Figure 2 in Chapter 2, are the same for a multinational enterprise as for other international companies. The constituent entry plan always focuses on a single product (or product line) and a single foreign target market. What is different in the multinational enterprise is the *context* or internal system environment of worldwide operations in which managers make entry decisions. In such a system, managers can use experience acquired in one country for entry decisions in a second country, and they can improve the cost-effectiveness of entry decisions by coordinating them across countries.

Multinational Entry Planning Model

A multinational enterprise system influences entry decisions through (1) a multinational corporate philosophy and strategy, (2) information transfers, (3) resources, and (4) decision-making support.

In making entry decisions, managers are guided by an overall corporate philosophy and strategy, which expresses goals for the entire enterprise system. Constituent entry strategies must support those goals if they are to optimize profit contributions to the system; otherwise, entry strategies that are cost-effective in isolation may nonetheless be suboptimum for overall operations. In sum, planners need to fit new entry strategies into existing operations.[4]

Managers planning entry strategies in stage 4 companies obtain *information transfers* that originate in existing country operations.[5] Subsidiaries can provide corporate managers with information on host countries and local markets that may be difficult, costly, or impossible to obtain from other sources. Apart from providing information useful in selecting new target markets, subsidiaries (and other foreign operations) originate information pertinent to the choice of candidate products and entry modes. Again, existing country marketing programs offer valuable models in designing programs for new entry strategies. For instance, advertising campaigns that have proved successful in one or more countries should be considered by managers planning new entry strategies for the same product. In a multinational enterprise system, the parent company functions as the clearinghouse for system-wide information flows. Thus the immediate source of information originating in foreign operations is likely to be corporate staff departments. Those departments also originate information (and information assessments) that can be tapped by managers making entry decisions.

The availability of *system resources* exerts a powerful influence on entry decisions. We are speaking here not of financial resources but rather of the capabilities of multinational research, production, logistics, and marketing operations headed by experienced managers. The candidate product itself may originate in a subsidiary in a foreign country rather than in the parent company. Even when the global enterprise has no existing operations in a new target country, the availability of multiple-country production bases can make export entry or a mixed export/investment entry more profitable than otherwise. In countries where the global enterprise already has operations, their use can drastically enhance the cost-effectiveness of a new entry strategy.

Corporate managers can also obtain *decision-making support* from their worldwide system environment. Corporate staff and country managers are sources of advice as well as information. As we shall observe shortly, country managers also share in entry decisions within an interactive planning process. This support generates functional, product, and geographical inputs for entry decisions to a far higher degree than would be possible if corporate line executives acted on their own.

Figure 26 depicts entry strategy planning in a global enterprise system. Decisions on each element of the constituent entry strategy are influenced by the strategy, information transfers, resources, and decision-making support of the system. In designing entry strategies, managers have a twofold task of planning constituent strategies that will be effective in their target markets and will also make an optimum profit contribution to the worldwide system. This latter task encourages efforts to standardize entry strategies across country markets that form a group of similar markets, as shown in Figure 26. Entry strategy elements that cannot be standardized in a cost-effective way must be adapted to in-

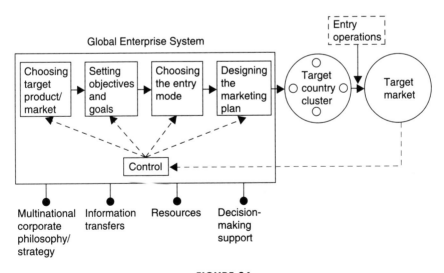

FIGURE 26

Planning Entry Strategy in a Multinational Enterprise System

dividual target country markets. We shall have more to say about grouping later on.

A multinational enterprise system can increase the profit contributions of constituent entry strategies by lowering incremental costs and raising incremental revenues. Information transfers make for better decisions; system resources can sharply cut incremental production and marketing costs; decision-making support brings functional, product, and country expertise to decisions; and multinational corporate strategy guides managers toward a full use of ongoing foreign operations in designing new entry strategies. But these benefits are not always obtained by managers. Blockages in system communication channels may impede information transfers and limit the availability of resources. Organization structures that emphasize product skills to the detriment of area skills, or vice versa, can weaken decision-making support. Overcentralization of decision making at the corporate level can ignore the knowledge and experience of subsidiary managers. In sum, the benefits of a multinational system for new entry strategies are dependent on an information network together with an organization structure that facilitates coordination across functions, products, and countries.

Benefits may also be constrained by a broad diversification of products with different technologies and end uses, although functional and geographical skills can serve all product groups in some measure. Products that must be closely adapted to individual country markets also limit the benefits of coordination across such markets. Another limitation deserves mention: exclusive reliance on information originating in existing foreign operations can cause corporate managers to ignore opportunities in new countries or new products, because country managers tend to scan only the environment in their own countries for existing product lines.

Centralizing and Decentralizing Entry Decisions

Entry strategy planning in a multinational system should be an interactive process involving managers at corporate, regional, and country levels. Interactive planning is vital to the design of effective entry strategies that take full advantage of existing worldwide operations. Highly centralized, top-down entry planning ignores the intimate knowledge of and experience in host countries and local markets possessed by country managers. Conversely, highly decentralized, bottom-up entry planning by autonomous country managers ignores the functional and product skills possessed by corporate managers and also fails to integrate entry strategies across countries and regions.

The argument for interactive entry planning or *shared decision making* in a multinational enterprise system does not necessarily imply that *all* entry decisions should be shared between corporate and subsidiary managers or shared in the same degree. Headquarters may reserve certain entry decisions to itself while delegating other entry decisions to country subsidiaries. But the great majority of entry decisions falls between these two extremes; they are made with the active participation of corporate, regional, and subsidiary managers.

Shared decision making takes many forms: the subsidiary recommends or proposes while headquarters approves or rejects; headquarters proposes while the subsidiary accepts or rejects; headquarters consults with the subsidiary and then decides; and so on.[6] In sum, corporate managers may recommend, propose, consult, review, approve, or reject, while country managers may recommend, propose, consult, accept, or reject. At times, shared decision-making turns into negotiations between corporate and country managers, with give-and-take by both sides. Even with shared decision making, all entry decisions are ultimately subject to corporate approval, because all planned expenditures by subsidiaries are subject to corporate review and approval in the annual budgeting process.

What factors determine whether a specific entry decision should be made by corporate managers, by country managers, or jointly by both? The main consideration is the potential contribution of the local skills and knowledge of country managers to that decision. If that contribution is modest or unnecessary, then corporate managers should make entry decisions on their own; on the other hand, if it is significant, then country managers should be brought into the decision-making process. To illustrate, country managers can seldom contribute much to decisions on entering new country markets in which the multinational enterprise has no current operations or to decisions on new world products, although in both instances they may provide valuable information. But country managers can contribute a great deal to decisions on the marketing program for new products in their respective countries. Because consumer products are generally more sensitive to local market conditions than industrial products, country managers assume a more prominent role in entry decision making in consumer-products companies than in industrial-products companies.

A second consideration is the size of the cash outlay required to carry out the entry decision. One can express this consideration with the following rule: corporate managers should make entry decisions when the probability times the cost of a bad decision made by a country manager exceeds a certain sum. It is hardly surprising, therefore, that investment entry decisions are highly centralized at the corporate level.

A third consideration is the degree of multinationality of the entry decision. Decisions involving transfers between two or more countries should be made by corporate managers, because only they can take an objective regional or global perspective. Hence decisions to source products in one country for export to another or decisions on intracorporate transfer pricing are properly centralized at headquarters. Decisions on world products that are marketed in several countries with common trademarks and brand names should also be the responsibility of headquarters. Conversely, decisions on "local" products that are sold only in single country markets should be shared between corporate and respective country managers. In brief, corporate managers should make entry decisions that have significant multinational dimensions, and they should share with country managers entry decisions that are primarily uninational in nature, unless the first two considerations indicate otherwise.

Because of these considerations, the multinational enterprise should centralize decisions on new international products. Entry mode decisions should also be centralized, because they involve two or more countries (sourcing decisions for export entry are an example), require substantial cash outlays (notably in the case of investment entry), or commit the corporation to long-term arrangements with foreign parties (as in licensing entry). In contrast, decisions on the design of the foreign marketing plan should be shared with managers in the target country, because channel, promotion, and pricing decisions are critically dependent on local country/market conditions. In concluding this section, it should also be noted that shared decision making among different corporate managers is necessary to provide the functional, product, and area skills that are vital to planning cost-effective entry strategies in a global enterprise system.

Grouping Country Markets for Standardized Marketing Strategies

The benefits of a multinational enterprise system for constituent entry strategies are most evident when managers can design a single effective marketing plan for a group of countries. But to do so, managers need to search for country markets that will respond to a standardized marketing program. When done right, grouping facilitates entry planning, in addition to enhancing the profit contributions of constituent entry strategies.

It is correct to assert that each country, each market, and each consumer or user is unique at some level of analysis. It is easy, therefore, for managers to deny the usefulness of country grouping. This is particularly true for country managers who are quick to proclaim the uniqueness of their own countries and markets in opposing corporate marketing plans. But at issue is not the ultimate uniqueness of country markets, but rather whether certain country markets are similar enough to justify a common marketing strategy. To find out, managers should look for country groups on a global basis, because some country markets may be similar across regional lines.

Figure 27 offers a sequential model for grouping country markets. It allows managers to determine, first, broad primary groups and, second, secondary groups within each primary group. Starting with all countries, managers determine a small number of primary groups by using statistical indicators of market behavior with respect to a candidate product. Although the purpose of this model is to group countries rather than choose a target country, the same multicountry statistics used for preliminary screening (such as those listed on pages 59 and 60) may be used here. Indeed, the grouping model in Figure 27 is intimately related to the target selection model presented in Chapter 3. Managers should

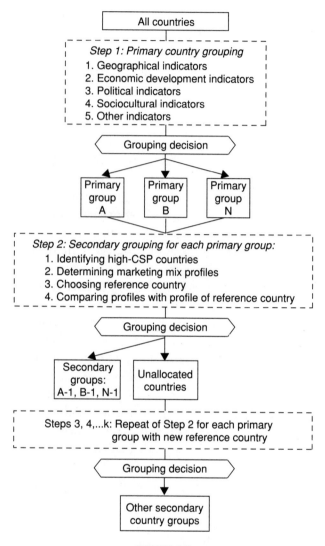

FIGURE 27

A Model for Grouping Country Markets

regard statistical indicators as "proxies" for direct measures of market behavior, and they should select them for that purpose.

For administrative reasons, managers generally group countries by geographical area, but there is no a priori reason why countries in the same geographical area should respond to a standardized marketing program in the same way. Nor is there any a priori reason why countries in different geographical areas should have different market responses. For example, markets in Australia are much more similar to markets in Canada than to markets in Indonesia, which is a geographical neighbor. In planning entry strategies, therefore, managers should not be constrained by geographical country groups used for administrative purposes. At times, certain geographical groups may be sensible from a marketing perspective, but then the reason is seldom mere physical contiguity. Most of the Western European countries form a natural market grouping not because they are next to each other but for other reasons, including membership in the EC or European Free Trade Area (EFTA) (which are joined together in an industrial free-trade area) and a common level of economic development.

In classifying countries into primary groups, managers may use several kinds of indicators: geographical (apart from mere contiguity), level of economic development, political, sociocultural, and others. Since a country's level of economic development exerts a pervasive influence on market behavior, many managers will determine country groups by using per capita income and other indicators of economic development. Countries may also be grouped by sociocultural similarities, such as language, religion, education, and other attributes that influence market behavior. In placing countries in primary groups, managers may use one or more of these categories of indicators. Generally, the use of multiple indicators covering more than one category is superior to the use of a single indicator or a single category.

The number of primary country groups depends on the range of indicator values covering all countries and the ranges selected by managers to demarcate one group from another. Since primary groups are intended to be broad, their number would seldom exceed five.

The second step of the model starts the sequential process of determining secondary groups within each primary group. This step focuses only on countries with high company sales potential (CSP) that have been identified by using the target selection model presented in Chapter 2. These countries justify the time and effort to ascertain their marketing mix profiles for the candidate product, as was done for a single target country/market in Chapter 8 (Figure 18). Next, managers choose one of the high-potential countries in each primary group as a *reference* country, whose marketing mix profile is used as a standard. This reference country is likely to be a country in which the global company is already marketing the candidate product or the country with the highest CSP. The marketing mix profiles of other high-CSP countries are then compared with the marketing profile of the reference country in the respective primary groups. On the basis of these pair comparisons, managers classify countries into a secondary group whose members have profiles judged similar to the reference profile, and into unallocated countries. Managers then go on to allocate all countries to secondary groups by repeating step 2 in successive steps with new reference countries.

How many steps are needed to classify all countries into secondary groups depends on the diversity in marketing mix profiles as judged by managers. At one extreme, managers may decide that common marketing strategies for *any* two countries would not be successful; in effect, each country is the sole member of its secondary group. At the other extreme, managers may judge a product so insensitive to local market conditions that they can place all countries in a single secondary group. Most products fall between these two extremes: the number of secondary groups is greater than the number of primary groups but smaller than the number of high-CSP countries.

This model is intended to help managers group country markets in a systematic but economical fashion. It makes use of the natural inclination of managers to ask whether new country markets are similar to old country markets. By using, whenever possible, reference countries in which the company has ongoing marketing programs for the candidate product, the model should aid managers in making sequential choices of target markets as well as in designing common marketing strategies. But other approaches to country grouping may also prove useful, including formal methods that use computer-assisted clustering techniques such as factor analysis, discriminant analysis, and multidimensional scaling. Managers should understand that no grouping method, however sophisticated, can possibly account for all the many factors that may influence marketing effectiveness in a group of countries. Ultimately, only managers make grouping decisions, and therefore they should use a grouping method (or methods) that makes sense to them, given constraints of time and of information resources. Moreover, they should be ready to revise grouping decisions in the light of actual marketing performance.

Country grouping is the starting point for the design of marketing programs common to each country group. If grouping is done well, managers have an empirical basis for judging whether a common strategy in an overall marketing program or in any one of its individual elements is likely to be cost-effective for a target group.

In Chapter 3 we first discussed adapting products for foreign markets, pointing out that few companies can profitably follow a pure version of a product adaptation strategy or a product standardization strategy. That observation also pertains to other elements of the marketing mix: pricing, promotion, and distribution channels. That is to say, few companies can offer the same product lines at the same prices through the same distribution channels supported by the same promotion to a group of countries. No group of country markets is likely to show similar responses to *all* elements of a marketing program. Conversely, many companies can offer, say, the same product lines or the same promotion to a group of countries while adapting other policies to national differences. Therefore country grouping usually leads to different degrees of standardization across the several elements of the marketing mix. The issue for managers is not whether to standardize the entire marketing mix across national markets, but how to adjust specific mix elements as their business responds to global markets and competition.[8]

In the face of national differences, the only reason for managers to standardize marketing policies for a group of countries is the higher profit contribution of common policies as compared to separate national policies. Earlier in this chapter we discussed the benefits a multinational enterprise can achieve by fitting constituent entry strategies into its worldwide operations. But this cannot be done by ignoring national differences; it calls for informed judgments that involve trade-offs among effectiveness, costs, and risks in support of standardization/adaption decisions.

General observation suggests that multinational companies err on the side of little standardization rather than too much, because

Parker Pen Company (U.S.) is one of the world's best-known firms in the writing instrument industry. In 1982 Parker was making top-of-the-line pens in 500 styles in eighteen plants, with its foreign subsidiaries creating their own advertising and packaging for national markets. Hence subsidiaries had broad and diverse product lines, and collectively they utilized some forty different advertising agencies. About four-fifths of Parker's sales were outside the United States. In the early 1980s, Parker began losing market share to A.T. Cross (U.S.) and Montblanc (Germany). In 1982 a new president and CEO took over the direction of Parker; based on his successful experience with global brands at R. J. Reynolds (notably the Marlboro man), this person decided that a global marketing strategy was needed to restore Parker's sales and market share. All of its pens would have "one look, one voice" as directed by U.S. headquarters, representing a drastic shift from Parker's traditional multidomestic strategy featuring local product adaptation. He quickly cut the product line from 500 to 100, consolidated manufacturing operations, and hired Ogilvy and Mather to take sole control of Parker's advertising throughout the world. Also, the new CEO decided to go after the low end of the market: Parker would continue to market an upscale line (called Premier), but most profits were to come from a roller-ball pen (called Victor) selling for $2.98. By 1984 Parker was marketing 100 pen styles (produced in eight plants) with a single ad campaign, translated into the world's languages but using the same copy, layout, illustration, and bottom location of the Parker logo in all country markets.

This grand experiment in standardization lasted only one year; a disastrous fall in profits forced the CEO's resignation in 1985. What went wrong? The strategy of marketing pens the same way everywhere was strongly opposed by many Parker country managers and distributors. They argued that country markets were different; for instance, French and Italian consumers wanted fancy, expensive pens, while Scandinavians liked ballpoint pens. In retrospect, Parker was an extreme example of a company moving too fast and too far toward global standardization in marketing. Successful standardization rests on real similarities in buying behavior across countries—not assumed similarities, as in Parker's case. But it also needs the support of local country managers encouraged to participate in developing marketing strategies and given control over their own marketing budgets. Such participation by country managers is likely to lead in most companies to product portfolios that include local as well as global brands. In 1986 a group of British managers bought Parker's pen business and—shifting back to a multidomestic marketing strategy—made it profitable again.

Adapted from "Parker Pen Company" in Michael R. Czinkota and Ilkka A. Ronkainen, *International Marketing*, 2nd ed. (Chicago: Dryden Press, 1990), pp. 778–782; and "Marketers Turn Sour on Global Sales Pitch Harvard Guru Makes." *Wall Street Journal*, May 12, 1988, p. 1.

they let country managers plan, as well as manage, local marketing programs. But as multinational companies become more global in their orientation, standardized marketing policies will gradually replace purely local policies through a process of interactive planning. This shift, however, will fall far short of full global standardization as managers continue to cope with many significant national differences.[9]

Controlling Entry Strategies

In Chapter 2, Figure 2 depicts a control system as the fifth element of an international market entry strategy. Our intent here is to alert readers to the need for controlling entry strategies rather than describe control systems in any detail.

A management control system has three functions: (1) monitoring operations to identify variances between actual and planned performance; (2) diagnosing the causes of variances, with particular emphasis on negative variances; and (3) devising courses of action to eliminate or reduce variances. Managers exercise control, therefore, to make the results of operations conform to planning goals. Control is intimately involved with planning, because without control, planning becomes merely an intellectual exercise. Moreover, control may bring about remedial changes in a plan and, in any event, provides vital information for the ongoing planning process. In contrast, control is meaningless without a planning process that creates standards against which performance can be measured by managers.[10]

Control is an essential element of a constituent entry strategy focused on a single product and a single target country/market.

The execution of an entry strategy requires translation of the international marketing plan into a tactical operating plan or budget, which usually covers the first year of the strategic plan. The budget therefore becomes the principal control instrument, with its goals and objectives serving as control standards. In establishing the budgets of country subsidiaries through interactive planning, it is the responsibility of corporate managers to make certain that those budgets are consistent with longer-term entry strategies; otherwise, the budgets of country subsidiaries are likely to be based on short-term objectives and amount to little more than an extension of last year's budgets. In sum, annual country budgets should be viewed as the current-period expression of the strategic entry plan.

International managers should control not only the performance of foreign subsidiaries but also the performance of licensees, agents, distributors, and other contractual parties in target markets. Admittedly control cannot be as comprehensive for the latter as for the former, but some degree of control can always be achieved using reports about key performance variables, such as profitability, sales, and market share. Our observations here, however, apply particularly to controlling country subsidiaries.

To exercise control over the performance of country subsidiaries, corporate managers must overcome several difficulties peculiar to international business. Information for control purposes must cross many cultural, economic, political, legal, and other differences that create obstacles to effective communication between corporate and country managers. Another problem arises when corporate managers simply extend domestic control systems to cover foreign subsidiaries. When that happens, country managers are commonly burdened by reporting requirements that contribute little or nothing to control.

To illustrate the control process, Figure 28 offers a product/country matrix to help corporate managers control constituent entry strategies as well as compare them across countries and products. Let us look first at a single row in Figure 28 that reports the operating results in the budget period for a particular product and country market.

The third-column entry is the variance in profit contribution. By itself this variance means little, but it can be allocated to a

Country market	Profit contribution			Subsidiary's sales in units			Contribution margin			Industry unit sales			Market share (%)			Ratios
	A	P	V	A	P	V	A	P	V	A	P	V	A	P	V	
1																
2																
3*																
4																
5																
n																

Products

*Reference country.
General Note: A is actual results, P is planned results, and V is variance (A–P).

FIGURE 28

Multicountry/Multiproduct Matrix for Controlling Entry Strategies *volume variance* (the variance in the unit sales of the company's product) and a *price/cost variance* (the variance in profit contribution per unit or contribution margin). This allocation may be expressed algebraically as follows:

$$(R_a - R_p) = (S_a - S_p)C_p + (C_a - C_p)S_a$$

where R represents profit contribution, S represents the subsidiary's unit sales volume, C represents the contribution margin, and the subscripts a and p represent actual and planned results.[11]

The price/cost variance may be decomposed into a *price variance* and a *cost variance* according to the following equation:

$$(C_a - C_p) = (P_a - P_p) + (K_p - K_a)$$

where P represents price and K represents the unit variable cost. The cost variance may be further decomposed into specific cost variances.

The volume variance may be decomposed into a *market size variance* (the variance in industry unit sales of the candidate product type by all sellers) and a *market share variance*. The market size variance may be expressed as $(M_a - M_p)E_pC_p$, where M represents total industry sales in units, E the subsidiary's market share, and C the contribution margin. The market-share variance becomes $(E_a - E_p)M_aC_p$.

After corporate managers have allocated the profit-contribution variance to variances in price, cost, market size, and market share, they are prepared to raise "why" questions—to ask about the causes of these variances. Ultimately, managers must decide whether negative variances are attributable to poor *planning* or to poor *performance*. Was the entry strategy for this country faulty in one or more of its elements, or was its execution inadequate, or both? There is no easy quantitative answer to this question. Somehow corporate managers must evaluate the performance of a country manager in the light of *ex post* information, some of which is quantitative and some of which is qualitative. That is to say, they must answer the question: what should this manager have accomplished in the actual circumstances of the budget period? Any remaining variance is traceable to the strategy itself.

Corporate managers must distinguish between strategy variance and performance variance if they are to undertake the proper remedial action.

The primary focus of a control system is on the individual country program for a candidate product. But in a multinational enterprise, comparisons of programs across countries for the same product and comparisons across products within countries are also part of the international control system. Just as systematic comparisons of market and sales potentials are needed to choose the most attractive target markets, so are systematic comparisons across countries and products needed for effective control. By spotting country and product variations in the several performance measures, control comparisons can raise important questions with respect to market and sales potentials, weaknesses and strengths in country/product performance, new opportunities, the design of entry strategies, and other issues. Such comparisons offer corporate managers another way to apply experience in one country or product to another country or product. It may also be argued that a comparative control standard is more objective than a standard confined to a single country market or product. But for comparisons to be meaningful, the corporate control system should be standardized across countries and products.

Comparative performance assessments should not be misused by corporate managers in rewarding or punishing country managers. Country managers are inclined to resent any form of country comparisons, but they will surely sabotage a control system that generates unfair comparisons. Hence corporate managers need to be objective in distinguishing performance variances from strategic planning variances. For that reason, comparisons between countries belonging to the same secondary group with similar marketing mix profiles are most defensible, as well as most meaningful.

Returning to Figure 28, comparisons down the columns reveal differences in results among country subsidiaries. Comparisons may be facilitated by using one country's program as a reference program or, alternatively, by using "average" results. Ratio comparisons among country programs that relate specific inputs to marketing results can be particularly useful, because discrepancies trigger further inquiry.[12] Why is advertising for the candidate product 1.5 percent of sales in one country while it is no higher than 1 percent in other countries? Are we spending too much on advertising in that country or too little in other countries? Or is there another explanation? Enlightening comparisons may also be made across different products, as indicated by the arrow marked "products" in Figure 28.

Once corporate managers have correctly diagnosed the cause or causes of variances in a foreign subsidiary's performance, they must decide on remedial action. Performance variances call for improvement in local management; planning variances call for a revision of entry strategy.

Any or all of the elements of entry strategy (the target product/market, objectives, entry mode, or the marketing plan) may be the source of planning variances. Accordingly, remedial action may lead to a revision of any or all of these elements. For example, if the source of negative variance is a lower industry market potential than the one assumed in the entry plan, remedies may range from abandoning the market entirely to simply lowering sales objectives in a revised strategy. Or again, if the negative variance proceeds from market share, remedies may include a step-up in total marketing effort and/or a shift in the composition of the marketing mix (say, a drop in price together with a lower advertising expenditure). If the cause of a negative variance is new import or investment restrictions, the appearance of a strong competitor, or political instability, then remedial action may include a change in the entry mode, such as moving from export to investment entry or from investment entry to export or licensing entry.

Corporate managers should respond to positive variances as well as negative variances. A positive planning variance carries an opportunity cost, because it means that corporate planners have not taken full advantage of market opportunity in a target country: they underestimated the overall market size, the market share, or the contribution margin. Persistent positive variances are almost a sure sign of poor planning.

The revision of entry strategies to eliminate variances is necessary but not sufficient to achieve good strategies. As pointed out in Chapter 2, entry planning is a continuous process: entry strategies should be periodically reviewed to take account of changes both external and internal to the global enterprise. Such reviews keep entry strategies more closely attuned to new circumstances and thereby minimize future planning variances. Only in this way can international companies design cost-effective strategies in a turbulent world.

Entry Strategies for Global Competitive Advantage

In this section we offer a conceptual framework to help managers design global entry strategies for competitive advantage. We start by returning to the "where in the world" questions at the beginning of this chapter and by raising two additional questions in the context of the value-added chain of an MNE's business.[13]

Configuring and Coordinating the MNE's Value-Added Chain

As used here, a company's value-added (VA) chain designates the sequence of activities necessary to move the products (goods and services) of a business from their creation to their ultimate consumption. Each activity—or link—in the VA chain adds value to products, although some activities add more value than others. Each activity also adds costs to products.

The MNE's value-added chain is depicted in Figure 29. Strategic VA decisions for a global MNE require consideration of three questions: (1) Where should the MNE locate individual activities? (2) What activities should the MNE own? (3) How should the MNE coordinate activities along the VA chain? Answers to these questions create the *geographical configuration,* the *ownership configuration,* and the *coordination pattern* of the VA chain, which in turn provide the platform for the design of global entry strategies. The VA chain is broken into two parts: *upstream activities* covering the development and production of products and *downstream activities* covering marketing and customer service.

Geographical configuration on a global scale enables the MNE to exploit national factor endowments (natural resources, labor, capital, and technology) by locating upstream activities in low-cost countries. Geographical configuration is a key source of global competitive advantage based on cost.[14]

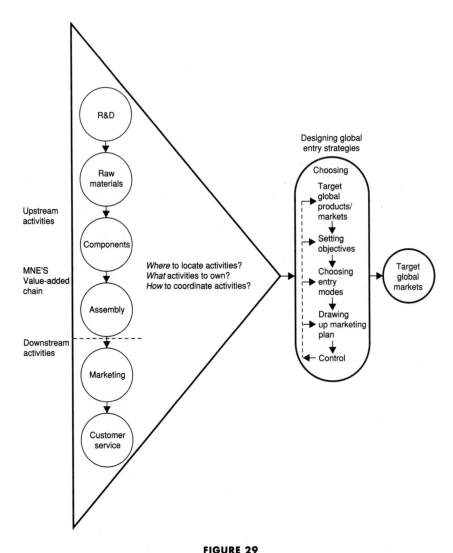

FIGURE 29

*Designing Global Entry Strategies: Configuring and
Coordinating the MNE's Value-Added Chain*

Ownership configuration enables the MNE to get the most effective exploitation of its proprietary assets: technology, managerial skills, and other capabilities. Proprietary assets can give the
MNE a global competitive advantage based on differentiated
products, as well as a lower-cost advantage based on economies of
scale and cumulative international experience. The MNE is able

Cummins Engine Company, the world's foremost independent manufacturer of heavy-duty diesel engines, and Komatsu Ltd., Japan's leading construction equipment manufacturer, have formed a strategic partnership. This collaboration is occurring less than a decade after Komatsu and other Japanese engine manufacturers tried to gain a strong foothold in the U.S. market with an aggressive marketing effort. Although this attempt failed, it forced Cummins to lower costs with deep cuts in its operations. Before attacking the U.S. market, Komatsu had been a customer and licensee of Cummins. The restoration of ties between Cummins (whose revenues were $3.8 billion in 1992) and Komatsu (whose size is twice that of Cummins, but which is more diversified) demonstrates the pressures on companies to compete globally. The first step in the Cummins\Komatsu alliance is to make in one of Komatsu's plants in Japan the popular 3.9-liter and 5.9-liter Cummins engines that range in horsepower from 70 to 200. Komatsu will use much of the output in its own construction equipment, and Cummins will market the rest in Asia. A second step is the formation of a joint venture to manufacture the big 30-liter Komatsu engine with horsepower of 1,100 in one of Cummin's U.S. plants and to market it through Cummin's U.S. dealer network. These steps will help Komatsu stay competitive with Caterpillar and will help Cummins compete with Caterpillar in the engine market for large off-road construction equipment. The two companies plan to start production of Cummins engines in Japan by 1995. The alliance does not involve any investment by either company in the other.

Adapted from "Cummins, Komatsu Form Pact," *New York Times*, February 17, 1993, p. D1.

to "leverage" proprietary assets by keeping control through ownership of the value-added activities in which it excels compared to competitors (core competencies) and by contracting out activities that outside firms can do better or at a lower cost. In this way, the MNE allocates scarce resources to activities that provide the highest profit contribution.[15]

With VA activities located in many different countries and with some performed by the MNE while others are contracted to outside firms, coordination along the VA chain becomes vitally important to achieve global competitive advantage based on cost and/or differentiation advantages.[16] Without coordination, operations would fragment and fall short of optimal global performance. While coordination is not easy even when the MNE has control over country operations through ownership, it becomes much harder when some VA activities are outsourced to independent contractors.

Entry strategies are intimately related to the configuring and coordinating of VA activities. In a global MNE, entry strategies require decisions on upstream as well as downstream VA activities. Indeed, global entry strategies become indistinguishable from corporate-level strategy seeking to optimize performance in global markets. A challenge to managers is the design of entry strategies that are sensitive to national environments and yet allow for the global exploitation of upstream VA activities. Fundamentally, there are only two sources of competitive advantage: lower costs than rival firms and product differentiation. Configuration and coordination of the VA chain enhance the MNE's competitive advantage, which entry strategies then put to work in global markets. Because the global environment is turbulent, the MNE frequently needs to adjust its configuration and coordination patterns and related entry strategies in response to—or better yet, in anticipation of—changes in that environment. Indeed, MNE managers can gain critical competitive advantages by being quicker than rival managers in adjusting VA chains and complementary entry strategies.

Entering Strategic Alliances

In the past decade, MNEs have turned increasingly to cooperative arrangements known as *international strategic alliances* to become more competitive in global markets. Even managers in the biggest MNEs have concluded that "going it alone" is no longer a viable strategy.

An international strategic alliance is a long-term collaboration between two or more companies (usually MNEs) that combine the core competencies of the partners to build global competitive advantages. *Long-term* does not refer to any specific period of time, but rather a duration that exceeds that of arm's-length,

In 1986, General Motors (U.S.) and Daewoo Group (South Korea) started a joint venture to build an automobile in Korea for sale in the United States based on a design by General Motor's Opel subsidiary in Germany. But the fifty-fifty joint venture has not worked out. Sales of the subcompact Pontiac LeMans, which the joint venture manufactured, have been very weak in the United States. In retrospect, it can be seen that the failure was attributable to shifts in the goals and strategies of the two partners that reflected changes going on in the economies and markets of the United States and South Korea. Originally GM wanted to use Korea's low-wage workers to build an inexpensive auto for the U.S. market, and Daewoo wanted to become a major auto manufacturer through exports. The joint venture began poorly because the LeMans cars shipped to the United States were poor in quality. Eventually GM sent its own manufacturing expert to Daewoo. Then wages rose sharply in Korea, its currency (the won) appreciated against the U.S. dollar, and frequent strikes interrupted Daewoo's production. Hence Korea was losing its advantage as a low-cost sourcing country for General Motors, and Daewoo was losing its reputation as a reliable supplier. Shifts in strategic focus compounded the joint venture's problems. Daewoo turned from exports to the dynamic domestic market, where it faced rivals introducing models with new technology. When GM rejected Daewoo's request for newer models to meet competition in the Korean market, Daewoo reached a technology-sharing agreement with Suzuki Motor (Japan).

Today each side blames the other for the joint venture's troubles. Daewoo charges that General Motors did not promote the LeMans enough in the U.S. market while General Motors argues that the auto's initial low quality and interrupted supplies turned off U.S. dealers. To the outside observer, Daewoo could not deliver as a reliable supplier, and General Motors could not deliver as a seller. Both companies failed to assess the other's strengths and weaknesses when the joint venture was formed, and both failed to reassess the joint venture when the partners' strategies and circumstances changed.

Adapted from "Why GM and Daewoo Wound Up on the Road to Nowhere," *Business Week*, September 23, 1991, p. 55.

Many companies are now avoiding vertical integration of their value-added chains. Instead they are concentrating on core activities—designing products or marketing, for instance—while letting outside firms take care of other activities, such as parts manufacture or assembly. In this way, companies become hubs of networks that are intended to include the world's best suppliers, best assemblers, and so on. Outsourcing offers two main advantages: (1) it holds down the core company's unit costs and the investment needed for fast product innovations, and (2) it allows the core company to allocate its scarce resources to value-added activities in which it has competitive advantages ("core competencies"). Using the network model, a company can get rapid growth with relatively small amounts of capital and a small management group.

Nike and Reebok are U.S. companies that design and market high-tech footwear. Nike owns a small plant that makes some sneaker parts; Reebok owns no plants. Both firms contract almost all footwear production to independent companies in Asia. This outsourcing enables Nike and Reebok to keep up with changing consumer preferences, because their suppliers can quickly retool for new products. Quantum (U.S.) develops new computer disk drives, but when they are ready for mass production, Quantum transfers manufacturing to Matsushita-Kotobuki Electronics (MKE) in Japan. Collaboration between the two firms is very close: during the design phase, Quantum sends its newest drawings to a MKE production team that gets ready for the production phase, constantly proposing changes to Quantum to make the new disk drives easier to manufacture. When a disk drive is ready for manufacture, Quantum engineers go to Japan for a month or so to work with MKE engineers. This cooperative arrangement has made Quantum a strong competitor in the U.S. market for desktop computers. Such arrangements are now commonplace in electronics. American Telephone and Telegraph Company (AT & T) joined with Matsushita Electric Industrial Company (Japan) to jumpstart production of its Safari notebook computer designed by Henry Dreyfuss Associates (U.S.). Not having the capacity to manufacture its entire line of PowerBook notebook computers and needing to launch it quickly to exploit a short life cycle, Apple Computer Company (U.S.) arranged with Sony Corporation (Japan) in 1991 to manufacture its least-expensive model. Having served its purpose, the arrangement was ended by Apple one year later.

A big potential disadvantage of networks for core companies is the loss of control over some operations. Intel (U.S.) contracted two Japanese firms (NMB Semiconductor and Sharp) to make flash memory chips so that Intel could avoid the huge investment necessary to keep its share of a fast-growing market. But the Japanese firms were unable to supply Intel with enough chips, so Intel saw its market share drop by 20 percent in one year. The message of such failures is clear: for networks to work well, core companies need to find trustworthy partners.

Adapted from "The Modular Corporation," *Fortune*, February 8, 1993, pp. 106ff.; and "The Virtual Corporation," *Business Week*, February 8, 1993, pp. 98–103.

open-market transactions. Strategic alliances can involve collaboration on any set of VA activities. Specific motivations of partners include gaining access to key markets, filling out product lines, acquiring technology, reducing investment in new plant and equipment, utilizing excess capacity, and achieving scale economies. These motivations may classified as *resource sharing* or *market access*.

The extraordinary growth of strategic alliances shows no signs of slowing down. For instance, in the 1980s the biotechnology sector formed 847 alliances; the computer software sector, 344; the telecommunications sector, 366; and the chemicals sector, 410.[17] This proliferation is blurring the boundaries of MNE systems: alliances between core MNEs and their suppliers, customers, and competitors can create so much organizational overlap that it becomes impossible to say where the core enterprise begins and where it ends.

Proliferation is also generating doubts about the continuation of the vertical, hierarchical organization structures described earlier in this chapter. Strategic alliances raise several management issues. Who is to manage the alliance? How is the alliance to be managed? How is the "output" of the alliance to be shared between or among partners? How are disputes to be resolved? In responding to these issues, centralized MNE structures appear to be giving way to horizontal, cooperative *global networks* that can accommodate strategic alliances and are quick to adjust to a global economy of dynamic technology and competition. By their very nature, networks are continuously in a process of renewal. But how far can networks go in dispersal of authority? Global strategies require a high degree of coordination of activities along the VA chain. Can the necessary degree of coordination be achieved through cooperation and persuasion instead of hierarchical authority? As yet, the record of international strategic alliances is too short to provide answers to these questions. In sum, global networks promise flexibility and competitive power, but they also run the risk that the core MNE will lose control of the network.

Tomorrow's Global Managers

We started this book by looking at the challenges and opportunities of a new global economy. We end it by offering some remarks on the skills that managers will need to succeed in that economy.

The current generation of senior managers grew up in multidomestic business environments that are vanishing in the wake of forces propelling a global economy. It is hardly surprising that these managers are often uncomfortable and awkward in thinking about global enterprises, to say nothing of running them. But tomorrow's senior managers will not have multidomestic pasts; they will have to cope with global business environments from the start of their careers. To do so successfully, two broad skills are vital: (1) a global perspective on technology, markets, and competition; and (2) an ability to manage people of diverse national and corporate cultures within and outside and global enterprise.

The progressive transformation of national markets into global markets intensifies the need for managers to understand their business environments. Global environments are more complex, more dynamic, and more "surprise intensive" than local business environments. A global economy demands sophisticated managers who understand political, economic, technological, and competitive "discontinuities" and know how to use them to gain competitive advantage over their rivals.

The spread of strategic alliances brings to the fore the need to manage people within cooperative arrangements. Experience shows that the success of alliances depends on the imagination and skills of managers who must handle day-to-day operations.[18] MNE managers need to ensure that the partner company continues to benefit from the alliance in a spirit of give-and-take. At the same time, they must protect their company's own core competencies and not let the partner take over the alliance. Most important, they need to cooperate with international partners in a common learning experience. In sum, tomorrow's manager will be a person who can work with people throughout the world in designing entry strategies that exploit the MNE's global competitive advantage.

Summary

1. The multinational enterprise is a company that (1) enters markets throughout the world by establishing its own sales and production subsidiaries in several countries and by using other entry modes, (2) exercises control over its subsidiaries, and (3) strives to design and execute corporate strategies in marketing, production, finance, and other functions from an international perspective that transcends national and regional boundaries.

2. Management and technology transfers from the parent company to subordinate system members are essential features of the multinational enterprise system. When managers at the parent company design foreign market entry strategies from a global perspective, they act to build up intersubsidiary transfers at regional and global levels.

3. When managers perceive their company as competing in separate national markets, they create a multidomestic variant of the multinational enterprise system. When they perceive the boundaries of their company's markets and competition as coextensive with the world, they create a global system.

4. Global strategies have no inherent superiority over multidomestic strategies. A strategy's superiority depends on its net advantages in specific circumstances. The emergence of a global economy described in Chapter 1 suggests that managers are more likely to err by failing to globalize than the opposite.

5. As an enterprise becomes more international, its organization structure also evolves in response to shifts in international strategies. The principal organizational alternatives for the multinational enterprise are the international division, the product-based global structure, the area-based global structure, and mixed structures.

6. A multinational enterprise system influences entry decisions through (1) a global corporate philosophy and strategy, (2) information transfers, (3) resources, and (4) decision-making support. In these ways, a global enterprise system can increase the profit contributions of constituent entry strategies by lowering incremental costs and raising incremental revenues. But these benefits are dependent on an information network together with an organization structure that facilitates coordination across functions, products, and countries.

7. Entry strategy planning in a global enterprise system should be an interactive process involving managers at corporate, regional, and country levels. Shared decision making among different corporate managers is also necessary to provide functional, product, and area skills.

8. The benefits of a multinational enterprise system for constituent entry strategies are most evident when managers can design an effective marketing plan for a group of countries. A model is offered to help managers group country markets in a systematic but economical fashion.

9. Country grouping is the starting point for the design of marketing programs common to each country group. In the face of national differences, the only reason for managers to standardize marketing policies for a group of countries is the higher profit contribution of common policies as compared to separate national policies. General observation suggests that multinational companies err on the side of too little standardization rather than too much, because they let country managers plan as well as manage local marketing programs.

10. Control is an essential element of a constituent entry strategy. A control system (1) monitors operations to identify

variances between actual and planned performance, (2) diagnoses the causes of variances, and (3) devises courses of action to eliminate variances. Corporate managers must distinguish between planning variance and performance variance if they are to undertake the proper remedial action.

11. In a multinational enterprise, comparisons of programs across countries for the same product and comparisons across products within countries are also part of the international control system. Planning variances may lead to a revision of any or all of the elements of a constituent entry strategy.

12. A company's value-added (VA) chain designates the sequence of activities necessary to move products (goods and services) of a business from their creation to their ultimate consumption. Each activity in the chain adds both value and cost to products.

13. Strategic VA decisions for a global MNE require consideration of three questions: (1) Where should the MNE locate individual activities? (2) What activities should the MNE own? (3) How should the MNE coordinate activities along the VA chain? Answers to these questions create the geographical configuration, the ownership configuration, and the coordination pattern of the MNE's VA chain, which in turn provide the platform for the design of global entry strategies.

14. Geographical configuration is a key source of global competitive advantage based on cost. Ownership configuration enables the MNE to get the most effective exploitation of its proprietary assets that give it a global competitive advantage based on differentiated products. Without coordination, MNE operations would fragment and fall short of optimal global performance.

15. A challenge to managers is the design of entry strategies that are sensitive to national environments and, at the same time, allow for the global exploitation of upstream VA activities.

16. An international strategic alliance is a long-term collaboration between two or more companies (usually MNEs) that

combines the core competencies of the partners to build global competitive advantages.

17. The proliferation of strategic alliances is blurring the boundaries of MNE systems and is generating doubts about the continuation of traditional MNE organization structures. Centralized MNE structures appear to be giving way to horizontal, cooperative global networks that can accommodate strategic alliances.

18. Two broad skills are vital for tomorrow's global managers: (1) a global perspective and (2) an ability to manage people of diverse national and corporate cultures both within and outside their own enterprises.

| Notes |

Chapter 1

1. Louise A. Girifalco, "The Dynamics of Technological Change," *Wharton Magazine,* Fall 1982, pp. 31–37.

2. See Figure 9–1 in Franklin R. Root, *International Trade and Investment,* 7th ed. (Cincinnati: South-Western Publishing Company, 1994), p. 214.

3. See Table 23–4 in Franklin R. Root, op. cit., p. 604. Foreign direct investment (FDI) is equity investment by an enterprise (called the parent company) in an entity (called a branch, subsidiary, or affiliate) located in a foreign country that gives managerial control to the parent company.

4. "The New Face of American Power," *Fortune,* July 26, 1993, p. 72.

5. Franklin R. Root, "U.S. High Technology Industry and International Competitiveness," *Journal of High Technology Management Research,* no. 1, 1990, p. 98.

6. The product life cycle is described in Chapter 3.

7. The twelve EC member countries are Belgium, Denmark, France, Germany, Greece, Ireland, Italy, Luxembourg, the Netherlands, Portugal, Spain, and the United Kingdom.

8. *Global Economic Prospects and the Developing Countries* (Washington, D.C.: World Bank, 1992), Table E8, p. 64.

9. The flow of products in multinational enterprise systems (comprising a parent company and its foreign subsidiaries) is described in Chapter 10.

10. United Nations Center on Transnational Corporations, *World Investment Report: The Triad in Foreign Direct Investment* (New York: United Nations, 1991), Table 12, p. 70.

11. United Nations Center on Transnational Corporations, op. cit., Figure 7, p. 56.

12. See Don P. Clark, "Recent Changes in Non-Tariff Measure Use by Industrial Countries," *International Trade Journal,* Spring 1992, Table 2, p. 317.

13. For two recent studies of Japan and its economy, see John Hunter Boyle, *Modern Japan: The American Nexus* (Fort Worth, TX: Harcourt Brace Jovanovich, 1993); and Edward J. Lincoln, *Japan's Unequal Trade* (Washington, D.C.: Brookings Institution, 1990).

14. The EC started in 1958 with six members: Belgium, France, Germany, Italy, Luxembourg, and the Netherlands. It now has twelve members, which were identified in note 7.

15. It also established a common agricultural program (CAP) with price supports, export subsidies, and tight import restrictions. The CAP remains a bone of contention between the EC and the United States because it limits the sale of U.S. farm products in the EC market.

16. For recent publications on Europe '92, see "A Rude Awakening: A Survey of the European Community," *Economist,* July 3, 1993, pp. 5–20; Commission of the European Communities, *The Single Market in Action* (Luxembourg: Office of Official Publications of the European Communities, 1992); Timothy M. Devinney and William C. Hightower, *European Markets After 1992* (Lexington, Mass.: Lexington Books, 1991); John A. Quelch, Robert D. Buzzell, and Eric R. Salama, *The Marketing Challenge of 1992* (Reading, Mass.: Addison-Wesley Publishing Co., 1990); and John W. Dudley, *1992: Understanding the New European Market* (Chicago: Dearborn Financial Publishing, 1989).

17. This account of Whirlpool and Maytag drew on the following publications: "Where Whirlpool Flies and Maytag Sputters," *New York Times,* January 3, 1993, p. F5; "Whirlpool to Control Philips Unit," *New York Times,* August 19, 1988, p. D1; "Whirlpool Plots the Invasion of Europe," *Business Week,* September 5, 1988, p. 70; and "Whirlpool Finds Success Abroad," *Philadelphia Inquirer,* December 20, 1992, p. F1.

18. For a discussion of several NAFTA studies, see Nora Lustig, Barry P. Bosworth, and Robert Z. Lawrence, eds., *North American Free Trade* (Washington, D.C.: Brookings Institution, 1992). See also Gary C. Hufbauer and Jeffrey J. Schott, *North American Free Trade* (Washington, D.C.: Institute for International Economics, 1992).

19. "How NAFTA Will Help America," *Fortune,* April 19, 1993, p. 96.

20. The information on foreign companies in Japan is drawn from "Apple? Japan Can't Say No," *Business Week,* June 29, 1992, pp. 32–33; "To Sell in Japan Just Keep Trying," *Fortune,* January 25, 1993, pp. 103–104; "American Business Starts a Counterattack in Japan," *New York Times,* February 24, 1992, p. 1; "Under the Wing of Japan, Inc., A Fledgling Enterprise Soared," *New York Times,* January 15, 1992, p. 1; "You Can Make Money in Japan," *Fortune,* February 12, 1990, p. 85; and "Myth and Marketing in Japan," *Wall Street Journal,* April 6, 1989, p. 31.

21. Eastern Europe is here defined to include Poland, the Czech and Slovak republics, Hungary, Romania, Bulgaria, and the fifteen republics of the former Soviet Union (collectively designated as the Commonwealth of Independent States or CIS).

22. Some recent publications on China's reform are "When China Wakes: A Survey of China," *Economist,* November 28, 1992, pp. 11–18; Richard Pomfret, *Investing in China: Ten Years of Open Door Policy* (Ames: Iowa State University Press, 1991); and Mario Blejer and others, *China: Economic Reform and Macroeconomic Management,* Occasional Paper 76 (Washington, D.C.: International Monetary Fund, January 1991).

23. The remainder of this section draws on "China, the Emerging Economic Powerhouse of the 21st Century," *Business Week,* May 17, 1993, pp. 55–69; "When China Wakes: A Survey of China," *Economist,* November 28, 1992, pp. 11–18; "Stirring Giant," *New York Times,* February 14, 1993, p. 1, and February 15, 1993, p. A1; "China Fever Strikes Again," *Business Week,* March 29, 1993, pp. 46–47; "The Awakening Chinese Consumer," *New York Times,* December 11, 1992, p. F1; and "U.S. Companies in China Find Patience, Persistence and Salesmanship Pay Off," *Wall Street Journal,* April 3, 1992, p. B1.

24. Some recent articles on reform in eastern Europe are "Rejoined: A Survey of Eastern Europe," *Economist,* March 13, 1993, pp. 3–22; Paul Lawrence and Charalambos Vlachoutsicos, "Joint Ventures in Russia: Put the Locals in Charge," *Harvard Business Review,* January–February 1993, pp. 44–54; "Russia Reborn: A Survey of Russia," *Economist,* December 5, 1992, pp. 3–26; Ed Hewett, *Open for Business: Russia's Return to the Global Economy* (Washington, D.C.: Brookings Institution, 1992); and John Williamson, *The Economic Opening of Eastern Europe* (Washington, D.C.: Institute for International Economics, 1991).

25. Information on Unilever is drawn from "The Subtleties of Detergent Sales in East Europe," *New York Times,* February 18, 1991, p. D1.

26. There is no hard and fast rule to classify countries as NICs. Two criteria, however, are important: (1) a fast, sustained rise in gross domestic product for a decade or more, and (2) a sharp increase in exports of mature but high-technology industrial products. The indisputable NICs are the four "little dragons" of Asia: Hong Kong, South Korea, Singapore, and Taiwan. Other countries sometimes designated as NICs include Argentina, Chile, and Mexico in Latin America. Likely additions to the NICs in the 1990s are India, Malaysia, Indonesia, and Thailand. China qualifies as a NIC, but we have chosen to treat it as a transitional economy moving from a command to a market economy. For entertaining accounts of the Asian NICs, see Simon Winchester, *Pacific Rising* (New York: Simon & Schuster, 1991); and Brian Kelly and Mark London, *The Four Little Dragons* (New York: Simon & Schuster, 1989).

27. See "Asia's High-Tech Quest," *Business Week,* December 7, 1992, pp. 126–130.

28. The information on Motorola is taken from "Future Perfect," *Economist,* January 4, 1992, p. 61; "Asia Beckons," *Economist,* May 30, 1992, pp. 63–64; "How Motorola Took Asia by the Tail," *Business Week,* November 11, 1991, p. 68; and "Beating Japan at Its Own Game," *New York Times,* July 13, 1990, p. D1.

29. See the World Bank, *World Development Report 1987* (New York: Oxford University Press, 1987), pp. 78–112. The World Bank is now promoting a

"market-friendly approach" to economic development. See the World Bank, *World Development Report 1991* (New York: Oxford University Press, 1991), pp. 6–9.

30. "India: Look Out, Asia," *Economist,* June 26, 1993, pp. 34–35; and "India is Opening for Business," *Fortune,* November 16, 1991, pp. 128–130.

Chapter 3

1. For an elaboration of the international product life cycle, see Sak Onkvisit and John J. Shaw, "An Examination of the International Product Life Cycle and Its Application Within Marketing," *Columbia Journal of World Business,* Fall 1983, pp. 73–79.

2. This injunction calls to mind Finagle's Law on Information: (1) the information you have is not what you want; (2) the information you want is not what you need; (3) the information you need is not what you can obtain; and (4) the information you can obtain costs more than you can afford! Preliminary screening is intended to soften—if not eliminate—the impact of Finagle's Law on the selection of target country markets.

3. U.S. Department of Commerce, Bureau of the Census, *Foreign Trade Reports,* FT 410, monthly. A reference publication, Schedule B, is the index that describes the numbered export categories.

4. These and other statistics on 160 countries appear in the following United Nations publications: *Commodity Trade Statistics, Monthly Bulletin of Statistics, Statistical Yearbook, Yearbook of International Trade Statistics, and Yearbook of National Accounts Statistics.* Other sources of international statistics are listed in the annotated bibliography at the end of this chapter.

5. Another conception of IMP is the upper limit of demand for a product type as the marketing effort of all sellers approaches infinity. Although this conception indicates that IMP depends on marketing effort as well as external demand factors, we regard it as too theoretical for practical use in the selection of foreign target markets.

6. Another definition of company sales potential is the upper limit of demand for a company's product as the company's marketing effort increases relative to that of competitors in the designated market. Our definition may be regarded as a pragmatic adaptation of this definition to foreign markets.

Chapter 4

1. Empirical studies confirm the proposition that exporting is a development process. See, for example, Warren J. Bilkey and George Tesar, "The Export Behavior of Smaller-Sized Wisconsin Manufacturing Firms," *Journal of International Business Studies,* Spring/Summer 1977, pp. 93–98; Jan Johanson and Jan-Eric Vahlne, "The Internationalization Process of the Firm—A Model of Knowledge Development and Increasing Foreign Market Commitments," *Jour-*

nal of International Business Studies, Spring/Summer 1977, pp. 23–32; and Jean-Emile Denis and Daniel Depelteau, "Market Knowledge, Diversification, and Export Expansion," *Journal of International Business Studies,* Fall 1985, pp. 77–89. For export entry considered as an innovation process, see Stan R. Reid, "The Decision-Maker and Export Entry and Expansion," *Journal of International Business Studies,* Fall 1981, pp. 101–112.

2. See Figure 4.

3. The distinction between a branch and a subsidiary is legal rather than operational: a branch does not have a legal identity separate from the parent company, whereas a subsidiary has its own legal identity, usually as a corporation.

4. The direct export channel using home-based representatives who travel abroad to make sales to final buyers avoids some of the fixed costs of the foreign branch/subsidiary but may incur higher variable costs, particularly travel. Also this channel may fail to meet the manufacturer's performance specifications. Direct mail-order export avoids some (if not all) the fixed costs of the foreign branch/subsidiary but incurs higher variable costs of transportation, communication, and catalog publications.

5. An agent who guarantees customer credit is known as a *del credere* agent.

6. If a branch/subsidiary channel is used, then a company must choose a manager to head the facility.

7. Based on an analysis of forty-one companies in Canada and the United Kingdom, one study finds that high performance is associated with shared decision making (reciprocity) between manufacturers and their foreign distributors. See Philip J. Rosson and I. David Ford, "Manufacturer-Overseas Distributor Relations and Export Performance," *Journal of International Business Studies,* Fall 1982, pp. 57–72.

8. The International Chamber of Commerce publishes *Incoterms* that defines the terms and *Guide to Incoterms* that explains how buyer and seller share the risks and obligations of specific terms of sale.

9. Several other government agencies are involved in export promotion. The Trade Promotion Coordinating Committee, chaired by the U.S. Secretary of Commerce, has representatives of ten cabinet departments and six other government agencies. Although we are discussing U.S. export promotion, it should be noted that many foreign governments also provide export promotion services to encourage national firms to start or sustain export activities.

10. The *Export Yellow Pages* directory of the U.S. Department of Commerce contains the names of EMCs in the United States. See also *Directory of Leading U.S. Export Management Companies* (Fairfield, Conn.: Bergano Book Company).

Chapter 5

1. Another provision of the convention obligates each member country to grant the same patent and trademark treatment to nationals of other member countries as it grants to its own nationals. Each member country is free to deter-

mine its own industrial property laws, however, and there has been little cross-national harmonization of those laws.

2. The Patent Cooperation Treaty (PCT) has been ratified by most industrial countries and a few developing countries; it became effective in 1978. The PCT extends the Paris Union's priority filing period for patents from one year to twenty months, and it provides for a single search and preliminary examination procedure for patent coverage in the member countries. Application for a patent, however, must still be made in each country. The European Patent Convention went into force in 1977 for countries of the European Community, Switzerland, and Sweden. Patent applications are administered by a European Patent Office. If search and examination procedures are satisfactory, then the patent is published in the *European Patent Bulletin* eighteen months after the date of application. The public has nine months to file an opposition. After that time, a patent is issued and is effective in all the member countries for twenty years from the filing date.

3. A foreign firm can register its trademark in the United States by demonstrating commercial use outside the United States, but to secure ownership, it is well advised to offer a token shipment of merchandise for sale in the United States prior to registration.

4. For a description of counterfeiting methods and actions to curb counterfeiting, see Michael G. Harvey and Ilkka A. Ronkainen, "International Counterfeiters: Marketing Success Without the Cost and the Risk," *Columbia Journal of World Business,* Fall 1985, pp. 37–45.

5. Under the Madrid Convention, trademark registration in one member country is automatically extended protection in all other member countries. But there are only twenty-one, mostly European, signatory countries. Although the United States is not a signatory, U.S. companies can take advantage of the Madrid Convention by using branches or subsidiaries in a signatory country.

6. See Chapter 7.

7. When industrial property rights are assigned instead of licensed, or when they are used to acquire equity in the licensee firm, capitalization is explicit. But it is based on the negotiated value of the rights, not on their development costs.

8. See Chapter 9.

9. If one drops the assumption that the prospective licensee is ethical, the bid ceiling price may be determined by a fourth value: the cost of patent infringement or other illegal acquisition of the licensor's technology.

10. For elaboration and empirical testing of this pricing model, see Franklin R. Root and Farok J. Contractor, "Negotiating Compensation in International Licensing Agreements," *Sloan Management Review,* Winter 1981, pp. 23–32.

11. A licensing venture may involve separate agreements on patents, trademarks, technical know-how, and technical services. For expositional convenience, however, we shall use *licensing contract* to cover all the agreements between the licensor and licensee pertaining to a particular venture.

12. Political risks are discussed at some length in Chapter 6.

13. U.S. Companies can get political risk insurance from the Overseas Private Investment Corporation (a U.S. government agency), but only for developing countries.

14. Joint ventures are discussed in Chapter 6.

15. For recent information on countertrade, see Aspy P. Palia, "Countertrade Practices in Japan," *Industrial Marketing Management,* 22, 1993, pp. 125–132; Aspy Palia and Oded Shenkar, "Countertrade Practices in China," *Industrial Marketing Management* 20, 1991, pp. 57–65; Rolf Mirus and Bernard Yeung, "Countertrade: What Have We Learnt?" in Khosrow Fatemi, ed., *International Trade and Finance in the 1990s,* vol. 3 (Laredo, Texas: International Trade and Finance Association, 1991), pp. 779–795; and Matt Schaffer, "Countertrade as an Export Strategy," *Journal of Business Strategy,* May–June, 1990, pp. 33–38.

Chapter 6

1. In the economist's language, foreign direct investment allows a company to extend its monopolistic advantage into foreign markets and thereby earn a higher economic rent.

2. Services that allow a decoupling of production and consumption, such as computer software, are termed *hard* services. Like physical goods, such services can be exported. But services whose production and consumption cannot be decoupled because they occur simultaneously (such as health care, car rental, consulting, and advertising) are termed *soft* services. Such services cannot be exported, for they must be produced at the point of consumption.

3. Branch/subsidiary exporting also requires equity investment by the manufacturer. But the size of this marketing investment is ordinarily much smaller than the size of a manufacturing investment, and it is intended to facilitate export entry, not replace it. Hence we shall use the term *investment entry mode* to mean only entry through investment in local production.

4. Gerald D. Newbould, Peter J. Buckley, and Jane C. Thurwell, *Going International—the Experience of Smaller Companies Overseas* (New YorK: Wiley and Sons, 1978), p. 46. See also the discussion of exporting as a learning experience in Chapter 4.

5. Negotiations with acquisition candidates or joint-venture partners are subsumed in step 4.

6. For a study of how U.S.-based manufacturing multinational companies evaluate foreign investments, see Marie E. Wicks Kelly and George C. Philippatos, "Comparative Analysis of the Foreign Investment Evaluation Practices by U.S.-Based Manufacturing Multinational Companies, *Journal of International Business Studies,* Winter 1982, pp. 19–42.

7. Political risk is perceived by managers as a downside risk, but it must be recognized that political change may also benefit foreign investors. Witness, for example, the recent collapse of the communist regimes in Eastern Europe. Nonetheless, we shall discuss political risk as a downside risk.

8. See Stephen J. Kobrin, *Managing Political Risk Assessment* (Berkeley: University of California Press, 1982); Fariborz Ghadar and others, eds., *Managing International Political Risk: Strategies and Techniques* (Washington, D.C.: Bond Publishing Company, 1983); and Fariborz Ghadar and Theodore H. Moran, *International Political Risk Management* (Washington, D.C.: Ghadar

and Associates, 1984); Franklin R. Root, "Environmental Risks and the Bargaining Power of Multinational Corporations," *International Trade Journal*, No. 1, Fall 1988, pp. 111–124; and Peter Smith Ring and others, "Management of the Political Imperative in International Business" in Franklin R. Root and Kanoknart Visudtibhan, *International Strategic Management* (Washington, D.C.: Taylor & Francis, 1992), pp. 233–246.

9. Nationalization becomes confiscation when the government does not compensate the owners.

10. We are not concerned here with how the project is financed. Suffice it to say that the financing arrangements may be any of several possible mixes of the investor's own funds, funds borrowed anywhere in the world outside the target country, funds borrowed locally in the name of the project (affiliate), or equity funds of joint-venture partners.

11. Readers interested in a good exposition of capital budgeting for a foreign investment project are referred to David K. Eiteman and Arthur I. Stonehill, *Multinational Business Finance,* (Reading, Mass.: Addison-Wesley) latest edition.

12. The equation for net present values is:

$$\text{NPV} = \left[\frac{F_1}{(1+d)} + \frac{F_2}{(1+d)^2} + \cdots \frac{F_n}{(1+d)^n} \right] - I_o$$

where F represents net cash inflows; I the original investment; and d the discount rate. If the value of this equation is zero, then the rate of return equals the rate of discount (required rate of return or hurdle rate).

13. The internal rate of return (IRR) is the discount rate that equates the present value of net cash inflows with the original investment outflow. The equation is:

$$\frac{F_1}{(1+r)} + \frac{F_2}{(1+r)^2} + \cdots \frac{F_n}{(1+r)^n} = I_o$$

where F represents net cash inflows; I the original investment; and r the internal rate of return. Calculation of the IRR requires a trial-and-error procedure (using a present-value table) or a computer program.

14. See Figure 15.

15. Income that is not repatriated by the parent company is not subject to withholding taxes and (generally) enjoys a deferral of U.S. taxes. But if such income *could* be repatriated at the discretion of the parent company, then it should be counted as a dollar cash inflow.

16. A crude variant of this approach is to shorten the allowable payback period for foreign investments.

17. At this ceiling price, the investor would expect to make his or her required rate of return (hurdle rate), but if a new-venture entry would achieve his or her strategy objectives at a higher rate of return, then the latter should be used to de-

termine his ceiling price: he or she should not buy a company if it is cheaper to build one.

18. We are speaking here of joint ventures as an entry mode for a single target country. Joint ventures and other cooperative arrangements between two or more international firms to strengthen global competitive advantages—commonly called international strategic alliances—are taken up in Chapter 10.

19. For study of the use of international joint ventures by U.S. high-technology firms, see John D. Daniels and Sharon L. Magill, "The Utilization of International Joint Ventures by United States Firms in High Technology Industries," *Journal of High Technology Management Research,* no. 1, 1991, pp. 113–131.

20. For articles on the control and performance of international joint ventures and on the relative bargaining power of joint venture partners, see Syed Akmal Hyder and Pervez N. Ghauri, "Joint Venture Relationship Between Swedish Firms and Developing Countries: A Longitudinal Study," *Journal of Global Marketing,* no. 4, 1989, pp. 25–47; Erin Anderson, "Two Firms, One Frontier: On Assessing Joint Venture Performance," *Sloan Management Review,* Winter 1990, pp. 19–30; Jafor Chowdhury, "Performance of International Joint Ventures and Wholly Owned Foreign Subsidiaries: A Comparative Perspective," *Management International Review,* no. 2, 1992, pp. 115–133; and Linda L. Blodgett, "Toward a Resource-Based Theory of Bargaining Power in International Joint Ventures," *Journal of Global Marketing,* no. 1 and 2, 1991, pp. 35–54.

Chapter 7

1. A more extreme version of the naive rule is practiced when managers consider only a single way of exporting, a single way of investing, or a single way of licensing.

2. A "workable" entry mode is a mode that offers a company acceptable profits at an acceptable risk over its planning period.

3. Symbolically:

$$PC = \sum_{t=1}^{t=n} (R_t - C_t)$$

where PC is profit contribution, R_t is revenue in period t, and C_t is cost in period t. R_t and C_t are summed over all n planning periods.

Chapter 8

1. If the aggregate level of marketing effort falls short of the optimum level, then optimum allocation of effort among the mix elements requires an equality

of the incremental revenues generated by the last dollar spent on each of the mix elements.

2. Even test marketing or actual performance cannot prove that a marketing plan is optimum, although it may indicate a defective plan or (possibly) ways to improve a plan.

3. Empirical evidence suggests that the majority of U.S. exporters do not follow a systematic approach to entry pricing. For example, a study of sixty-five U.S. industrial exporters (representing 113 product lines in the electrical, machine tool, food processing, and fluid power industries) found that the export prices of more than three-fifths of the firms were the same as their domestic prices, while the export prices of one-sixth were somewhat higher and those of another one-sixth were somewhat lower than their domestic prices. See Bruce Seifert and John Ford, "Are Exporting Firms Modifying Their Product, Pricing and Promotion Policies?" *International Marketing Review* 6, no. 6, 1990, Table 2, p. 60.

4. Variable costs, as defined by the accounting profession, do not always coincide with incremental costs, especially over a planning period of three to five years. If, for example, foreign market entry requires new investment in plant facilities or new marketing overhead, then these costs (whether treated as capital or expense items) are incremental costs that should enter into the entry pricing decision.

5. An exception to this statement is the agent middleman, who has no pricing authority.

6. The Readers' Digest Association, Limited, *Products and People* (London, 1963).

7. Akira Nagashima, "A Comparison of Japanese and U.S. Attitudes Toward Foreign Products," *Journal of Marketing,* January 1970, pp. 68–74; and Akira Nagashima, "A Comparative 'Made-In' Product Image Survey Among Japanese Businessmen," *Journal of Marketing,* July 1977, pp. 95–100.

8. John R. Darling and Van R. Wood, "A Longitudinal Study Comparing Perceptions of U.S. and Japanese Consumer Products in a Third/Neutral Country: Finland 1975–1985," *Journal of International Business Studies,* third quarter 1990, pp. 427–450.

9. See Martin S. Roth and Jean B. Romeo, "Matching Product Category and Country Image Perceptions: A Framework for Managing Country-of-Origin Effects," *Journal of International Business Studies,* third quarter 1992, pp. 477–497.

10. There is widely scattered evidence that consumers and industrial users in developing countries view their own country's products as generally inferior to those of the industrial countries. Thus industrial-country exporters have a "made-in" advantage over local competitors in developing countries.

11. "U.S. Industrial Companies Spending Poor Overseas," *Industrial Marketing,* May 1980, p. 92. A more recent study (cited in note 3) found that almost nine-tenths of the sixty-five industrial exporters spent less on export advertising than on domestic advertising. Only 1 percent spent more on export advertising than on domestic advertising. See Bruce Seifert and John Ford, loc. cit., Table 3, p. 62.

12. International managers may be said to use personal selling to get agents or distributors to handle their products.

13. For a model of international sales negotiations, see Art Weinstein and Richard R. Still, "International Sales Negotiations: The Impact of Cross-Cultural Communications," *Journal of Global Marketing,* no. 3, 1990, pp. 73–85.

Chapter 9

1. Edward T. Hall, *Beyond Culture* (Garden City, N.Y.: Doubleday, 1977), p. 16.

2. See Edward T. Hall, *The Silent Language* (Greenwich, Conn.: Fawcett, 1959, chap. 5.

3. American culture belongs to Western culture. Hence the American culture traits listed in Table 11 are shared with Europeans. Within these fundamental shared traits, there are differences of degree between Americans and Europeans and among the Europeans themselves.

4. Communication also requires a medium or message carrier, such as voice, mail, or electronic channels. Hence communication failure can result from channel distortions and blockages as well as from incongruities in perception and coding/decoding errors. Of course, even when a receiver fully understands a message, he or she may not take the action desired by the sender—that is, communication may be *ineffective* even when it is successful.

5. For example, the Eskimo has several words for snow, while the American has only one. Thus the former can think of snow in several ways but the latter in only one way. See Benjamin Lee Whorf, *Language, Thought, and Reality* (New York: MIT Press/John Wiley & Sons, 1956).

6. We are speaking here only of *cultural* congruence. Even members of the same culture do not have identical perceptual fields and encoding/decoding behavior, which are also influenced by social status, personality, and knowledge. We all know how hard it can be to communicate with some persons who nonetheless share our culture.

7. The distinction between low-context and high-context cultures is drawn from Edward T. Hall, *Beyond Culture* (Garden City, N.Y.: Doubleday, 1977), p. 91.

8. Ibid., p. 127. See also Ronald E. Dulek and others, "International Communication: An Executive Primer," *Business Horizons,* January–February 1991, pp. 20–25.

9. Japanese multinationals appear to be transferring their management philosophies and practices to their U.S. subsidiaries with good results. See Clair Brown and Michael Revich, "When Does Union-Management Cooperation Work: A Look at NUMMI and General Motors-Van Nuys," *California Management Review,* Summer 1989, pp. 26–44.

10. Even the same spoken words can convey several different meanings depending on their loudness, pitch, timbre, and rate of articulation.

11. Edward T. Hall, *The Hidden Dimension* (Garden City, N.Y.: Doubleday, 1969), pp. 135–136. This entire book is devoted to the language of space.

12. Ibid., p. 147.

13. Ibid., p. 150.

14. Paul Norbury and Geoffrey Bownas, *Business in Japan* (New York: Halstead, 1975).

15. Hall, op. cit., p. 155.

16. See, for example, John L. Graham, "The Influence of Culture on the Process of Business Negotiations: An Exploratory Study," *Journal of International Business Studies,* Spring 1985, pp. 81–96.

17. Edward T. Hall, "The Silent Language in Overseas Business," *Harvard Business Review,* May–June 1960, p. 92. This now-classic article was the first to describe the influence of *covert* cultural behavior on international business.

18. For a lively explanation of American negotiating style, see John L. Graham and Roy A. Herberger, Jr., "Negotiators Abroad—Don't Shoot from the Hip," *Harvard Business Review,* July–August 1983, pp. 160–168.

19. Howard F. Van Zandt, "How to Negotiate in Japan," *Harvard Business Review,* November–December 1970, p. 53. This article remains one of the most insightful ever published on this subject. For another depiction of the Japanese negotiation style, see J. Stewart Black and Mark Mendenhall, "Resolving Conflicts with the Japanese: Mission Impossible?" *Sloan Management Review,* Spring 1993, pp. 49–59.

Chapter 10

1. The present discussion of system transfers is confined to nonfinancial transfers. The system members are also connected by a wide variety of financial transfers, including product payments, capital funding, interest and dividend payments, royalties, and management fees, that finance and pay for nonfinancial transfers. Clearly, both nonfinancial and financial transfers depend on information transfers among system members.

2. For an empirical study confirming that the market-boundary perceptions of MNE managers form a reliable indicator of strategic focus at the business level (a positive association of market-boundary perceptions and intrasystem product transfers), see Franklin R. Root and Kanoknart Visudtibhan, "Defining and Measuring the International Strategic Focus of Multinational Corporations," in Franklin R. Root and Kanoknart Visudtibhan, *International Strategic Management: Challenges and Opportunities* (Washington, D.C.: Taylor & Francis, 1992), pp. 43–54.

3. For the most part, European companies do not establish international divisions as they evolve into global enterprises. Lacking the large domestic market of U.S. companies, European companies become so international as exporting companies that by the time they invest abroad, all their top executives have assumed international responsibilities.

4. For an empirical study indicating that a firm's entry mode choice is significantly influenced by global strategic variables as well as by environmental and transaction-specific factors relating to the target market, see W. Chan Kim and Peter Hwang, "Global Strategy and Multinationals' Entry Mode Choice," *Journal of International Business Studies,* first quarter 1992, pp. 29–54.

5. In a study of "environment scanning" by corporate executives in international companies, Keegan found that 67 percent of all important international information came from human sources, of which 81 percent was transmitted by voice. The most important human source of external information was company managers in foreign operations. As a consequence, corporate managers have much more information on countries and markets in which they have operations than on others. To remedy this imbalance, managers should make use of distributors, agents, licensees, and other contractual parties as information sources for entry decisions. See Warren J. Keegan, *Multinational Marketing Management,* 3rd ed. (Englewood Cliffs, N.J.: Prentice-Hall, 1984), pp. 218–221.

6. The presence of separate regional organizations adds to the variety and complexity of shared-decision-making arrangements.

7. Managers may choose to define markets as segments within national markets. Grouping may be viewed as segmenting a global market, and much of what I have to say about segmenting a target market in Chapter 8 is pertinent to country grouping. But to avoid confusion I shall continue to use *segmentation* to refer only to submarkets within a national market.

8. John A. Quelch and Edward J. Hoff, "Customizing Global Marketing," *Harvard Business Review,* May–June 1986.

9. An extreme argument urging companies to offer only standardized products in homogenized global markets is made by Theodore Levitt in "The Globalization of Markets," *Harvard Business Review,* May–June 1983, pp. 92–102. For other articles relating to the standardization issue, see Subhash C. Jain, "Standardization of International Marketing Strategy: Some Research Hypotheses," *Journal of Marketing,* January 1989, pp. 70–79; Kamran Kashani, "Beware the Pitfalls of Global Marketing," *Harvard Business Review,* September–October 1989, pp. 91–98; and Ugur Yavas and others, "Global Consumer Segmentation Versus Local Market Orientation: Empirical Findings," *Management International Review* 32, no. 3, 1992, pp. 265–272.

10. For a general review of control systems in multinational corporations, see B. R. Baliga and Alfred M. Jaeger, "Multinational Corporations: Control Systems and Delegation Issues," *Journal of International Business Studies,* Fall 1984, pp. 25–40; and Yves Doz and C. K. Prahalad, "Patterns of Strategic Control Within Multinational Corporations," *Journal of International Business Studies,* Fall 1984, pp. 55–72.

11. To illustrate, suppose the profit contribution variance is $-\$200$, S_a is 200, S_p is 215, C_a is \$4.9985, and C_p is \$5.58. Then $(200 - 215)\$5.58 + (\$4.9985 - \$5.58)200 = (-\$83.7) + (-\$116.3) = -\$200$.

12. Commonly used ratios include profit contribution to marketing assets (inventories, distribution facilities, net working capital), marketing costs/sales, advertising costs/sales, personal selling costs/sales, and inventory turnover.

13. A "business" constitutes a set of products or product lines that are sold in the same market, such as ethical pharmaceuticals or processed foods. Each international business is influenced by its own mix of multidomestic and global forces. A business is the highest level of a company's operations for which it is reasonable to plan entry strategies built on the constituent strategies taken up in

Chapters 2 through 8. Commonly, MNEs establish *strategic business units* to manage each of their businesses. To simplify the discussion here, we assume that the MNE has only a single business, such as computers, motor vehicles, or chemical specialities.

14. For a thorough study of competitive advantage derived from national location, see Michael E. Porter, *The Competitive Advantage of Nations* (New York: Free Press, 1990). The following article offers an approach to creating a global network of capabilities through facility location decisions: Andrew Bartmess and Keith Cerny, "Building Competitive Advantage Through a Global Network of Capabilities," *California Management Review,* Winter 1993, pp. 78–103.

15. For a survey of the current status of international subcontracting in manufacturing, see E. P. Hibbert, "Global Make-or-Buy Decisions," *Industrial Marketing Management* 22, 1993, pp. 67–77.

16. For a pioneering effort demonstrating how the VA chain can be used to analyze sources of international strategic advantages, see Bruce Kogut, "Designing Global Strategies: Comparative and Competitive Value-Added Chains," *Sloan Management Review,* Summer 1985, pp. 15–28. Michael E. Porter introduced the terms *configuration* and *coordination* for VA analysis in his *Competition in Global Industries* (Boston: Harvard Business School Press, 1986).

17. "Everybody's Favorite Monsters, a Survey of Multinationals," *Economist,* March 27, 1993, Table 5. For recent articles on strategic alliances, see Riad A. Ajami, "Global Strategic Alliances: The New Transnationals," *Journal of Global Marketing,* no. 1 and 2, 1991, pp. 55–69; David Lei and John W. Slocum, Jr., "Global Strategic Alliances: Payoffs and Pitfalls," *Organizational Dynamics,* Winter 1991, pp. 44–62; Michel Robert, "The Do's and Don'ts of Strategic Alliances," *Journal of Business Strategy,* March–April 1992, pp. 50–53; and David Lei and John W. Slocum, Jr., "Global Strategy, Competence-Building and Strategic Alliances," *California Management Review,* Fall 1992, pp. 81–97.

18. Robert W. Haigh, "Building a Strategic Alliance," *Columbia Journal of World Business,* Spring 1992, pp. 61–74. This article traces the evolution of the collaboration between Ford Motor Company (U.S.) and Mazda Motor Corporation (Japan).

| Supplementary Readings |

Chapter 1

The following publications look at competition in the global economy of today and tomorrow.

Competitiveness Policy Council. *Annual Report to the President and Congress.* Washington, D.C.: U.S. Government Printing Office.

Kelly, Brian, and Mark London. *Four Little Dragons.* New York: Simon & Schuster, 1989.

Ohmae, Kenichi. *The Borderless World.* New York: Harper Perennial, 1990.

Porter, Michael E. *The Competitive Advantage of Nations.* New York: Free Press, 1990.

Reich, Robert B. *The Work of Nations.* New York: Vintage Books, 1992.

Thurow, Lester. *Head to Head: The Coming Economic Battle Among Japan, Europe and America.* New York: William Morrow and Company, 1992.

Wendt, Henry. *Global Embrace.* New York: HarperBusiness, 1993.

Womack, James P., and others. *The Machine That Changed the World: The Story of Lean Production.* New York: Harper Perennial, 1991.

Chapter 2

Introductory texts in international marketing are complementary to *Entry Strategies for International Markets*. From the several texts now available to students, we have selected the latest editions of six to illustrate this complementarity. Individual chapters of these texts are cited as supplementary readings throughout this book.

Albaum, Gerald, Jesper Strandskov, Edwin Duerr, and Laurence Dowd. *International Marketing and Export Management.* Reading, Mass.: Addison-Wesley Publishing Company.

Czinkota, Michael R. and Ilkka A. Ronkainen. *International Marketing.* Chicago: Dryden Press.

Jain, Subash C. *International Marketing Management.* Boston: Kent Publishing Company.

Jeannet, Jean-Pierre, and Hubert D. Hennessey. *International Marketing.* Boston: Houghton-Mifflin Company.

Onkvisit, Sak, and John J. Shaw. *International Marketing.* New York: Macmillan Publishing Company.

Terpstra, Vern. *International Marketing.* Chicago: Dryden Press.

Chapter 3

Albaum, Gerald, Jesper Strandskov, Edwin Duerr, and Laurence Dowd. *International Marketing and Export Management.* Reading, Mass.: Addison-Wesley Publishing Company, 1989, chaps. 4 and 7.

Czinkota, Michael R., and Ilkka A. Ronkainen. *International Marketing.* Chicago: Dryden Press, 1990, chaps. 8 and 9.

Douglas, Susan P., and others. "Approaches to Assessing International Marketing Opportunities for Small- and Medium-Sized Companies," *Columbia Journal of World Business,* Fall 1982.

Green, Robert T., and Ajay K. Kohli. "Export Market Identification: The Role of Economic Size and Socioeconomic Development," *Management International Review,* no. 1, 1991.

Jain, Subash C. *International Marketing Management.* Boston: Kent Publishing Company, 1993, chaps. 10 and 12.

Jeannet, Jean-Pierre, and Hubert D. Hennessey. *International Marketing.* Boston: Houghton-Mifflin Company, 1988, chaps. 5, 6, 7, and 11.

Koh, Anthony C. "An Evaluation of International Marketing Research Planning in United States Export Firms," *Journal of Global Marketing,* no, 3, 1991.

Onkvisit, Sak, and John J. Shaw. *International Marketing.* New York: Macmillan Publishing Company, 1993, chaps. 8, 10, and 11.

Terpstra, Vern. *International Marketing.* Chicago: Dryden Press, 1994, chaps. 7, 8, and 9.

Chapter 4

Albaum, Gerald, and others. *International Marketing and Export Management.* Reading, Mass.: Addison-Wesley Publishing Company, 1989, chaps. 5 and 6.

Cooper, Robert G., and Elko J. Kleinschmidt. "The Impact of Export Strategy on Sales Performance," *Journal of International Business Studies,* Spring 1985.

Czinkota, Michael R., and Ilkka A. Ronkainen. *International Marketing.* Chicago: Dryden Press, 1990, chaps. 7 and 12.

Exporter's Encyclopaedia. New York: Dun & Bradstreet International, annual.

Ingram, Thomas N., Thomas R. Day, and George H. Lucas, Jr. "Dealing with Global Intermediaries: Guidelines for Sales Managers," *Journal of Global Marketing 5,* no. 4, 1992.

Jain, Subash, C. *International Marketing Management.* Boston: Kent Publishing Company, 1993, chap. 17.

Jeannet, Jean-Pierre, and Hubert D. Hennessey. *International Marketing.* Boston: Houghton-Mifflin Company, 1988, chaps. 12 and 19.

Onkvisit, Sak, and John J. Shaw. *International Marketing.* New York: Macmillan Publishing Company, 1993, chaps. 12 and 13.

Rosenbloom, Bert. "Motivating Your International Channel Partners." *Business Horizons,* March–April 1990.

Samiee, Saeed, and Peter G. P. Walters. "Rectifying Strategic Gaps in Export Management." *Journal of Global Marketing 4,* no. 1, 1990.

U.S. Department of Commerce. *A Basic Guide to Exporting,* latest edition. Washington, D.C.: U.S. Government Printing Office.

U.S. Department of Commerce. *Business America,* biweekly.

U.S. Small Business Administration. *The World Is Your Market,* latest edition. Washington, D.C.: U.S. Government Printing Office.

Chapter 5

Ayal, Igal, and Dove Izraeli. "International Market Expansion for New High Tech Products Through Franchising." *Journal of High Technology Management Research,* no. 2, 1990.

Butler, Alison. "The Trade-Related Aspects of Intellectual Property Rights: What Is at Stake?" *Review* (Federal Reserve Bank of St. Louis), November–December 1990.

Contractor, Farok J. *Licensing in International Strategy.* Westport, Conn.: Quorum Books, 1985.

Czinkota, Michael R., and Ilkka A. Ronkainen. *International Marketing.* Chicago: Dryden Press, 1990, chaps. 13 and 22.

Eroglu, Sevgin. "The Internationalization Process of Franchise Systems: A Conceptual Model," *International Marketing Review,* no. 5, 1992.

World Intellectual Property Organization. *Licensing Guide for Developing Countries,* latest edition. Geneva: United Nations.

Chapter 6

Czinkota, Michael R., and Ilkka A. Ronkainen. *International Marketing.* Chicago: Dryden Press, 1990, chap. 14.

Jeannet, Jean-Pierre, and Hubert D. Hennessey. *International Marketing.* Boston: Houghton-Mifflin Company, 1988, chap. 9.

Onkvisit, Sak, and John J. Shaw. *International Marketing.* New York: Macmillan Publishing Company, 1993, chap. 9.

Poynter, Thomas A. *Multinational Enterprises & Government Intervention.* London: Croom Helm, Ltd., 1985.

Terpstra, Vern. *International Marketing.* Chicago: Dryden Press, 1994, chap. 10.

Chapter 7

Erramilli, M. Krishna, and C. P. Rao. "Choice of Foreign Market Entry Modes by Service Firms: Role of Market Knowledge." *Management International Review,* no. 2, 1990.

Hill, Charles W., and others. "An Eclectic Theory of the Choice of International Entry Mode." *Strategic Management Journal* 2, 1990.

Minor, Michael, and others. "A Proposition-Based Approach to International Entry Strategy Contingencies." *Journal of Global Marketing,* no. 3, 1991.

Okoroafo, Sam C. "Effects of Repatriation Risk on the Choice of Entry Modes Used by U.S. Manufacturing Firms in LDCs." *Journal of Global Marketing,* no, 2, 1989.

Chapter 8

Albaum, Gerald, and others. *International Marketing and Export Management.* Reading, Mass.: Addison-Wesley Publishing Company, 1989, chaps. 8 and 10.

Czinkota, Michael R., and Ilkka A. Ronkainen. *International Marketing.* Chicago: Dryden Press, 1990, chaps. 10, 11, 17 and 19.

Jain, Subash C. *International Marketing Management.* Boston: Kent Publishing Company, 1993, chaps. 13, 15, and 16.

Jeannet, Jean-Pierre, and Hubert D. Hennessey. *International Marketing.* Boston: Houghton-Mifflin Company, 1988, chaps. 13, 14, and 15.

Mooij, Marieke K., de, with Warren J. Keegan. *Advertising Worldwide.* New York: Prentice Hall, 1991.

Onkvisit, Sak, and John J. Shaw. *International Marketing.* New York: Macmillan Publishing Company, 1993, chaps. 14, 15, 16, and 17.

Terpstra, Vern. *International Marketing.* Chicago: Dryden Press, 1994, chaps. 12, 13, and 14.

Chapter 9

Czinkota, Michael R., and Ilkka A. Ronkainen. *International Marketing.* Chicago: Dryden Press, 1990, chap. 5.

De Mente, Boye. *How To Do Business with the Japanese.* Lincolnwood, Ill.: NTC Business Books, 1991.

Harris, Philip R., and Robert T. Moran. *Managing Cultural Differences,* 3rd ed. Houston: Gulf Publishing Company, 1991.

Hofstede, Geert. *Cultures and Organizations.* New York: McGraw-Hill Book Company, 1991.

Jain, Subash C. *International Marketing Management.* Boston: Kent Publishing Company, 1993, chap. 7.

Jeannet, Jean-Pierre, and Hubert D. Hennessey. *International Marketing.* Boston: Houghton-Mifflin Company, 1988, chap. 3.

Onkvisit, Sak, and John J. Shaw. *International Marketing.* New York: Macmillan Publishing Company, 1993, chap. 6.

Ricks, David A. *Blunders in International Business.* Cambridge, Mass.: Blackwell Publishers, 1993.

Terpstra, Vern, and Kenneth David. *The Cultural Environment of International Business.* Cincinnati: South-Western Publishing Company, 1991.

Chapter 10

Aaker, David A. *Strategic Market Management,* 3rd ed. New York: John Wiley & Sons, 1992.

Bartlett, Christopher A., and Sumantra Ghoshal. *Transnational Management.* Homewood, Ill.: Richard D. Irwin, 1992.

Buzzell, Robert D., John A. Quelch, and Christopher Bartlett. *Global Marketing Management,* 2nd ed. Reading, Mass.: Addison-Wesley Publishing Company, 1992.

Contractor, Farok J., and Peter Lorange. *Cooperative Strategies in International Business.* Lexington, Mass.: Lexington Books, 1988.

Czinkota, Michael R., and Ilkka A. Ronkainen. *International Marketing.* Chicago: Dryden Press, 1990, chaps. 16 and 20.

Douglas, Susan P., and C. Samuel Craig. "Evolution of Global Marketing Strategy: Scale, Scope and Synergy," *Columbia Journal of World Business,* Fall 1989.

Jain, Subash C. *International Marketing Management.* Boston: Kent Publishing Company, 1993, chaps. 18 and 19.

Jeannet, Jean-Pierre, and Hubert D. Hennessey. *International Marketing.* Boston: Houghton-Mifflin Company, 1988, chaps. 16 and 17.

Porter, Michael E. *Competition in Global Industries.* Boston: Harvard Business School Press, 1986.

Root, Franklin R., and Kanoknart Visudtibhan, eds. *International Strategic Management, Challenges and Opportunities.* Washington, D.C.: Taylor & Francis, 1992.

Terpstra, Vern. *International Marketing.* Chicago: Dryden Press, 1994, chaps. 7, 8, and 9.

| Index |